Visuality in the Novels of Austen, Radcliffe, Edgeworth and Burney

ANTHEM NINETEENTH-CENTURY SERIES

The **Anthem Nineteenth-Century Series** incorporates a broad range of titles within the fields of literature and culture, comprising an excellent collection of interdisciplinary academic texts. The series aims to promote the most challenging and original work being undertaken in the field, and encourages an approach that fosters connections between areas including history, science, religion and literary theory. Our titles have earned an excellent reputation for the originality and rigour of their scholarship, and our commitment to high-quality production.

Series Editor
Robert Douglas-Fairhurst – University of Oxford, UK

Editorial Board
Dinah Birch – University of Liverpool, UK
Kirstie Blair – University of Stirling, UK
Archie Burnett – Boston University, USA
Christopher Decker – University of Nevada, USA
Heather Glen – University of Cambridge, UK
Linda K. Hughes – Texas Christian University, USA
Simon J. James – Durham University, UK
Angela Leighton – University of Cambridge, UK
Jo McDonagh – King's College London, UK
Michael O'Neill – Durham University, UK
Seamus Perry – University of Oxford, UK
Clare Pettitt – King's College London, UK
Adrian Poole – University of Cambridge, UK
Jan-Melissa Schramm – University of Cambridge, UK

Visuality in the Novels of Austen, Radcliffe, Edgeworth and Burney

Jessica A. Volz

ANTHEM PRESS

Anthem Press
An imprint of Wimbledon Publishing Company
www.anthempress.com

This edition first published in UK and USA 2020
by ANTHEM PRESS
75–76 Blackfriars Road, London SE1 8HA, UK
or PO Box 9779, London SW19 7ZG, UK
and
244 Madison Ave #116, New York, NY 10016, USA

First published in the UK and USA by Anthem Press 2017

Copyright © Jessica A. Volz 2020

The moral right of the authors has been asserted.

All rights reserved. Without limiting the rights under copyright reserved above,
no part of this publication may be reproduced, stored or introduced into
a retrieval system, or transmitted, in any form or by any means
(electronic, mechanical, photocopying, recording or otherwise),
without the prior written permission of both the copyright
owner and the above publisher of this book.

British Library Cataloguing-in-Publication Data
A catalogue record for this book is available from the British Library.

Library of Congress Cataloging-in-Publication Data
Library of Congress Control Number: 2019953385

ISBN-13: 978-1-78527-253-0 (Pbk)
ISBN-10: 1-78527-253-5 (Pbk)

This title is also available as an e-book.

For Mom, Dad and Adrian

CONTENTS

Foreword
Caroline Jane Knight — ix

Preface — xi

Introduction. Visuality in Profile — 1

1. Jane Austen's Aesthetic Vocabulary of Character — 27
2. Ann Radcliffe's Gothic Reconstructions of Female Identity and Experience — 87
3. The Gendered Gaze and 'Made-up' Women in Maria Edgeworth's *Castle Rackrent*, *Ennui* and *Belinda* — 137
4. Optical Allusions in Frances Burney's *Evelina* and *The Wanderer* — 173

Conclusion — 209

Selected Bibliography — 215

Index — 233

FOREWORD

A storyteller wants the audience to imagine a character, scene or situation in their mind's eye. The clearer the mental image is, the greater the connection and engagement with the story. A vague picture with little recognition is unlikely to hold a reader's interest. Detailed descriptions can be used to create a precise image, or a writer can achieve a similar outcome by allowing the audience to paint a picture that empowers a subjective frame of reference. In today's world, storytellers tend to rely more heavily on 'high-resolution' visual aids than on telling silhouettes. We have witnessed images of natural wonders, cultures, inventions and disasters and are able to envision lives and situations that are far removed from our own. We are bombarded with a constant stream of graphics, photographs and moving pictures. Some of these images are designed to build relationships, while others are destined to provoke a reaction.

Storytelling has always been about visualization and vicarious experiences. The level of detail needed to communicate has changed as culture and technology have developed. *Visuality in the Novels of Austen, Radcliffe, Edgeworth and Burney* is the first book to analyse how four of the most prolific late eighteenth- and early nineteenth-century women novelists were able to articulate certain thoughts and conjure particular images through self-conscious narration. Despite their individual perspectives and distinct contributions to the evolution of the novel, Jane Austen, Ann Radcliffe, Maria Edgeworth and Frances Burney all relied on visuality – a continuum linking the visual and the verbal in a way that creates a shortcut between communication and understanding. As this book explores, their use of visuality served as a form of strategic communications, making their novels relevant to disciplines ranging from literature and diplomacy to art history and film.

Austen confined her writing to characters, situations and surroundings that her audience would be familiar with. She was a minimalist when it came to descriptive details, granting her readers the artistic license to paint their own mental images. We are merely given the following verbal portrait of Mr Darcy: 'Mr. Darcy soon drew the attention of the room by his fine, tall person, handsome features, noble mien'. Readers are left to fill in the blanks when imagining his face, hair, eyes and clothes. Austen does not ask us to picture her idea of the perfect man but to imagine our own. Perhaps that is why, 200 years later, Darcy is considered to be one of the best-drawn and most universal romantic heroes of all time.

As the last of the Austen descendants to grow up in the Great House in Chawton, the country manor belonging to Jane's brother Edward (my fourth great-grandfather), I have known about Mr Darcy for as long as I can remember. Austen's characters are, through her use of visuality, immediately recognizable. Almost every reader can relate to the essence of her characters, skilfully painted with a few carefully chosen words, and identify similar traits in their friends and family. For readers in some countries, the limited rights and earning opportunities that women faced during the late eighteenth and early nineteenth centuries are readily translatable.

If Austen, Radcliffe, Edgeworth and Burney had not been able to read and write, the world would be a more lacklustre place without their novel contributions. Inspired by Great-Aunt Jane's success, I started the Jane Austen Literacy Foundation (JALF) in her honour. JALF works with the Jane Austen community and industry to raise funds to provide literacy resources for communities in need across the world. Reading and writing are essential skills that empower individuals to participate in society and pursue their dreams. As *Visuality in the Novels of Austen, Radcliffe, Edgeworth and Burney* attests, literacy and self-expression are fundamental forces that change the way we see and perceive the world around us, in literature and in life.

Caroline Jane Knight
Founder and Chair, Jane Austen Literacy Foundation
Raising funds to buy literacy resources, in honour of Jane

PREFACE

'If adventures will not befall a young woman in her own village, she must seek them abroad.' And with *Northanger Abbey*'s opening axiom echoing in my mind, I set out from the Highlands of Denver to explore visuality and its intriguing inherence in late eighteenth- and early nineteenth-century British women's novels. Visuality, which functions as a continuum linking visual and verbal modes of communication and understanding, empowered women novelists at a time when self-expression was particularly constrained for their sex, allowing them to control the gaze and speak through pictures. My analysis of the novels of Jane Austen, Ann Radcliffe, Maria Edgeworth and Frances Burney demonstrates that visuality provided them with a coded methodology capable of depicting and negotiating the ways in which women 'should' see, appear and think in a society in which the reputation was image based.

    I have relished writing a book that offers fresh insights into a particularly beguiling chapter in British literature. My research unfolded in a small, tea-stocked room in St Andrews that though draughty, featured a mesmerizing view of the mercurial North Sea, with its frothy tempests and righteous rainbows. Like the Scottish weather, my doctoral studies were a subject of total immersion and the substance of which novels are made. My quest for understanding the dynamics between the visual and the verbal, the 'seeable' and the describable in women's novels published between 1778 and 1815 prompted productive pilgrimages to a number of key destinations: Chawton House Library, Jane Austen's House Museum, the Wallace Collection, the Royal Academy of Arts, the National Portrait Gallery, the British Museum, the British Library, the National Library of Scotland, the Bodleian Libraries, King's College (Cambridge) Library, Blenheim Palace, King's Lynn, the Musée Jacquemart-André, the Château de Malmaison and even Buckingham Palace. Perhaps nothing could have surpassed the thrill of speaking at Lucy Cavendish College, Cambridge's *Pride and Prejudice* bicentenary conference, which culminated in a proper Regency ball led by renowned dance master Stuart Marsden.

I am thankful for the scholars, writers, artists and actors who, directly or indirectly, knowingly or unknowingly, helped me find my path – a path that straddles literature, art, strategic communications and international relations. Without the encouragement and enthusiasm of Dr Joe Bray, Professor Janet Todd, Professor Sir Hans Kornberg and Professor Rosanna Warren, this book would not have been possible.

Above all, I am grateful to my parents and brother for their loving support at every stage of my work's progression and for their confidence in the direction of my dreams. My book is also indebted to Kyra Brenzinger for enabling me to visit a number of inspirational exhibitions in Paris, and to John Bingley, Robin Ellis and Meredith Wheeler, whose friendship I also treasure.

I hope that this book will convey the measure of my admiration for late eighteenth- and early nineteenth-century women novelists who, whether famed or forgotten, harnessed the powers of visuality to become heroines of their own limitations, in literature and in life.

Introduction

VISUALITY IN PROFILE

At the opening of Jane Austen's 'The Mystery', Corydon halts a conversation before one has begun, exclaiming, 'But Hush! I am interrupted.'[1] The three-page 'UNFINISHED COMEDY' highlights the role of unfinished sentences that shift from verbal to visual modes of expression. Austen spells out 'the mystery' only once, not through dialogue but rather through the inaudible *act* of speech.[2] Whereas the reader of the playlet sees the script, the spectator reads it from the actors' countenances. Drawing upon the interplay between well-chosen words and visual communication, the novelist dramatizes the enduring influence of what Joseph Addison decreed in the *Spectator* nearly a century before:

> Words, when well chosen, have so great a Force in them, that a Description often gives us more lively Ideas than the Sight of Things themselves. The Reader finds a Scene drawn in stronger Colours, and painted more to the Life in his Imagination, by the help of Words, than by an actual Survey of the Scene which they describe. In this case the Poet seems to get the better of Nature.[3]

According to Addison's theory and Austen's burlesque, a well-crafted, even if undetailed, verbal sketch has the potential to theatricize in the mind's eye what complete visual impressions would limit, enhancing the view beyond the reality. Novels, more than drama, compel the reader to 'see' the images that he or she paints in the mind's eye from the text that appears on the printed page, allowing the aesthetic functioning of descriptions to produce a more lively impression in the imagination than sight alone could offer.

---

1 Jane Austen, *Minor Works*, ed. R. W. Chapman (Oxford: Oxford University Press, 1954; 1963), 55.
2 On Jane Austen and brevity, see Bharat Tandon's *Jane Austen and the Morality of Conversation* (London: Anthem Press, 2003), 61–63.
3 Joseph Addison, 'On the Pleasures of the Imagination', *Spectator* 416, no. 27 (June 1712), 290–93 (292).

Lionel Trilling's landmark essay 'Manners, Morals, and the Novel' (1961) proposes that 'well-chosen' words are as much in dialogue with manners as they are with their linguistic roots:

> What I understand by manners, then, is a culture's buzz of implication. I mean the whole evanescent context which is made up of half-uttered or un-uttered or unutterable expressions of value. They are hinted at by small actions, sometimes by the arts of dress or decoration, sometimes by tone, gesture, emphasis, or rhythm, sometimes by the words that are used with a special frequency or a special meaning.[4]

David Lodge points out in *Language of Fiction* (1966) that Trilling's survey explains how manners – the link between the visible and the audible – operate in actuality.[5] In literature, however, they take on a more complex status because even the 'half-uttered, un-uttered or unutterable' must be redrawn through verbal expression.

Seizing upon 'the mystery' that lies at the conjunction of the visual and the verbal, this book demonstrates how late eighteenth- and early nineteenth-century women novelists relied on visuality to circumvent the constraints on expression in literature and in life. As James Fordyce's *Sermons to Young Women* (1766) makes explicit, women were required to keep up certain appearances and censor their comments in order to preserve their reputations.[6] Codes of conduct and the trending public–private divide between the 'made-up' self and the intrinsic self scripted the drama of womanhood in the late eighteenth and early nineteenth centuries. The language that women novelists had to employ reveals the self-consciousness that resonated between the author and her fictional women. Writing to her father, Elizabeth Montagu rationalized her hesitation to publish her work because she was uncertain how it would be received. As she explained, 'There is a general prejudice against female Authors especially if they invade those regions of literature which the Men are desirous to reserve to themselves.'[7] While novels were sometimes considered improper reading material for unmarried women because of their potentially salacious plots, it was one genre that women could get their hands on and identify with, both as readers and as writers – a fact that is frequently acknowledged in

---

4 Lionel Trilling, *The Liberal Imagination: Essays on Literature and Society* (London: Mercury Books, 1961), 206–7.
5 David Lodge, *Language of Fiction: Essays in Criticism and Verbal Analysis of the English Novel* (London: Routledge and Kegan Paul, 1966), 100.
6 James Fordyce, *Sermons to Young Women* (London: J. Williams, 1767).
7 An extract from a letter, dated 10 September 1769, from Elizabeth Montagu to her father, Matthew Robinson (MO 4767, Huntington Library, San Marino, CA).

women's novels published between the start of the Anglo-French War in 1778 and the end of the Napoleonic Wars in 1815. In Maria Edgeworth's *Belinda* (1801), for instance, Lady Delacour taunts the heroine, remarking, ' "You are thinking that you are like Camilla, and I like Mrs. Mitten – novel reading […] novel reading for young ladies is the most dangerous" '.[8] During an era that played witness to the French Revolution, empires in transition, cultural suspicions and changing attitudes towards freedom of expression, women novelists, more than women novel-readers, were seen as possible threats to patriarchal society and its system of knowledge transfer.

Alongside the complications of language specific to the late eighteenth and early nineteenth centuries, women writers confronted the tension between how their sex saw and had to be seen. Returning to Montagu's concession, it is clear that she was also concerned how her literary reputation would affect her social image. The correspondence between the ways in which women were seen in print and in life appears in discussions addressing 'good taste' from an artistic perspective. In her *Enquiry Concerning the Principles of Taste, and of the Origin of Our Ideas of Beauty &c.* (1785), Frances Reynolds, Sir Joshua Reynolds's younger sister, who was a talented artist in her own right, explains that 'in cultivated nations, every precept for exterior appearance […] has for its object […] a desire to impress upon the spectator a favourable idea of our mental character'.[9] By extension, exteriors, whether animate or inanimate, have the potential to communicate qualities that are hidden from view.

In this context, visuality – a methodology involving the use of visual cues, analogues and references to the gaze – played a crucial role in illustrating women's difficulties, polite society's anxieties and the problems inherent in judging by appearances. This book's originality lies in its exploration of visuality's many facets as they apply to late eighteenth- and early nineteenth-century representations of women by women novelists. While my investigation highlights particular influences from visual culture, including portraiture, the looking glass, architecture and landscape painting, it does not feature illustrations, for to do so would defeat my point that novelists painted with words. The critique focuses on the oeuvres of four women novelists of the period who were simultaneously influential and well-received interpreters of their respective social contexts: Jane Austen, Ann Radcliffe, Maria Edgeworth and Frances Burney. The discussion illuminates why British women novelists publishing their oeuvres during a period shaped by cross-Channel tensions and

---

8   Maria Edgeworth, *Belinda*, ed. Siobhán Kilfeather ([1801] London: Pickering & Chatto, 1993), 57.
9   Frances Reynolds, *An Enquiry Concerning the Principles of Taste, and of the Origin of Our Ideas of Beauty &c.* (London: [n.p.], 1785), 26.

protectionist tendencies relied heavily on visuality as a powerful tool for communicating character, constructing plots and commenting on socio-economic topics, such as the estate. Since these authors embodied the conflict between woman-as-viewer and woman-as-subject/object-on-view, their fictional works provide authentic accounts of how different women interrogated gender politics and cultural expectations of self-presentation.

While 'visuality' is a broad concept that lends itself to multiple definitions, scholars from disparate disciplines offer valuable explanations of its dependency on biological sight and the visible world. As Fraser MacDonald has proposed, visuality exposes culture's manner of influencing perceptions of oneself and one's surroundings: 'Visuality refers to the acculturation of sight. It starts from the premise that vision is cultural as much as biological.'[10] Despite the term's recent proliferation in interdisciplinary subjects, it is not a novelty. Nicholas Mirzoeff contends that Thomas Carlyle was one of the first to use 'visuality' to refer to '"a succession of vivid pictures"' appearing within a culturally inspired analytical frame.[11] While optical devices have the potential to enhance eyesight, they do not necessarily improve the mind's ability to interpret 'clear' visual messages.

In contrast to Carlyle's quasi-cinematic application of the term, recent reassessments define visuality as the nexus of multiple perceptual elements, such as 'the gaze', 'scopic regime' and 'ocularcentrism'. Peter de Bolla's 'The Visibility of Visuality' (1996) breaks down these subcomponents of eighteenth-century habits of looking into their simplest forms. His analysis reasserts culture's influence on the look, or appearance, of the gaze:

> In point of fact, looking represents just one option within a range of possible insertions into visuality; other activities within the domain of the scopic are delimited by terms such as 'gazing' or 'glancing.' The period in question worked out an entire metaphorics of the eye in which these different activities were distinguished. For example, in the activity of viewing a landscape the eye might be 'cast' to a particular point or 'thrown' toward an object in the landscape known as an 'eye-catcher.' The eye might become 'exhausted' or 'sated'; sometimes it is described as being 'hungry', at others 'restless' […] In all these cases eighteenth-century culture images to itself the organ of sight as both actively participating in the visual field and its passive recorder.[12]

---

10 Fraser MacDonald, 'Visuality', in *International Encyclopedia of Human Geography*, ed. Rob Kitchin and Nigel Thrift (London: Elsevier Books, 2009), 151–56 (151).
11 Ibid.
12 Peter de Bolla, 'The Visibility of Visuality', in *Vision in Context*, ed. Teresa Brennan and Martin Jay (Abingdon: Routledge, 1996), 63–82 (69).

De Bolla's claim suggests that the quality of looking depends as much on the viewer's state of mind as on the eye's *manner* of viewing. His statement reconfirms that visuality pertains to the interplay between the somatic, the cognitive and the cultural. In the literary dimension, these traits take on the features of a methodology. De Bolla draws from René Descartes's philosophy that human embodiment is a prelude to sight: the eyes of the body reify the eye of the mind.[13] For de Bolla, the gaze is simultaneously passive and active; it conveys cultural expectations of looking as it selectively scans and interprets the visual field. The imagined Other's perceptions operate in conjunction with the cultural conscience to predetermine the look of the gaze in a particular context. The imagination thus provides the link between visual and bodily experiences that are partly shaped by the viewpoint of another person with whom we can sympathize. The sights that we see reflect our position as subjects as well as our ability, or willingness, to look, study, recognize, review and/or ignore the objects around us according to cultural habits of censoring the visible world.

Complicating vision's need for human embodiment is its rapport with the cultural site of sight. As de Bolla's and Thomas's studies illustrate, mid-eighteenth-century Britain witnessed a 'culture of visuality' that was obsessed with 'visibility, spectacle, [and] display'.[14] From the novel entertainments of Vauxhall Gardens to the ubiquity of portraiture exhibitions, seeing became distinctly self-conscious and culturally choreographed. With publications like the *Spectator* and *The Female Spectator* in vogue, looking itself became visible.

Whereas by 1831 England had become, as Edward Bulwer declared, a 'Staring Nation',[15] tasteful spectatorship in the late eighteenth and early nineteenth centuries involved a more indirect manner of looking. The tension between literal and imagined spectatorship, self-determination and self-preservation, dominates women's novels published between 1778 and 1815. Certain 'polite' appearances had to be maintained, as did gender-specific modes of seeing and being seen. This premise also applied to female typologies in fiction, including the strong-willed romantic, the damsel in distress, the lady of fashion and the role model inspired by conduct literature. In *Belinda*, Edgeworth uses Harriet Freke to caricaturize a woman who is a 'freak' of nature. She wears men's clothing and craves an attention disassociated with her sex: 'there was a wild oddity in her countenance which made one stare at her, and she was delighted to be stared at'.[16] The

---

13 For a detailed discussion on the 'eye of the mind', see Sybille Krämer's 'The "Eye of the Mind" and the "Eye of the Body": Descartes and Leibniz on Truth, Mathematics, and Visuality', in *Sensory Perception*, ed. F. G. Barth (Vienna: Springer-Verlag, 2012), 369–82 (377).
14 De Bolla, 'The Visibility of Visuality', 69.
15 See Sophie Thomas, *Romanticism and Visuality: Fragments, History, Spectacle* (Abingdon: Routledge, 2008), 30.
16 Edgeworth, *Belinda*, 37.

heroine's need to deflect the gaze and its penetration represents a fundamental preoccupation in the novel that I examine in relation to the image control that women impose on themselves – or that men impose on women – and the theatrical relationship between viewing/being viewed and happiness. The pervasive use of visuality in women's novels of the era highlights the extent to which visual and verbal modes of self-expression were consistently constrained.

Throughout the late eighteenth and early nineteenth centuries, women were forever subject to what Mary Daly calls '"an invisible tyranny"',[17] or the threat of being seen out of countenance. While Adam Smith's *The Theory of Moral Sentiments* (1759) is notionally gender neutral, it helps to understand the complications that women encountered in being simultaneously spectators and spectacles:

> Two different models, two different pictures, are held out to us, according to which we may fashion our own character and behaviour; the one more gaudy and glittering in its colouring; the other more correct and more exquisitely beautiful in its outline: the one forcing itself upon the notice of every wandering eye; the other, attracting the attention of scarce any body but the most studious and careful observer.[18]

Here, Smith's language and imagery are suggestive of idealized feminine roles within a context of visual conformity. Whereas ostentatious display would attract 'every wandering eye', a woman who blended in with the crowd, like Alexander Pope's female 'chameleons', would need to be looked for. The preoccupation with modesty and passivity encouraged women to preserve their reputations by yielding to the visual presentation of the 'norm'.

In this frame, women in late eighteenth- and early nineteenth-century life and literature were particularly shaped by the influence of what Smith calls the 'impartial spectator'. According to Smith's definition, this type of viewer is an imaginary extension of the self that sees that same self through the eyes of the imagined 'other':

> We can never survey our own sentiments and motives, we can never form any judgment concerning them; unless we remove ourselves as it were, from our own natural station and endeavour to view them as at

---

17 See LeRoy W. Smith, *Jane Austen and the Drama of Woman* (London: Macmillan, 1983), 23.
18 Adam Smith, *The Theory of Moral Sentiments*, ed. D. D. Raphael and A. L. Macfie ([1759] Oxford: Clarendon Press, 1976), 1.3: 29. Reproduced by permission of Oxford University Press.

a certain distance from us. But we can do this in no other way than by endeavouring to view them with the eyes of other people, or as people are likely to view them.[19]

Smith concludes that the self is as influenced by the literal gaze as it is by the imagined, or 'moral gaze', which seeks praiseworthiness over praise from actual spectators. Although his claim is not gender specific, it had acute significance for women at that time because it implied men's 'moral' power over women's appearances. As a result, the tension between woman-as-viewer and as subject/object-on-view was a product of internal and external pressures.

Sir Joshua Reynolds's method of portraiture offers one of the best illustrations of the process of seeing oneself objectified. De Bolla explains that Reynolds often arranged his studio with a mirror so that his sitter would be able to see him or herself coming into being in another frame.[20] James Beattie recorded the sensation in his account of August 1775:

'I sat to him five hours, in which time he finished my head and sketched out the rest of my figure. The likeness is most striking, and the execution most masterly. The figure is as large as life. Though I sat five hours, I was not in the least fatigued, for, by placing it in my power to see every stroke of his pencil; and I was greatly entertained to observe the progress of the work, and the easy and masterly manner of the artist'.[21]

As the spectator is partly reshaped by an imaginary mirror, the gender of the literal spectator, and thus the imaginary spectator, plays a determining role in meeting the gaze of the 'other'.

The following scene from Austen's *Emma* (1815) illustrates the extent to which contextual associations elicited certain 'looks' from men and women:

Some change of countenance was necessary for each gentleman as they walked into Mrs. Weston's drawing-room; – Mr. Elton must compose his joyous looks, and Mr. John Knightley disperse his ill-humour. Mr. Elton must smile less, and Mr. John Knightley more, to fit them for the

---

19 Adam Smith, *The Theory of Moral Sentiments*, 3.1: 2. Reproduced by permission of Oxford University Press.
20 De Bolla, 'The Visibility of Visuality', 73.
21 Ibid.

place. – Emma only might be as nature prompted, and shew herself just as happy as she was. To her, it was real enjoyment to be with the Westons.[22]

Austen's narrator points to how the drawing room's feminine connotations oblige each gentleman to undergo a 'change of countenance' in order to meet the public gaze. Unlike her male companions, however, Emma does not have to alter her expression; the drawing room allows her to be 'as nature prompted' according to the visual expectations of her sex. Whereas the female spectators of Emma's male drawing-room companions inspire them to 'feminize' their appearances, her 'impartial' spectator – the masculine 'moral' gaze – allows her to remain as she is.

Recent scholarship drawn from multidisciplinary subjects has alluded to the relationship between gendered vision and self-presentation in conjunction with Smith's *The Theory of Moral Sentiments*. While Smith's theory of spectatorial subjectivity is not gender specific, it imposes male ideals through a male viewpoint that, as Anna Despotopoulou observes, 'compromises the female consciousness'.[23] Karen Horney offers a similar view, claiming that in a patriarchy 'women have adapted themselves to the wishes of men and felt as if their adaptation were their true nature'.[24] Since the publication of Laura Mulvey's influential study, 'Visual Pleasure and Narrative Cinema' (1975), the male gaze has attracted a greater degree of scholarly attention. Regardless of the disparities between film and prose, her discussion, compiled in *Visual and Other Pleasures* (2009), is particularly relevant to women's novels published between 1778 and 1815. Mulvey's theory, which assumes the individuation of sight from other senses, proposes that the woman in film is 'a signifier for the male other'.[25] Rather than a creator of sense, she is the bearer of the actual and/or imagined 'male gaze', which shapes her experience as a woman accordingly. Whereas Mulvey's claim acknowledges that gender shapes cultural expectations of women's appearances, Smith's theory implies the same truth through an aesthetic rationale.

In the literary field, scholars frequently cite Mulvey's theory of the penetrating male gaze in relation to female subjection. Some critics, including

---

22 Jane Austen, *Emma*, ed. Richard Cronin and Dorothy McMillan, *The Cambridge Edition of the Works of Jane Austen* ([1815] Cambridge: Cambridge University Press, 2006), 111. © Cambridge University Press 2005, reproduced with permission.
23 Anna Despotopoulou, 'Fanny's Gaze and the Construction of Feminine Space in Mansfield Park', *Modern Language Review* 99, no. 3 (July 2004): 569–83 (571).
24 LeRoy W. Smith, *Jane Austen and the Drama of Woman*, 15.
25 See Laura Mulvey, 'Visual Pleasure and Narrative Cinema', *Screen* 16, no. 3 (Autumn 1975): 6–18.

MacDonald, find Mulvey's binary of woman as objectified image and man as active viewing subject/deliverer of the look to be myopic.[26] Mulvey's reductive correlation denies the coexistence of female and male spectatorship. In fictional and actual experience, vision does not alternate between viewers but rather allows for simultaneous subjective viewpoints and perceptions. The polyphony of valid viewpoints includes the perspectives of the fictional characters, as well as those of the author and reader. While visuality is not characteristically oppressive of women, its inherence in women's novels of the late eighteenth and early nineteenth centuries points to the fragility of the female reputation in a society of patriarchal authority and fault-seeking gazes.

More recent theories have abandoned the attempt to fit women within the moulds of male expectations. The man-made notion that women are passive rather than observant subjects has finally lost its resonance. Instead, scholars often embrace what Jacqueline Labbe defines as the 'feminine and disenfranchised perspective'.[27] Catherine Nash and Elaine Showalter claim that women are part of a microcosm wherein 'the occupations, interactions, and consciousness of women' have power.[28] LeRoy W. Smith's analysis of the power of the female spectator specifically draws from Mary Wollstonecraft's declaration, 'I do not wish [women] to have power over men; but over themselves':[29]

> [S]he attacks those women who construct their outer and inner selves according to the male gaze, and who are preoccupied more with their social projection than their private education and improvement.[30]

The conflict between expressed and concealed dimensions of the female self governs the plots of women's novels of the late eighteenth and early nineteenth centuries. The conduct book-inspired heroine of Burney's *Evelina* (1778) is one of the many fictional women to admit to the pressure of men's watchful eyes: 'But, not once, – not a moment, did I dare meet the eyes of Lord Orville! All consciousness myself, I dreaded his penetration, and directed mine every way – but towards his.'[31] For D. W. Harding and Marvin Mudrick, the drama of womanhood is comprised of what Simone de Beauvoir claims 'lies in this conflict between the fundamental aspirations of every subject (ego) – who

---

26 See MacDonald, 'Visuality.' In *Human Geography*, 154.
27 Jacqueline M. Labbe, *Romantic Visualities: Landscape, Gender and Romanticism* (Houndmills: Palgrave Macmillan, 1998), ix.
28 See MacDonald, 'Visuality'. In *Human Geography*, 54.
29 LeRoy W. Smith, *Jane Austen and the Drama of Woman*, 16.
30 LeRoy W. Smith, *Jane Austen and the Drama of Woman*, 16. Reproduced with permission of Palgrave Macmillan.
31 Burney, *Evelina*, 287.

always regards the self as the essential – and the compulsions of a situation in which she is the inessential'.[32] I would argue that the same applies to all women, past and present, who see themselves as similarly divided.

Thomas suggests that given the inseparability of vision and envisioning, the unseen had the potential to animate the seen. While most scholarship, including Jonathan Crary's *Techniques of the Observer: On Vision and Modernity in the 19th Century* (1992), contends that this was a Victorian phenomenon,[33] Sophie Thomas correctly identifies that the invisible represented a significant cultural anxiety from as early as 1780:

> The prominence of figurative and metaphoric uses of sight in literary texts of the period argues […] for an interest in acts of seeing that intersected, often producing conflicting effects, with a correspondent interest in acts of the imagination.[34]

The relationship between the seen and the unseen, the said and the unsaid, complicates the plots of women's novels of the late eighteenth and early nineteenth centuries. Edgeworth's *Belinda* provides another lucid example. When Lady Boucher reveals that Belinda's favoured suitor, Clarence Hervey, is to marry a 'nobody', she tries to make out the change that occurs in the young woman's face. She fails to understand why her companion's countenance is impenetrable: 'Was it because she had not the best eyes, or because there was nothing to be seen? To determine this question, she looked through her glass […] to take a clearer view; but Lady Delacour drew off her attention.'[35] Readers thus become invisible eyewitnesses to the ways in which women in novels published between 1778 and 1815 negotiated the tensions between concealing and revealing.

Christopher Rovee's *Imagining the Gallery: The Social Body of British Romanticism* (2006) examines the rise of visuality in literature through an artistic lens. In visual culture, he finds an index of imagining national identity similar to the one reserved for portraiture. According to his theory, the social body 'gets re-imagined as an object of representation and collective fantasy'.[36] Vision becomes embroiled in

---

32 See LeRoy W. Smith, *Jane Austen and the Drama of Woman*, 25–26.
33 Jonathan Crary, *Techniques of the Observer: On Vision and Modernity in the 19th Century* (Cambridge, MA: MIT Press, 1992).
34 Thomas, *Romanticism and Visuality*, 3. For a discussion on Eliza Haywood's *The Female Spectator* (1744–46), see Elizabeth Eger and Lucy Peltz's *Brilliant Women: 18th-Century Bluestockings*, 47–48.
35 Edgeworth, *Belinda*, 276.
36 Christopher Rovee, *Imagining the Gallery: The Social Body of British Romanticism* (Stanford: Stanford University Press, 2006), 8.

the duality of spectatorship and display, the epistemologies of seeing and being seen, a status that Radcliffe dramatizes through her use of the supernatural. Near the opening of *A Sicilian Romance* (1790), Julia 'almost fancied that the portrait breathed, and that the eyes were fixed on hers with a look of penetrating softness'.[37] As Edgeworth records a decade later in *Belinda*, '"Miss Portman's blushes [...] speak for her."'[38] Both examples represent what anthropologist Tim Ingold defines as 'looking-and-listening', or communicating inaudibly.[39] His analysis of ekphrasis, or what James Heffernan calls 'the verbal representation of visual representation', strengthens my point that visuality operates as a functional continuum linking the limits of visual description and verbal depiction.[40] Visuality – like soft diplomacy – resists prescriptive formulas. It depends as much on the viewer's subjectivity as on the gendered and cultural associations of the object of the gaze.

Ancient Greek references to ekphrasis suggest that it was initially used to articulate the emotional experience of an object to an audience that could only picture its existence.[41] Whereas in 1715 ekphrasis meant 'a plain declaration or interpretation of a thing', by 1814 the term became indicative of 'the florid effeminacies of style'.[42] The stark shift in ekphrasis's gendered and stylistic associations implies that visuality was also regarded as a feminine mode of expression and rhetorical control during the Age of Enlightenment. Women novelists self-consciously incorporated the pictorial capacity of 'description by omission' in their oeuvres in order to convey the otherwise inexpressible.[43] Their use of visuality enacts what W. J. T. Mitchell calls 'ekphrastic hope', or the premise that verbal encounters can produce visual impressions that reflect upon the describer.[44] By inviting the reader to translate sight and speech

---

37 Ann Radcliffe, *A Sicilian Romance*, ed. Alison Milbank ([1790] Oxford: Oxford University Press, 1993), 27.
38 Edgeworth, *Belinda*, 179.
39 See Tim Ingold's *The Perception of the Environment: Essays on Livelihood, Dwelling and Skill* (London: Routledge, 2000).
40 For an analysis of ekphrasis, refer to James A. Heffernan's *Museum of Words: The Poetics of Ekphrasis from Homer to Ashbery* (Chicago and London: University of Chicago Press, 1993). Visuality, more than ekphrasis, encompasses perceptual elements pertaining to the gendered gaze.
41 See Peter Wagner, ed., *Icons–Text–Iconotexts: Essays on Ekphrasis and Intermediary* (New York: de Gruyter, 1996), 5–13.
42 *OED* Online, s.v. 'ecphrasis', accessed 7 November 2013. See also Shadi Bartsch's *Decoding the Ancient Novel: The Reader and the Role of Description in Heliodorus and Achilles Tatius* (Princeton: Princeton University Press, 1989), 8–10.
43 On Lorraine Daston's 'description by omission', see Joanna Stalnaker's *The Unfinished Enlightenment: Description in the Age of the Encyclopedia* (New York: Cornell University Press), 8.
44 W. J. T. Mitchell, *Picture Theory* (Chicago: University of Chicago Press, 1994), 152.

simultaneously, visuality allows for the cross-exploration of reading and spectatorship, description and depiction.

Given its importance in elucidating the gender politics of late eighteenth- and early nineteenth-century social contexts, it is surprising how few studies discuss visuality's role as a multifaceted methodology inherent in novels of the period. While Crary's *Techniques of the Observer* (1992) and *Suspensions of Perception* (2001) chronicle how scientific advances, from the kaleidoscope to the stereoscope, reshaped the visible world, his findings primarily address the Victorians' acute fascination with physiognomic detail. He explains that in contrast to the eighteenth century, which preferred transparency to opacity, the nineteenth century esteemed the reality effect of microscopic detail and moving pictures:[45]

> If vision previously had been conceived as an experience of qualities (as in Goethe's optics), it is now a question of differences in quantities, of sensory experience that is stronger or weaker. But this new valuation of perception, this obliteration of the qualitative in sensation through its arithmetical homogenization, is a crucial part of modernization.[46]

Crary cites Charles Wheatstone's stereoscope as a device that conflated the actual with optical illusion, reproducing the depth of 'natural vision' through artifice.[47] His studies seek to demonstrate that with the Industrial Revolution, the speed of time and the pace of life accelerated, rendering the camera obscura's linear optical system obsolete.

Unlike Crary, Teresa Brennan and Martin Jay address non-scientific factors that shape perception. Their compendium, *Vision in Context: Historical and Contemporary Perspectives on Sight* (1996), claims that recent interpretations of 'the eye' and 'the gaze' (or 'the look') move away from the universality of visual experience wherein the appearance of the real becomes representative of the culturally symbolic.[48] By exploring the analyses of Peter de Bolla, Gillian Beer and other luminaries, *Vision in Context* resists sweeping generalizations about ekphrasis. Even if much of the survey focuses on dissimilar times and topics, it demonstrates a universal truth: context, gender and 'the optical unconscious'[49]

---

45 Crary, *Techniques of the Observer*, 62. For a complementary account of the recasting of visual perception and ekphrasis during the Victorian period, see Crary's equally insightful *Suspensions of Perception: Attention, Spectacle, and Modern Culture* (Cambridge, MA: MIT Press, 2001).
46 Crary, *Techniques of the Observer*, 147.
47 Ibid., 122.
48 Teresa Brennan and Martin Jay, eds., *Vision in Context: Historical and Contemporary Perspectives on Sight* (Abingdon: Routledge, 1996), 3.
49 Ibid.

influence the interdependency of the visual and the rhetorical in perceptible and imperceptible ways.

Sophie Thomas's *Romanticism and Visuality: Fragments, History, Spectacle* (2008) clarifies the connection between visual and verbal communication that predated Crary's age of optical revolution. In contrast to Brennan and Jay, Thomas allows the perspectives of male writers to dominate her survey of the crosscurrents, or translative process, between inexpressibility and vision. For Thomas, the Romantic poets, including William Wordsworth and Lord Byron, supplied the most intriguing depictions of ruins, or those fragments that are simultaneously present and absent from the visual field; they blur the distinction between past and present, the visible and the visualizable.[50] Despite its constricted analysis of the picturesque, Thomas's exploration of visuality lends itself to my study of the identity crisis to which women of the period were subjected and why much that could have been described or expressed of their visible appearances and innermost selves was not.

Like the fragments that lay the foundation for Thomas's argument, women straddled the seen and the unseen, the describable and the ineffable. The boundaries of the sayable/unsayable were temporally defined. According to Murray Cohen, the stigma that 'language is too poor for great literature' was a late eighteenth-century phenomenon:

> But where early eighteenth-century writers routinely commend the wealth, or riches, or power of their language and words, later eighteenth-century writers speak of its poverty. The aristocratic vocabulary of Augustan poetics – rich, wealthy, luxuriant, powerful – is unlikely to appeal to many Romantic writers for ideological reasons, but this sense of impoverishment is not just a matter of vocabulary, for it represents a change in the conception of language, which involves a recognition of limits past which words cannot go.[51]

Cohen's observation that ideological transformations sparked the 'change in the conception of language' points to the invisible cultural forces that shaped society's perception of the limits of language at that time. He finds that at the turn of the nineteenth century, writing was preoccupied with the ways in which feeling could be inspired by visual effect within and beyond language. The era's cultural conditions empowered visuality by allowing it to operate

---

50 Thomas, *Romanticism and Visuality*, 19.
51 Murray Cohen, *Sensible Words, Linguistic Practice in England, 1640–1785* (Baltimore: Johns Hopkins University Press, 1977), 81. © 1977 The Johns Hopkins University Press. Reprinted with permission of Johns Hopkins University Press.

as a 'language within language' and therefore an efficient alternative to what modern readers would interpret as straightforward speech. As subsequent chapters of this book demonstrate, the interdependency of the unseeable/unsayable was of particular interest to women novelists, who knew the risks of having their words and looks misinterpreted. Visuality gave them the liberty to challenge the authority of the male gaze and the male word through a methodology that seamlessly circumvented the strictures on self-expression in literature and in life.

James Thompson's study begins where Cohen's ends. He claims that the trope of expressed inexpressibility that the late eighteenth and early nineteenth centuries witnessed was not uniform. Instead, the constrictions of language differed by gender:

> In Austen, as in Wordsworth, there is a vast difference between 'will not tell' and 'cannot tell'; not saying covers a wide range of circumstances, from a rhetorical disinclination, to the failure of language to convey emotion, thought, or experience. In Austen, we find a similar range of denials; *Mansfield Park* includes twenty-four separate instances where the narrator tells us that characters experience feelings which they cannot express or which cannot be clothed in words: their happiness or gratitude or horror is 'indescribable' or 'unspeakable' or 'indefinable.'[52]

While Thompson disregards the linguistic differences between poetry and prose, his point that 'will not tell' and 'cannot tell' complicate conversations and illustrations holds true in the novels of Austen's predecessors and contemporaries. As discerning as Cohen and Thompson are, they undervalue the impetus behind the shrinking scope of effable language: the rise of a culture that returned to the early eighteenth-century formulation of 'taste', which associated classical aesthetics with the virtues of the Aristotelian golden mean. The non-chronological ordering of my book's chapters strengthens this view by identifying overlapping themes and influences rather than a false sense of definitive evolution.

The attractiveness of tastes rooted in earlier contexts simultaneously influenced modes of verbal expression and visual display. One of the leading figures at the beginning of the eighteenth century was Anthony Ashley Cooper, Third Earl of Shaftesbury, whose *Characteristicks* (1711) earned him the title of the father of 'The Rule of Taste'.[53] Also influential was Addison, whose

---

52 James Thompson, 'Jane Austen and the Limits of Language', *Journal of English and Germanic Philology* 85, no. 4 (October 1986): 510–31 (517).

53 See Bernard Denvir's discussion on the rise of *Taste in the Eighteenth Century: Art, Design and Society 1689–1789* (London: Longman, 1983).

musings in the *Spectator* advanced the notion that 'the Taste is not to conform to the Art, but the Art to the Taste'.[54] Shaftesbury's theories travelled still farther, decreeing that the power of moral aesthetics transcends all visible and invisible boundaries. In 1731, his view of taste's universal applications was disseminated to readers of the *Weekly Register*:

> Taste is a peculiar relish for an agreeable object, by judiciously distinguishing its beauties; is founded on truth, or veri-similitude at least, and is acquired by toil and study, which is the reason so few are possessed of it [...] It heightens every science, and is the polish of every virtue; the friend of society and the guide to knowledge; 'tis the improvement of pleasure, and the test of merit; it enlarges the circle of enjoyment, and refines upon happiness; it distinguishes beauty, and detects error; it obliges us to behave with decency and elegance, and quickens our attention to the good qualities of others; in a word 'tis the assemblage of all propriety, and the centre of all that's amiable.
>
> Truth and beauty include all excellence, and with their opposites are the objects of censure and admiration. The rightly distinguishing them is the proof of a good Taste; to acquire which we must be impartial in our enquiry, cool in our judgement, quick to apprehend, and ready to determine what is an error, and what a beauty.
>
> A good Taste is not confined only to writings, but extends to paintings and sculpture, comprehends the whole circle of civility and good manners, and regulates life and conduct as well as theory and speculation.[55]

Shaftesbury's all-encompassing understanding of 'good Taste', or 'a true Taste', changed more than 'the whole circle of civility and good manners': it distinguished between the desirable and the undesirable, the ethical and the unethical, in a way that allowed truth and its affectation to benefit society. For Shaftesbury, 'good Taste' was a form of human sympathy that required effort and observation to acquire. Its desirability and influence over the seeable/sayable strengthened the connection between the visual and the verbal, the eye of the body and the eye of the mind. As perceptions of 'improvement' and connoisseurship altered, so did the visible world and the 'look' of looking, in fiction and in actuality. Real and imagined physiognomies became indicative of moral attributes, encouraging the conception and representation of beauty to metamorphose along cultural lines. The triumph of nature over art changed the way in which cosmetics were seen. After England declared war on France

---

54 Addison, *Spectator*, no. 29 (3 April 1711), 7.
55 Shaftesbury, *Weekly Register*, no. 43 (6 February 1731), 55.

in 1778 – when delegates of King Louis XVI signed the Treaty of Amity and Commerce and the Treaty of Alliance with the United States – painted faces became fashion statements connotative of deception, adulteration and 'Frenchification'.[56]

In his *Language of Fiction*, Lodge notes that patterns of experience had come to replace the preference for particulars. As he puts it, a tasteful 'vocabulary of discrimination' comprised of vague words still allowed for communication, albeit through a categorical means.[57] According to Ludwig Wittgenstein, the mind is able to acclimate to changes in the grammar of communication that result from changes in taste. His theories explain how the shifts in the balance of power between the visual and the verbal can be left undetected:

> 'Let us imagine a picture story in schematic pictures, and thus more like the narrative in a language than a series of realistic pictures [...] Let us remember too that we don't have to translate such pictures into realistic ones in order to "understand" them, any more than we ever translate photographs or film pictures into coloured pictures, although black-and-white men or plants in reality would strike us as unspeakably strange and frightful.'[58]

Wittgenstein's observation that understanding does not come through '"realistic pictures"' alone has significant implications for discussions of ekphrasis. As Joanna Stalnaker explains, whereas seventeenth-century naturalists had favoured minute descriptions of individuals, Carl Linnaeus and his followers preferred concise reports that omitted individual idiosyncrasies.[59] In literature and in life, data that suggests ideas in visual terms allows for recognition by enabling the mind's eye to interpolate characteristics that look familiar. Visuality, like ekphrastic hope, taps into the powerful connection between the aesthetic functioning of verbal suggestion and the essence of that which it depicts.

Wittgenstein's premise that viewers use what they can and cannot see to represent what cannot be said lends itself to understanding the irony in Pope's 'To a Lady; of the Characters of Women' (1743). Both writers suggested that minute details could be dispensed with in the effective communication of

---

56 For a discussion on cosmetics, see Lynn Festa's 'Cosmetic Differences: The Changing Faces of England and France', *Studies in Eighteenth Century Culture* 34 (2005): 25–54.
57 Lodge, *Language of Fiction*, 99.
58 Cited in Martin Price's 'Manners, Morals, and Jane Austen', *Nineteenth-Century Fiction* 30, no. 3, Jane Austen 1775–1975 (December 1975): 261–80 (261).
59 Stalnaker, *The Unfinished Enlightenment*, 12.

ideas. Pope's presentation of the binary division between woman-as-viewer and woman-as-object-on-view highlights its implications for female character:

> Nothing so true as what you once let fall,
> 'Most Women have no Characters at all.'
> Matter too soft a lasting mark to bear,
> And best distinguish'd by black, brown, or fair.[60]

Pope contends that because his contemporary society saw women as 'too soft', their characters were deemed of no 'matter'. In representation and actuality, a well-defined self cannot take shape if its 'body' resists cultural practices of individualization. To advance his Lockean argument that identity involves more than the eye can see, Pope downplays the notion of 'character' as distinguished by particular marks, signs or features.[61] His satire on the appearances of women's characters theatrically exposes the conflict between expressed and concealed selves that women's novels published between 1778 and 1815 continued to highlight through visuality. The poem emphasizes that drawing out the character buried within the 'soft matter' requires more than descriptive analysis. As Myra Stokes writes in *The Language of Jane Austen* (1991), a more accurate delineation calls for a degree of dramatic, as well as discursive, description. Like the portrayal of physical features, the representation of non-physical qualities demands what she defines as a 'conceptual schema or grid: that is, some general theory or notion of what the range and nature of these non-physical aspects of person are'.[62]

While there is certainly more to a woman's character than schematized description can depict, the question of whether character is something that is bestowed (stamped upon the object of the gaze) or created autonomously by the subject is an enigma that Pope's poem brings into view. His epistle plays with the duality of character, which can mean both the intrinsic self, or natural disposition, and the report that society gives of a person, implying moral virtue or vice. The ensuing satire sketches out the 'classical' ways in which eighteenth-century men perceived women:

---

60 Alexander Pope, 'Epistle to a Lady', in *Alexander Pope: Selected Poems*, ed. Pat Rogers (Oxford: Oxford University Press, 1998), 1.2–4. Reprinted by permission of Oxford University Press.
61 Pope's perception of 'character' relates to John Locke's explanation of the term in his *An Essay Concerning Human Understanding*, ed. Roger Woolhouse ([1689] London: Penguin, 1997).
62 Myra Stokes, *The Language of Jane Austen* (Houndmills: Macmillan, 1991), 28.

> How many pictures of one Nymph we view,
> All how unlike each other, all how true!
> Arcadia's Countess, here, in ermin'd pride,
> Is there, Pastora by a fountain side.
> Here Fannia, leering on her own good man,
> And there, a naked Leda with a Swan.
> Let then the Fair one beautifully cry,
> In Magdalen's loose hair and lifted eye,
> Or drest in smiles of sweet Cecilia shine,
> With simp'ring Angels, Palms, and Harps divine;
> Whether the Charmer sinner it, or saint it,
> If Folly grows romantic, I must paint it.[63]

Pope's panorama of types of fictional women points to how even with non-physical qualities in view, their characters remain abstractions; they have been framed as schematized types rather than as fully characterized individuals.

In his thirteenth stanza, Pope abandons his initial lament that 'women have no characters'. He concedes that some of the fault lies in the poet–painter's eyes. According to Pope, depicting women as 'variegated Tulips' and 'simp'ring Angels' indicates the artist's lack of skill rather than his subject's insubstantiality:

> Pictures like these, dear Madam, to design,
> Asks no firm hand, and no unerring line;
> Some wand'ring touches, some reflected light,
> Some flying stroke alone can hit 'em right:
> For how should equal Colours do the knack?
> Chameleons who can paint in white and black?[64]

Pope claims that since women are inherently changeful, no 'firm' hand can capture them. In 'Cosmetic Differences: The Changing Faces of England and France' (2005), Lynn Festa seizes upon this premise, explaining that eighteenth-century women were exchanging cosmetics for other forms of fiction.[65] By extension, women's novels of the period have a tendency to emphasize how natural and contrived appearances often looked alike. The novels that this book discusses all feature women who need to obtain and/or retain

---

63 Pope, 'Epistle to a Lady', 2.5–16. Reprinted by permission of Oxford University Press.
64 Pope, 'Epistle to a Lady', 12.151–56. Reprinted by permission of Oxford University Press.
65 On cosmetics and women's identity crises, see Lynn Festa's 'Cosmetic Differences: The Changing Faces of England and France', 25–54.

control of their characters through the way in which they are portrayed and portray themselves.

Whereas 'good taste' did not prevent men from displaying their 'bolder Talents' in public, Pope observes that women's characters were revealed in private alone:

> But grant, in Public Men sometimes are shown,
> A Woman's seen in Private life alone:
> Our bolder Talents in full light display'd,
> Your Virtues open fairest in the shade.
> Bred to disguise, in Public 'tis you hide;
> There, none distinguish 'twixt your Shame or Pride,
> Weakness or Delicacy; all so nice,
> That each may seem a Virtue, or a Vice.[66]

Pope's comparison applies Addison's conception of taste to women. Like art, a woman's display of character must conform to the 'true' taste. Given the need for self-defence against the public eye, women had to maintain a 'type' of appearance that masked excessive exposure of individuality. Only in the shade of the boudoir were women at liberty to be their natural selves.

Lodge considers the tension between how a woman in the eighteenth century should appear and how she sees herself to be at the heart of her difficulties. He contends that subjecting the self to such an unforgiving code of conduct and strict aesthetic ideology was not easy to live with:

> It demands a constant state of watchfulness and self-awareness on the part of the individual, who must not only reconcile the two scales of value in personal decisions but, in the field of human relations, must contend with the fact that an attractive or unexceptionable social exterior can be deceptive.[67]

While a trompe l'œil preserved a woman's reputation, it complicated judging by appearances in a way that often produced undesirable consequences. The tension between a woman's self-awareness and woman as subject/object-on-view explains the titles of many women's novels of the period, like Burney's *The Wanderer; or, Female Difficulties* (1814).

Pope's 'Epistle II. To A Lady' confirms the power that taste and the framing of character had over people and their portraits during the late eighteenth and

---

66 Pope, 'Epistle to a Lady', 16.199–206. Reprinted by permission of Oxford University Press.
67 Lodge, *Language of Fiction*, 103.

early nineteenth centuries. The half-revealed, half-concealed state of womanhood presents a schema similar to that which art historian E. H. Gombrich discovers in the visual arts. He insists that artists do not merely paint 'what they see'; rather, they see individual elements in relation to conventional visual representations.[68] His theory also applies to verbal sketches of a woman's character. The accuracy of the scheme is negligible as long as it adheres to a vocabulary of discrimination. The schemas that late eighteenth- and early nineteenth-century women novelists adopted offer critical insight into how they used visuality to circumvent the constraints of verbal expression out of societal preference and gendered necessity.

While depictions of heroines in Victorian fiction have been the subject of extensive scrutiny, those in the novels of Austen, Radcliffe, Edgeworth and Burney have received less critical attention through an artistic lens. In her article 'The Heroine of Irregular Features: Physiognomy and Conventions of Heroine Description' (1981), Jeanne Fahnestock explains the apparent absence of women's characters through the stark shift that occurred in heroine depiction between the Regency and Victorian periods. As she suggests, features of an 'irregular characteristic cast' refashioned the faces of the industrial age: 'The minutely described heroine has a much harder time being perfectly beautiful; she is often a heroine of irregular features instead.'[69] Her study chronicles how by the mid-nineteenth century, Pope's type-face fictional women had evolved into individuals with recognizable physiognomies. As subsequent chapters of this book explore, character depiction was already changing in the novels of Austen, Radcliffe, Edgeworth and Burney, though in less obvious ways. Their visual techniques and manipulation of self-referential coordinates show that societal perceptions of 'model' heroines were beginning to allow for some display of human fallibility and self-directed views, even if the preference for classical conceptions of taste prevailed.

Like language, art experienced equivalent fluctuations in the level of detail deemed necessary, or appropriate, to communicate. Since the face was seen as a mirror of character in novels published between 1778 and 1815, examining portraiture offers valuable insight into what constituted 'recognizable' character in the visible world. At the time, German aesthetician Johann Winckelmann was a leading authority on Johann Caspar Lavater's physiognomic writings and asserted that beauty required certain proportions. His studies contain a template for the face of 'Grecian', 'perfect' and 'regular' dimensions that

---

68 E. H. Gombrich, *Art and Illusion: A Study in the Psychology of Pictorial Representation* (New York: Phaidon, 2002).
69 Jeanne Fahnestock, 'The Heroine of Irregular Features: Physiognomy and Conventions of Heroine Description', *Victorian Studies* 24, no. 3 (Spring 1981): 325–50 (329).

Burney particularly idealized.[70] In her darkest novel, *The Wanderer; or, Female Difficulties*, she advertises the Incognita's appearance in a fashion that preserves the heroine's visual anonymity:

ELOPED from HUSBAND,
 'A young woman, tall, fair, blue-eyed; her face oval; her nose Grecian; her mouth small; her cheeks high coloured; her chin dimpled; and her hair of a glossy light brown.'[71]

According to Winckelmann, a face of such qualitative attributes was exactly three noses long and two noses wide, while the distance between the eyes had to measure one-half of one-third the length of the face, or half the nose length.[72] Even if this were the case, faces in literature were proportioned through more discreet figures of speech. Society's absorption of Lavater's physiognomic principles was important in novels of the period because they provided a vocabulary of discrimination that could be culturally understood. In Austen's novels, physiognomic portraits and structures invite her heroines to 'stare' at a correlative of a man's character so that they may see and judge him truly.

 Britain's taste for the unfinished portrait during the late eighteenth and early nineteenth centuries mirrors its overarching preference for the well chosen but indistinct. In *Brilliant Women: 18th-Century Bluestockings* (2008), Elizabeth Eger and Lucy Peltz offer a valuable analysis of the relationship between exceptional women of the period and how artists controlled their images. Though Austen and Burney are mentioned only in passing, the text's findings on portraiture indicate the connection between visual and verbal sketches of women at the time. Eger and Peltz use Richard Samuel's *Portraits in the Characters of the Muses in the Temple of Apollo (The Nine Living Muses of Great Britain)*, painted in 1778, as a case study.[73] The highly romanticized tableau features nine female luminaries of the period: Elizabeth Carter, Anna Laetitia Barbauld, Angelica

---

70 Johann Joachim Winckelmann, *The History of Ancient Art*, trans. G. Henry Lodge, 4 vols. (Boston: J. R. Osgood, 1872), 4: 292. The passage is also quoted in Thomas, *Romanticism and Visuality*, 79
71 Fanny Burney, *The Wanderer; or, FEMALE DIFFICULTIES*, ed. Margaret Anne Doody, Robert L. Mack and Peter Sabor ([1814] Oxford: Oxford University Press, 1991), 756. Reprinted by permission of Oxford University Press.
72 Winckelmann, *The History of Ancient Art*, 4: 292.
73 See Eger and Peltz's *Brilliant Women: 18th-Century Bluestockings*, 59–62. As well as critiquing Samuel's oil on canvas, which is part of the National Portrait Gallery's collection, they discuss the dissimilar engraving of it, which appeared in the *Ladies New and Polite Pocket Memorandum-Book for 1778*. Unlike its full-colour companion, the engraving spelled out the names of the women whom it featured.

Kauffmann, Elizabeth Sheridan, Charlotte Lennox, Hannah More, Elizabeth Montagu, Elizabeth Griffith and Catharine Macaulay.[74] According to Sir Joshua Reynolds's discourse of 1776, the timeless dignity of classical features '"not only attracts, but fixes the attention"'.[75] As Eger and Peltz assert, the uniform figures donning classical attire were as illegible to their owners as they were to the public eye. Carter famously objected that 'by the mere testimony of my eyes, I cannot very exactly tell which is you, and which is I, and which is anybody else'.[76] As one of the living 'worthies' of Samuel's painting, she did not wish to be denied self-recognition.

Brilliant Women highlights how, even when women were not reduced to classical 'incognitae', they appeared in 'feminine' attitudes. In contrast to most of his Jasper portraits of men, Josiah Wedgwood's likenesses of Montagu and Barbauld capture them in severe profile.[77] While Eger and Peltz allude to the women's politely averted gazes, they do not fully explore the implications of the veil that Wedgwood casts over Montagu's eyes. The veil – a necessity in Radcliffe's *The Mysteries of Udolpho* (1794) and Edgeworth's *Ennui* (1809) – shields women from penetration and filters their observations.

Women artists, like women writers, were more self-conscious of the portraits that they produced. They thus had to find polite avenues of navigating the tensions between different gazes. When fictional women stopped being seen as flawless beauties, they were also permitted to display character flaws.[78] As the exhibition of natural flaws became acceptable, visible imperfections no longer compromised a woman's moral character, allowing the authentic self to rise into view. While there was no definitive turning point, this book shows that heroine depiction was already shifting in the late eighteenth century. Visuality, more than free indirect discourse, provided women novelists with a discreet means of shifting views and viewpoints in order to show that even if their heroines conformed outwardly, they were beginning to see and think in ways that called appearances and patriarchal authority into question.

Fahnestock rightly contends that 'the system of meaning' had, like the concept of beauty, changed form.[79] The only condition, Fahnestock concedes, is that the code of character must be consistent in order for it to prove effective:

---

74 Ibid.
75 Ibid., 61.
76 Ibid.
77 Ibid., 65–66.
78 Fahnestock, 'The Heroine of Irregular Features', 325.
79 Ibid.

Of course this substitution only worked if writers and readers shared a system of meaning, a code for translating descriptive terminology into aspects of personality.[80]

The preference for a more complete inventory of physical features allows previously invisible character traits to become visible. As subsequent chapters of this book illustrate, the various authors whom I treat have their own ways of using visual reference to explore the difficulties of reading women and of women reading the world. While visuality's system of meaning in women's novels published between 1778 and 1815 differs from that found afterwards, it still functions by holding together communication and understanding.

In view of what has been established – women turned the terms of visuality in the late eighteenth and early nineteenth centuries to their advantage by controlling the gaze and speaking through pictures – it is necessary to recognize how these forms of rhetorical and perceptual power interrelate. This text explores how women novelists directed attention to the ways in which women saw and were seen and how they used visual cues to comment on emotions, socio-economic factors and patriarchal abuses. As Marianne Dashwood explains in *Sense and Sensibility* (1811), '"Sometimes I have kept my feelings to myself, because I could find no language to describe them in but what was worn and hackneyed out of all sense and meaning."'[81] This study investigates how seeing and being seen become the preoccupations of fictional women, who, like their authors, are torn between concealment and self-display. Visuality offered women writers, more than their male counterparts, a viable method of character depiction by allowing them to use the language of visual representation to say what could not be more directly said.

While each of the novelists I examine relied on visuality, its forms and functions vary according to the unique perspectives of the women behind their characters. Jane Austen, Ann Radcliffe, Maria Edgeworth and Frances Burney were culturally representative figures who also experimented with and contributed to different approaches to the novel: Austen modernized narration through her introduction of free indirect discourse; Radcliffe reinterpreted the Gothic novel and removed her plots to temporally and geographically disparate settings; Edgeworth imbued her narratives with political undertones that conveyed the situation in Ireland and was innovative in her theatrical experimentation with male narrators and cross-dressing; Burney's comparative visibility in society, from Samuel Johnson's circle to the court of Queen

---

80 Ibid.
81 Jane Austen, *Sense and Sensibility*, ed. Edward Copeland, *The Cambridge Edition of the Works of Jane Austen* ([1811] Cambridge: Cambridge University Press, 2006), 95.

Charlotte and the Battle of Waterloo, shaped her treatment of the courtship novel and influenced her transition from an epistolary to a third-person perspective. Given their relation to a wider network of women writers, Austen, Radcliffe, Edgeworth and Burney serve as optimal focal points in my study.

My critique moves from novels empowering the role of projections of character exterior to the self to the drama of reflections, fashion and the minutiae of coded self-display. The first chapter begins with a discussion of Austen's use of 'self-division' and the language of viewing as a means of exploring the limitations, opacities and potential transformations of communication and insight. By engaging with the theory that a vocabulary of discrimination allows for categorical communication, my investigation demonstrates that portraiture and architecture serve as physiognomic correlatives of character that encourage the reader to see the heroine's changing view of others and herself. Lavater's premise that a striking likeness and the actual self are interchangeable enables the novelist to 'fix' the viewer's prejudices through a silhouette that simultaneously simplifies observation and clarifies interpretation for the reader. Whereas Austen's heroines rely on visible portraiture in order to see men differently, her heroes must be able to picture women's characters in their mind's eye in order to detect their invisible attractions. Society's habit of projecting character traits onto external surfaces anticipates the connection between portraiture and architecture. The novelist's application of physiognomic features to architecture communicates her heroines' shifts in vision that lead to revised perspectives of the owner of the place. According to Roy Pascal, the novelist's preoccupation with the characters' changing attitudes towards one another creates the optimal conditions for the 'dual voice effect' that is achieved through free indirect discourse.[82] While he rightly acknowledges that Austen's technique conjoins expressed and self-confessed perspectives, he does not consider the way in which free indirect discourse operates alongside visuality to give voice to an intermediary point of view. By imbuing the physiognomies of structures and their surroundings with ideological associations, Austen encourages her readers to see the heroine's simultaneous attachment to a place and its owner.

After investigating Austen's treatment of benevolent portraiture and place in her marriage plots, the analysis turns to Radcliffe's use of visuality to explore sexual, religious and social forms of female subjection. Her recalibration of the Gothic novel and the Burkean sublime makes terror specific to women. She relies on five concentric visual realms to portray the inescapability of

---

82 For a discussion on the 'dual voice', see Roy Pascal's *The Dual Voice* (Manchester: Manchester University Press, 1977). According to Pascal, the 'dual voice' is 'neither simple narrator nor simple character' but rather a fusion of the two (32).

female persecution: portraiture, architecture, veils, sublime panoramas and the undefined. The discussion moves from man-made and natural thresholds of persecution in her fiction to that which is supernatural. Her heroines appear as imprisoned in two dimensions as they are in actuality. In contexts where the obscure makes wax and flesh indistinguishable, the novelist turns her heroines' perceptions into false impressions, life into death and dreams into the undying nightmare that is womanhood itself.

Leaving behind the dark worlds of Radcliffe's novels, the third chapter examines Edgeworth's use of visuality in *Castle Rackrent* (1800), *Ennui* (1809) and *Belinda* (1801) to show that the theatrical 'making up' of a woman's character occurs on material, perceptual and pictorial levels.[83] Her fictional accounts of Anglo-Irish life and unconventional experimentation with male narrators show that women's public images appear differently to different viewers, including themselves. Whereas male narrators see women's self-display in quantitative terms, the novelist's fictional women regard their contrived selves as a priceless even if suffocating means of protection. The analysis progresses from Edgeworth's use of male narrators in *Castle Rackrent* and *Ennui* to her dialogic treatment of 'made-up' women in *Belinda*, which realigns the reader with female subjectivity. Employing direct comparison and cross-dressing, the novelist transforms the constrictions of fashionable attire into visual metaphors for women's inability to move and speak freely within and beyond the glass-bound theatre of the domestic sphere.

The fourth and final chapter examines the relationship between Burney's acute self-consciousness as a woman novelist and her consistent use of coded visuality in her first and last novels. She moves between public and private spaces in order to question the correlation between the appearance and the essence. *Evelina*'s epistolary perspective empowers the gaze over other modes of somatic communication, inviting the reader of the novel to see society through the heroine's eyes. In *The Wanderer*'s third-person narrative structure and study of anonymity, the novelist shifts her visual technique to addressing manifest appearances through the complex language of colour.[84] Regardless of which mask she wears, Juliet's visual identity reads as an analogue for her unmarred reputation. Her enigmatic appearance – more than her exceptional natural beauty – captivates the gaze. While Burney is conventional in extolling authenticity over fakery and modest looks over penetrating gazes, her novels,

---

83 While Edgeworth's *Helen* (1834) also exposes the 'bauble insanity' that typified women, the chapter focuses on the three novels that more explicitly demonstrate her use of visuality for theatrical effect.
84 The chapter does not investigate *Cecilia* (1782) and *Camilla* (1796). Though they also demonstrate the relationship between the language of colours and third-person narratives, *The Wanderer* offers a clearer presentation of its feminist applications.

like those of Austen, Radcliffe and Edgeworth, actually highlight women's need to hide, paint, dissemble and look critically.

The non-chronological structuring of my chapters does not suggest that Austen's style of visuality is superior or that it is necessarily more advanced. Instead, it encourages readers to consider that the visual details in women's novels published between 1778 and 1815 are more nuanced and communicative about the gender politics and ambivalent tastes of an era shaped by changing perceptions of national identity than scholars have previously acknowledged.

In examining the oeuvres of four prolific late eighteenth- and early nineteenth-century women novelists, this book journeys through physiognomic, psychological, theatrical and codified styles of visuality to confirm that in fiction and actuality, women were subject to visible and invisible pressures that determined their looks and manners of looking. As the cultured continuum linking visual and verbal modes of communication and understanding, visuality granted women novelists of the period the power to become heroines of their own limitations by providing them with a methodology capable of negotiating the conflicting choices of concealing and revealing. In channelling the culturally unsayable through the politely visualizable, they diplomatically called attention to the frames, veils and typologies through which the female viewpoint and views of women were explicitly and implicitly constrained.

Chapter 1

JANE AUSTEN'S AESTHETIC VOCABULARY OF CHARACTER

Portraiture and architecture are often interconnected surfaces of the self in Jane Austen's use of visuality. Both have the power to convey the way in which characters' shifting perspectives reorient their prejudices and lead to marriages based on compatible views and values. Drawing upon David Lodge's theory that the 'vocabulary of discrimination'[1] allows for a categorical means of communication through a language within language, my discussion moves from two- to three-dimensional forms of aesthetic representation in her fiction. The analysis focuses on *Sense and Sensibility* (1811), *Pride and Prejudice* (1813), *Mansfield Park* (1814) and *Emma* (1815), which best demonstrate the novelist's manipulation of the gaze and correlatives of character.[2]

After contextualizing Austen's visual technique, the chapter first examines her novels' reliance on the physiognomic qualities of the likeness to compel the viewer, and thus the reader, to picture the subject differently. Unlike Ann Radcliffe, whose references to portraits show the permanence of female subjection, Austen uses the 'likeness' as a positive force for change in her plots: visible and metaphorical portraits improve characters' insights into themselves and others through perceptual substitution, or the replacement of one image with another, that inspires a change of heart. Like Radcliffe, however, Austen discriminates between the male and female experience of viewing and being

---

1 Refer to my Introduction and Lodge, *Language of Fiction*, 99.
2 Jane Austen, *Sense and Sensibility*, ed. Edward Copeland ([1811] Cambridge: Cambridge University Press, 2006); *Pride and Prejudice*, ed. Pat Rogers ([1813] Cambridge: Cambridge University Press, 2006); *Mansfield Park*, ed. John Wiltshire ([1814] Cambridge: Cambridge University Press, 2006); *Emma*, ed. Richard Cronin and Dorothy McMillan ([1815] Cambridge: Cambridge University Press, 2006). This analysis uses *The Cambridge Edition of the Works of Jane Austen*, which is based on the second versions of *Sense and Sensibility* and *Mansfield Park*. Wiltshire concedes to Sutherland's argument that the ' "so-called accidentals" [punctuation, italics and paragraphing] contribute to the meaning of a text, and cannot be dismissed as incidental "textual noise" '. However, for the purposes of my investigation, the influence of accidentals is inconsequential.

viewed. While the painted male gaze has the power to 'arrest' the heroine's eyes and heart, the heroine cannot control a male viewer's way of looking and feeling. The reader observes that in contrast to Austen's fictional women, who require visible portraits to alter their perceptions of men, her heroes must be able to 'picture' a woman's character in their mind's eye.

Society's absorption of the Lavaterian habit of looking and René Descartes's philosophy that 'the eyes of the body reify the eye of the mind'[3] anticipate the connection between portraiture and architecture, which comprises the second half of my analysis. Like portraiture, architecture provides characters with an external means of identification. By imbuing the physiognomies of structures and their surroundings with comparisons to the Aristotelian golden mean, Austen reasserts the early eighteenth century's investment in looks that speak. Rather than focusing on the novelist's ambivalence towards picturesque improvements and distaste for Reptonian 'destruction', as Alistair Duckworth, Beatrice Battaglia and Diego Saglia have done,[4] my discussion shows that Austen uses 'place' to convince her readers of the heroine's changing affections. The novelist's application of physiognomic features to architecture conveys the way in which her heroines' shifts in vision guide them to newfound perspectives of their simultaneous attachment to a place and its owner.

Several months after Austen's death in 1817, the *British Critic* praised her technique of characterization, which allowed conversations rather than appearances to produce universal recognition:

> Our authoress gives no definitions; but she makes her *dramatis personae* talk; and the sentiments which she places in their mouths, the little phrases which she makes them use, strike so familiarly upon our memory as soon as we hear them repeated, that we instantly recognize among some of our acquaintance, the sort of persons she intends to signify, as accurately as if we had heard their voices [...] She sees every thing just

---

3 For a detailed discussion on the 'eye of the mind', see my Introduction. I explore Sybille Krämer's 'The "Eye of the Mind" and the "Eye of the Body": Descartes and Leibniz on Truth, Mathematics, and Visuality', in *Sensory Perception*, ed. F. G. Barth (Vienna: Springer-Verlag, 2012), 369–82 (377).

4 For a focused investigation of the debate surrounding 'improvements' to nature, see Alistair M. Duckworth's *The Improvement of the Estate: A Study of Jane Austen's Novels* (Baltimore: Johns Hopkins Press, 1971), 42–44. Duckworth suggests that Austen's technical vocabulary of improvements owes much to Cowper's *The Task* (1785), which presents 'improvements' as the 'idol of the age'. See also *Redrawing Austen: Picturesque Travels in Austenland*, eds. Beatrice Battaglia and Diego Saglia (Napoli: Liguori, 2004), 17–18, 22 and 41. Battaglia examines Austen's preference for William Gilpin's treatment of landscape in her discussion of the 'paper war' against proponents of Capability Brown and Humphry Repton.

as it is; even her want of imagination (which is the principal defect of her writings) is useful to her in this respect, that it enables her to keep clear of all exaggeration, in a mode of writing where the least exaggeration would be fatal.[5]

For the anonymous reviewer, Austen's characters were more verbal than visual; their expressions of sentiment were spoken rather than seen. Even if the novelist was, as he suggests, attuned to the actual visual dynamics within her surroundings, she resisted detailing appearances because the 'least exaggeration would be fatal'. This disjointedness between what Austen saw and what she was at liberty to 'define' points to that which the reviewer's impression underestimates: the novelist's reliance on visuality as an indirect, coded method of communicating more elaborate messages. Even if conversation is 'not simply a vehicle for abstract content',[6] as Marilyn Butler rightly asserts, verbal dialogue is not the only form of the expression of character in Austen's plots. Instead, her use of physiognomic codes conveys nuances that reported speech can repress. As Bharat Tandon contends, the omissions between the sayable and the unsayable animate much of her narratives.[7] For him, Austen's transition to writing for publication adjusted her perspective, challenging the reader to find a voice within the novel. Through her use of an aesthetic vocabulary, the novelist communicates that which neither the counterbalances within words nor pictures could represent.

While Austen's ability to make her '*dramatis personae* talk' and her understanding of companionate marriage have persistently fascinated readers and scholars, her visual vocabulary of showing emotional change remains underexplored. Until the publication of Butler's *Jane Austen and the War of Ideas* (1975), scholars tended to assume that Austen and her novels were sheltered from the political tumult of the 1790s. Most critics accepted Reginald Farrer's 1917 theory that Austen was concerned 'only with the universal, and not with the particular'.[8] Butler's conclusion that the novelist's marriage plots reinforce the existing social order identified her as an implicitly conservative author. Subsequent critics, including Claudia Johnson and Nancy Armstrong, have challenged this position, arguing that Austen radically exposes women's

---

5 'Art V. *Northanger Abbey* and *Persuasion*', *British Critic*, 9 (March 1818): 296–97; emphasis in original.
6 Butler, *Jane Austen and the War of Ideas*, 173.
7 Refer to Tandon's *Jane Austen and the Morality of Conversation* (London: Anthem Press, 2003), which explores the relationship between voice and voicelessness.
8 See Janine Barchas, *Matters of Fact in Jane Austen: History, Location, and Celebrity* (Baltimore: Johns Hopkins University Press, 2012), 7.

unequal power in the marriage market and creates quietly subversive narratives in which exploitative male behaviour is exposed and checked.[9] Austen's use of visuality to create attachments based on similar views and values indicates that, while conforming outwardly to the societal pressures on women to marry for economic security, her heroines pursue happiness more fervently than wealth.

An insightful beginning for theorizing the patterns that are concealed within Austen's narrative universe is offered in M. M. Bakhtin's *The Dialogic Imagination* (1975). As Katherine Green summarizes his theory of dialogism, individuation of characters is produced through the conflict between two categories of language: the language of patriarchal authority, which I redefine as Austen's vocabulary of aesthetic discrimination, and the language of internal persuasion, or subjectivity.[10] This premise has important implications for a study of the novelist's use of visuality. In *The Epistolary Novel: Representations of Consciousness* (2003), Joe Bray explores the theories surrounding eighteenth-century modes of communication. His reading of Bakhtin's 'Discourse in the Novel' highlights the need for the author's consciousness to choose a language that was culturally understood.[11] Drawing on John Mullan's and Janet Todd's works, Bray offers a survey of the relationship between heightened sensibility and silent speech, arguing that expression in late eighteenth-century epistolary novels tore writers between 'the fevered passion of the experiencing self and the calm reason of the narrating self'.[12] Mullan, referring to Richardson's novels, finds that the most 'natural' form of expression does not require words in conveying truthful feelings.[13] Todd offers a similar argument, contending that Austen's heroines convey their virtue and authentic emotions through their 'meaningful bodies'.[14] Though Bray convincingly highlights the overarching preference for non-verbal languages in late eighteenth-century epistolary novels, he does not pursue the theme of physiognomy in Austen's work. From a dialogic perspective, traditionally 'male' and 'female' vocabularies clash in her fiction, presenting a conflict between different modes of viewing

---

9 See Claudia Johnson's *Jane Austen: Women, Politics and the Novel* (Chicago: University of Chicago Press, 1990) and Nancy Armstrong's *Desire and Domestic Fiction: A Political History of the Novel* (New York and Oxford: Oxford University Press, 1987).

10 Katherine Sobba Green discusses the influence of Bakhtin in relation to the courtship novel in *The Courtship Novel: 1740–1820* (Lexington: University Press of Kentucky, 1991), 5–6.

11 Refer to Joe Bray's *The Epistolary Novel* (London: Routledge, 2003), 83. See also John Mullan, *Sentiment and Sociability: The Language of Feeling in the Eighteenth Century* (Oxford: Clarendon Press, 1988), 74.

12 Bray, *The Epistolary Novel*, 81.

13 Ibid., 83.

14 Ibid. See also Janet Todd, *Sensibility: An Introduction* (London and New York: Methuen), 120.

and being viewed that are articulated through different surfaces of meaning physiognomies.

The post-Butler critical tradition has frequently positioned the novelist's fiction in relation to feminism and female destiny. Sandra M. Gilbert, Susan Gubar, Nancy Armstrong and Claudia Johnson are among the many scholars who have explored the relationship between sexual desire and the limitations on women's self-expression in Austen's fiction. In *The Madwoman in the Attic* (1975), Gilbert and Gubar praise the novelist for informing readers about the tensions resulting from 'grace under pressure'.[15] Armstrong's *Desire and Domestic Fiction: A Political History of the Novel* (1987) similarly considers the novelist's skill in making cultural shifts appear ordinary by teaching her readership how to act and adapt, implying a change in vision and perception.[16] Johnson's *Jane Austen: Women, Politics and the Novel* (1990) reinterprets the conflicting forces of self-determination and self-restraint in Austen's fiction. Her assertion that the novelist 'defended and enlarged a progressive middle ground' is a premise that I reconsider and endorse from the vantage point of aesthetics.[17]

Other scholars have examined the centrality of morals in Austen's texts. In *Jane Austen and Education* (1975), D. D. Devlin traces the trajectory of character 'improvement' in her novels, highlighting the distinctive relationship that she draws between ethics and clear vision.[18] While he does not specifically and fully investigate the novelist's use of visuality and its relation to physiognomic ideologies, his argument remains significant because it implies their linked importance. He cites Aristotle, who explained that 'perhaps the most distinguishing characteristic of the good man is his seeing the truth in every instance', and uses it as the foundation for his critique of the underlying ideologies behind the picturesque improvements in *Mansfield Park*.[19] Devlin suggests that 'Locke's "character" and Jane Austen's "disposition" mean what we are at any given moment, for better or worse, is a result of education'.[20] For Devlin, seeing clearly involves 'both seeing oneself clearly (self-knowledge) and seeing other people and the external world as existing in their own right and independently of the self'.[21] His study of Austen's aim to cultivate 'a new clarity

---

15 Sandra M. Gilbert and Susan Gubar, *The Madwoman in the Attic* (New Haven, CT: Yale University Press, 1984). See pages 584–85 for a discussion on women writers' pursuit of literary autonomy and the limitations of language.
16 Armstrong, *Desire and Domestic Fiction*, 134–60.
17 Claudia Johnson, *Jane Austen: Women, Politics and the Novel* (Chicago: University of Chicago Press, 1990), xvii.
18 D. D. Devlin, *Jane Austen and Education* (London and Basingstoke: Macmillan, 1975), 2.
19 Ibid.
20 Devlin, *Jane Austen and Education*, 22. Reproduced with permission of Palgrave Macmillan.
21 Devlin, *Jane Austen and Education*, 2. Reproduced with permission of Palgrave Macmillan.

of vision'[22] overlooks, however, a key factor: the distinction between 'will not tell' and 'cannot tell' that Austen negotiates through the didactic language of physiognomy.[23] Whereas *Sense and Sensibility*'s Lucy Steele does not choose to speak of her attachment to Edward Ferrars for over three years, Elinor Dashwood cannot express the effect that this disclosure has on her.

Glenda Hudson also explores the correlation in Austen between ethics and clear sight. She contends in *Sibling Love and Incest in Jane Austen's Fiction* (1999) that Austen's use of the courtship novel allowed her to alter the imbalances between male and female power through what she proposes are literally 'incestuous' couples.[24] While rejecting the notion of Austen's couples as incestuous, this chapter shares Hudson's view that the novelist esteems ideological compatibility over sexual attraction in marriage. To borrow Hudson's phrase, 'She posits a system of relations between individuals based on a hierarchy of moral qualities'.[25] Applying this framework to Austen's use of aesthetics, I look at the interconnected roles of portraiture and architecture in showing the reader that the novelist's ideal view of marriage elevates 'companionship' as a form of sexual attraction.

The pedagogical implications of portraiture, landscape and architecture have continued to occupy a vital place in Austen scholarship but not in discussions relating to the marriage plot. Duckworth's *Improvement of the Estate: A Study of Jane Austen's Novels* (1971), for instance, considers the analogous themes of social improvement and the picturesque in Austen's fiction. His analysis of the tendency towards 'relativistic impressionism', or landscape's subjective influence on individuals, remains insightful in the twenty-first century, presenting a theme that I reconsider in the context of portraiture.[26] In 'The Influence of Place: Jane Austen and the Novel of Social Consciousness' (1981), Ann Banfield departs from the themes that Duckworth discusses. Her focus lies in elucidating the novelist's departure from the Gothic tradition: 'place' reverts from the sublime and the beautiful to the English country house and the English landscape.[27] The role of what Banfield refers to as 'the shaping hand

---

22 Ibid., 3.
23 Refer to my Introduction for a discussion on Thompson's argument in relation to visuality.
24 Glenda Hudson, *Sibling Love and Incest in Jane Austen's Fiction* (Basingstoke: Palgrave Macmillan, 1999), 107.
25 Hudson, *Sibling Love and Incest in Jane Austen's Fiction*, 107. Reproduced with permission of Palgrave Macmillan.
26 Duckworth, *The Improvement of the Estate*, 10 and 40.
27 Ann Banfield, 'The Influence of Place: Jane Austen and the Novel of Social Consciousness', in *Jane Austen in a Social Context*, ed. David Monaghan (Totowa, NJ: Barnes and Noble, 1981), 28–40 (35).

or eye' is a notion that I examine from an alternate angle: the eye of the owner of a place reforms the viewer's perceptions and, by extension, the reader's perception of the viewer's prejudices.[28]

Criticism pertaining to landscape and architecture has also drawn attention to the 'place' of the heroine. Claire Lamont's 'Domestic Architecture' (2005), for instance, explores the depictions and descriptions of the heroine's home. She claims that Austen's explicit exposure of the interior organization of a residence compensates for the lack of detailed interior description in her novels.[29] From a complementary perspective, Barbara Britton Wenner's *Prospect and Refuge in the Landscape of Jane Austen* (2006) investigates how landscape trains the novelist's heroines by positioning them in the permeable 'continuum' that is neither outside nor inside.[30] Wenner suggests that 'the act of experiencing the landscape is a double one: helping the heroine – or, in this case, heroine-in-training – to interpret the world and to know her own "self", transforming both world and self'.[31] Lamont's and Wenner's arguments, while discerning, do not consider the continuum between interiors and exteriors as critical signifiers of characters' changing perspectives of others and themselves.

Other recent critics have touched upon the role of landscape in Austen's narrative technique but do so in passing. Bharat Tandon's *Jane Austen and the Morality of Conversation* (2003) analyses the relationship between habit and habitation in *Pride and Prejudice* and *Mansfield Park*. His account connects the moral connotations of the picturesque to the visibility of the self, asserting that prospects are *embodied* rather than 'static' visions.[32] Tandon's conclusion leads Janine Barchas to reason in *Matters of Fact in Jane Austen: History, Location and Celebrity* (2012) that the overlaps between the worlds of the author and her characters confirm Austen's recourse to polite metaphors that she achieves through the 'universal' language of physiognomy.[33]

Linked to discussions on the visibility of the self in Austen's novels are critiques of her characters' actual appearances. John Wiltshire's *Jane Austen and the Body: 'The Picture of Health'* (1992) is one of the few accounts that discusses the facial language of health as a form of cultural 'somatization' in Austen's texts. His discussion assumes that 'value exists only in appearance' and reads 'health

---

28 Ibid.
29 Claire Lamont, 'Domestic Architecture', in *Jane Austen in Context*, ed. Janet Todd (Cambridge: Cambridge University Press, 2005), 225–32 (229).
30 Barbara Britton Wenner, *Prospect and Refuge in the Landscape of Jane Austen* (Aldershot: Ashgate Publishing, 2006), 41.
31 Ibid.
32 See Tandon, *Jane Austen and the Morality of Conversation*, 184–86.
33 See Barchas, *Matters of Fact in Jane Austen*, 5–17.

and vigour as virtue' in connection with *Persuasion*.³⁴ Rather than drawing attention to somatic physiognomy, Joe Bray uses portraiture as a lens through which to contemplate visual definitions of character. In '*Belinda, Emma*, and the "Likeness" of the Portrait' (2011), he analyses portraiture's absorption of cultural anxieties about the truthfulness of appearances.³⁵ The 'untrustworthiness' of actual and artistic appearances inspires him to argue that Emma, like other heroines of her generation, must learn to negotiate the 'subjective slipperiness of interpretation'.³⁶ As Kathryn Sutherland agrees, portraits 'confront the issue of truthfulness of representation' much in the same way that biography does.³⁷ Bray's theory that the image 'often reflect[s] on the characters of those who observe them' is a premise that I return to in my analysis of the influence of subjectivity on physiognomic judgements.³⁸ Whereas Bray's article focuses on portraiture's role in *Emma*, I extend his discussion by offering a more panoramic study of Austen's novels that evaluates portraits as 'speaking characters'.

While many critiques, then, have pointed to Austen's need for visible indices of character, there remains much to explore regarding how portraits and places act as forces of perceptual and emotional change in her novels. During the late eighteenth and early nineteenth centuries, Johann Caspar Lavater's *Physiognomishche Fragmente* (1775–78) permeated the cultural consciousness of Austen's times.³⁹ The illustrated volumes of his *Essays on Physiognomy: Designed to Promote the Knowledge and Love of Mankind* (1789) presented a philosophy of association between visible features and inner character.⁴⁰ Lavater's examination

---

34 John Wiltshire, *Jane Austen and the Body: 'The Picture of Health'* (Cambridge: Cambridge University Press, 1992), 13 and 162–63. His discussion frequently cites the psychiatrist and anthropologist Arthur Kleiman.
35 Joe Bray, '*Belinda, Emma* and the "Likeness" of the Portrait', *Nineteenth-Century Contexts* 33, no. 1 (February 2011): 1–15 (1).
36 Ibid., 13.
37 Kathryn Sutherland, *Jane Austen's Textual Lives: From Aeschylus to Bollywood* (Oxford: Oxford University Press, 2005), 11. See also Richard Brilliant, *Portraiture* (London: Reaktion Books Ltd., 1991), 13; for David Piper, the evidence of portraits is always 'loaded', offering the 'record of a dialogue between sitter and artist' and subsequently extending to the 'beholder' (*Personality and the Portrait* (London: BBC Publications, 1973), 2).
38 Bray, '*Belinda, Emma* and the "Likeness" of the Portrait', 1.
39 Refer to Graeme Tytler, *Physiognomy in the European Novel: Faces and Fortunes* (Princeton, NJ: Princeton University Press, 1982), 126.
40 See Joan K. Stemmler, 'The Physiognomical Portraits of Johann Caspar Lavater', *Art Bulletin* 75, no. 1 (March 1993): 151–88. For an introduction to the interdisciplinary dynamic of physiognomic theory, see Ellis Shookman's 'Pseudo-Science, Social Fad, Literary Wonder: Johann Caspar Lavater and the Art of Physiognomy', in *The Faces of Physiognomy: Interdisciplinary Approaches to Johann Caspar Lavater* (Columbia, SC: Camden House, 1993) and Sharrona Pearl's *About Faces: Physiognomy in Nineteenth-Century Britain* (Cambridge, MA: Harvard University Press, 2010).

of the ideological implications of 'beauty and deformity'[41] is valuable to an analysis of the affective force of physiognomy in Austen's formation of companionate couples. By removing physiognomic interpretation to surfaces external to the self, Austen allows her fictional women, like her men, to gain clear sight. Attuned to the relationship between outward appearance and inner truth, the reader of the novel learns to see the ways in which characters' vision and perception change through the conflicting forces of subjectivity and internal persuasion.

Austen surveyed the characters of her surroundings with an artist's eye and was influenced by physiognomic trends in depiction. As Lavater explained, 'physiognomy is a poetic feeling', and the true artist, whatever his medium, must maintain physiognomic consistency to communicate.[42] Henry Austen recalled that his sister Jane '"had not only an excellent taste for drawing, but, in her earlier days, evinced great power of hand in the management of the pencil."'[43] She and her sister Cassandra had drawing lessons, most likely from John-Claude Nattes (1765–1822), who was one of the most successful watercolourists in Bath at the time.[44] Nattes's *Sydney Hotel: The Garden Façade* (1805) features a view of the rear of the building from Sydney Gardens and displays the structure's prominent Ionic columns framing the figure of Apollo.[45] The hand-coloured aquatint of a scene that Austen would have encountered exhibits elegant men and women in the midground. Their appearances comply with the well-proportioned simplicity of Charles Harcourt Master's structure. During the early nineteenth century, fashions were changing to favour full-length silhouettes in accordance with landscape trends, allowing individuals to blend into scenes displaying similar values. Based on the subject matter for which Nattes was renowned, it can be assumed that Jane and Cassandra would have executed landscape paintings under his instruction. In learning to paint, the young novelist was trained to see the physiognomic relationships in her surroundings. Her novels' reliance on physiognomies as universal indices of character shows that she, like Lavater and Nattes, was intrigued by the visual relationship between people's appearances and the look of landscapes.

---

41 John Caspar Lavater, *Essays on Physiognomy for the Promotion of the Knowledge and Love of Mankind*, trans. Thomas Holcroft, 3 vols., 5 bks. ([1775–78] London: John Murray, 1789–98), 1.1: 175.
42 Tytler, *Physiognomy in the European Novel*, 181.
43 David Selwyn, *Jane Austen and Leisure* (London: Hambledon Press, 1999), 78.
44 Ibid. The Holburne Museum in Bath houses a selection of his architectural views of the city.
45 John Nattes, *Sydney Hotel: The Garden Façade* (c. 1805), no. A296, Holburne Museum of Art, Bath (UK).

The trend for silhouettes, the invention of Etienne de Silhouette (1709–1769), followed the publication of Lavater's *Physiognomische Fragmente* and endured until the advent of photography in 1860.[46] Peggy Hickman draws attention to Austen's personal familiarity with silhouettes. She notes that Jane and her family sat for four leading profilists: Mrs Harrington (appointed by the Royal family), Mrs Collins, John Miers and William Wellings.[47] Like Miers, the most successful profilist of the period, Austen sought to produce verbal 'shades' that ' "convey the most forcible expression of character" '.[48] Hickman also proposes the existence of a self-portrait. She explains that the likeness resurfaced in 1936 when Miss Jessie Lefroy, Jane's great-grandniece, presented Winchester Cathedral with a manuscript poem and silhouette, which bears the inscription 'done by herself in 1815'.[49] For Lavater, the silhouette, or shade, made the essence of character visible:

> The silhouette exhibits only a single line of the figure which it represents. We see in it neither motion, nor light, nor colour, nor rising, nor cavity: the eyes, the ears, the nostrils, the cheeks – all this is lost; nothing appears but a small part of the lips – and this feeble sketch is not the less on that account, possessed of infinite expression.[50]

Austen's habit of eschewing detail when describing characters' appearances indicates her preference for using a single telling line that, like the silhouette, supplies 'infinite expression' through a profile that is not overshadowed by the particulars within it.

Not only was Austen 'successful in everything that she attempted with her fingers' but she was also an admirer of art and an avid social observer.[51] In London, she frequented watercolour exhibitions, the British Gallery and Somerset-House.[52] For her, the spectators were more interesting than the subjects on display: 'Her preference for Men & Women, always [inclined her] to attend more to the company than the sight'.[53] She nevertheless

---

46 Tytler, *Physiognomy in the European Novel*, 56–58.
47 Honoria D. Marsh and Peggy Hickman, *Shades from Jane Austen* (London: Parry Jackman, 1975), xv–xxii.
48 Ibid.
49 Ibid. Hickman explains that the golden age of the silhouette spanned from 1760 to 1860. Sittings for a 'shade' lasted only a few minutes, and the framed finished piece cost 'only between half-a-crown and a guinea'.
50 Lavater, *Essays on Physiognomy*, 2.1: 176.
51 Selwyn, *Jane Austen and Leisure*, 65.
52 Ibid.
53 Ibid., 68.

found specimens of interest by Francis Nicholson and his contemporaries at the May 1813 exhibition of the Society of Painters in Oil and Water Colours at Spring Gardens.[54] The 'likenesses' that the novelist recounted to Cassandra help explain her approach to depicting the fictional characters in her novels:

> It is not thought a good collection, but I was very well pleased – particularly (pray tell Fanny) with a small portrait of Mrs Bingley, excessively like her. I went in hopes of seeing one of her Sister, but there was no Mrs Darcy; – perhaps however, I may find her in the Great Exhibition [at Somerset House] which we shall go to, if we have time; – I have no chance of her in the collection of Sir Joshua Reynolds's Paintings which is now shewing in Pall Mall, & which we are also to visit. – Mrs Bingley's is exactly herself, size, shaped face, features & sweetness; there never was a greater likeness. She is dressed in a white gown, with green ornaments, which convinces me of what I had always supposed, that green was a favourite colour with her. I dare say Mrs D. will be in Yellow.[55]

In *Pride and Prejudice*, Mr Bingley observes that Elizabeth is 'very pretty'.[56] Mr Darcy, meanwhile, looks upon her with condescension: 'he looked for a moment at Elizabeth, till catching her eye, he withdrew his own and coldly said, "She is tolerable; but not handsome enough to tempt me."'[57] Austen's letters show that she enjoyed picturing her characters with visual exactitude regarding taste and colour; however, in her novels, much of the description of characters' physical appearances uses general terms, empowering readers to imagine the particulars for themselves.

Austen's use of an aesthetic vocabulary of character in her fiction directs the reader's attention to the act of viewing and its ultimate subjectivity in creating couples united in their affections. In his allusion to Lavater's physiognomic theories, Ludwig Wittgenstein explained,

> Let us imagine a picture story in schematic pictures, and thus more like the narrative in a language than a series of realistic pictures [...] Let us remember too that we don't have to translate such pictures into realistic

---

54 Marsh and Hickman, *Shades from Jane Austen*, xv–xxii.
55 Jane Austen, 'To Fanny', 24 May 1813, *Jane Austen's Letters, New Edition*, ed. Deirdre Le Faye (Oxford: Oxford University Press, 1995), 212–13. Reprinted by permission of Oxford University Press.
56 Austen, *Pride and Prejudice*, 12.
57 Austen, *Pride and Prejudice*, 12. © Cambridge University Press 2006, reproduced with permission.

ones in order to 'understand' them, any more than we ever translate photographs or film pictures into coloured pictures, although black-and-white men or plants in reality would strike us as unspeakably strange and frightful.[58]

The novelist's reliance on schematic verbal pictures 'speaks' in a way that, while 'realistic' in the reader's mind's eye, would be 'unspeakably strange and frightful' in actuality. In literature and art, understanding comes through the reader's habituation to categorical communication.

As writers of conduct literature, from the radical Mary Hays to the conservative James Fordyce, agreed, enduring affection in marriage depended on the union of minds more than sexual or financial attraction.[59] In 1809, the anonymous moralist of *The Whole Duty of Woman or A Guide to the Female Sex* advised women to exercise the 'eye of reason' when selecting a partner:

> Comply not to give your heart before you have well weighed and advised what you are about to undertake. Let not love blind you, but make your choice with the eye of reason [...] Consider not of riches and a high birth so much as of virtue and agreeableness.[60]

Writing in a complementary vein, the *New Guide to Matrimony*, published the same year, proposed that the 'NICE MAN's' inner virtue was evident in his commitment to maintaining his physical image:

> If the man you contemplate have thick red lips, he will be simple, good-natured and easily managed [...] If he speak quick but distinct, and walk firm and erect, he will be ambitious, active, and probably a good husband [...] If he be what is termed a NICE MAN, he will not have dirty nails, dirty shoes, a cravat soiled and hair like brush-wood: his stockings will be tight, his apparel dusted, and his gait not as if his limbs were at variance with his body.[61]

---

58 Ludwig Wittgenstein, *Zettel*, ed. G. E. M. Anscombe and G. H. von Wright (Berkeley: University of California Press, 1970), 241–42. © 1967 Basil Blackwell. Reprinted with permission of Wiley.

59 On affectionate marriages in conduct literature, see Vivien Jones's '"The Coquetry of Nature": Politics and the Picturesque in Women's Fiction', in *The Politics of the Picturesque: Literature, Landscape and Aesthetics*, ed. Stephen Copley and Peter Garside (Cambridge: Cambridge University Press, 1994), 120–44 (120–33).

60 Anon., *The Whole Duty of Woman or A Guide to the Female Sex* (Glasgow: W. M. Borthwick, 1809), 56–57.

61 Anon., *The New Guide to Matrimony* (London: T. Hughes, 1809), vii–viii.

Rather than adhering to these formulas for happy marriages, Austen uses physiognomy in a sophisticated way to emphasize moral qualities through physiognomic correlatives that remove the interpretation of character to portraits and places. While conduct books also advocated good moral qualities and habits, the novelist does not settle for their simplistic schemas for ideal character. The Crofts in *Persuasion*, for instance, represent a picture of happiness that is emblematic of the similar quality of 'feelings so in unison' that the novel's hero and heroine ultimately enjoy. Austen's visual technique shows the reader that even characters with discerning 'hazle eyes' can be blinded by the conduct book's visual prescription for 'a NICE MAN' and their own subjectivity.

The language of physiognomy serves a fundamental purpose in Austen's fiction and use of visuality: as a continuum linking visual and verbal modes of communication and understanding, it teaches her characters and readers how to see 'true' love. In his *Remarks on the Utility of Drawing and Painting* (1786), Richard Samuel emphasizes that '"in learning to draw, we LEARN TO SEE; and as all knowledge is acquired through the senses, whatever tends to improve any one of them, must be very beneficial to the mind"'.[62] As Lavater had postulated, 'Yes, the Physionomy [*sic*] is true, and its truth is incontestable. A single exterior line is clearly possessed of infinite expression – and if one line says so much, what must be the expressive power of a thousand, all uniting in the same face, which we are able to retrace, observe and study in so many different points of view?'[63] The more Austen's characters know one another and their moral worth, the more their appearances become invisible. By depicting her heroes and heroines as 'commonplace' silhouettes, she directs her characters and readers to portraits and places for a visible means of discrimination.

In tailoring her depictions of happy couples according to Lavater's physiognomic theories of portraiture, Austen circumvents social prescriptions for the politely sayable. In 1776, Lavater offered the following definition for the 'art of portrait painting': 'The presentation of a particular acting human being, or of a part of the human body – the communication, the preserving of his image; the art of saying in a moment all which one says of a partial form of human being and can really never say with words.'[64] His emphasis

---

62 See Selwyn, *Jane Austen and Leisure*, 77.
63 Lavater, *Essays on Physiognomy*, 2.1: 199.
64 Joan K. Stemmler, 'The Physiognomical Portraits of Johann Caspar Lavater', *The Art Bulletin* 75, no. 1 (March 1993): 151–88 (165). Reprinted by permission of Taylor & Francis Ltd, http://www.tandfonline.com. This is Stemmler's literal translation of the German in *Fragmente*, 2: 79; *Physiognomie*, 2: 215; *Physiognomy*, 2: 240. Henry Hunter offers a slightly different translation: 'It is the representation of a real individual, or of a part of his body only; it is the reproduction of our image; it is the art of presenting, on the first glance of the eye, the form of man, by traits, which it would be impossible to convey by words' (qtd. in Stemmler, 165).

on the communicative capacity of appearances helps to explain the way in which physiognomic portraits and places 'articulate' character in Austen's narratives, from Mr Darcy's portrait, with its expressive eyes, to Mansfield's feeling of being a home for Fanny. Since Austen is more concerned with the affective force of impressions than their details, it is hardly surprising that later novelists should have observed the unprepossessing appearances of her characters. Charlotte Brontë famously complained that 'no glance of a bright, vivid physiognomy' was to be found in Austen's descriptions; instead, her fiction presented 'an accurate daguerreotyped portrait of a commonplace face'.[65] Brontë did not recognize any use of Lavater in Austen because she treated physiognomy differently in her fiction. As Jonathan Crary explains, optical advances and changes in the visible world inspired nineteenth-century society's newfound appreciation for detail.[66] Changing perceptions of the level of detail deemed necessary to communicate made Austen's usage look subtler in comparison.

Love and Likenesses in *Sense and Sensibility*, *Emma* and *Pride and Prejudice*

In *Sense and Sensibility*, Austen uses a miniature to expose the one-sidedness of Lucy Steele's secret engagement. The sentimental significance of these tokens, together with their popularity, is evidenced by the number of practising miniaturists in England between 1790 and 1820, with at least 15 working in London alone.[67] In Austen's novel, Edward's extended absences from Lucy's side inspire him to provide her with a 'likeness' to keep her company. The weakness of the young lady's character overcomes her attempt to internalize the weight of their secret attachment. No longer able to conceal her engagement to Edward, she solicits a tête-à-tête with Elinor. Her confession presumes her confidante's sympathetic ear:

> 'Though you do not know him so well as me, Miss Dashwood, you must have seen enough of him to be sensible he is very capable of making a woman sincerely attached to him.'[68]

---

65 Charlotte Brontë, Letter to G. H. Lewes, 12 January 1848, *Life*, Gaskell (1857), 2: 52–54. Also quoted in Katie Halsey, *Jane Austen and Her Readers: 1786–1945* (London: Anthem Press, 2012), 101.
66 For a discussion on Crary's account of the 'optical revolution', refer to my Introduction.
67 Hazel Jones, *Jane Austen and Marriage* (London: Continuum Books, 2009), 72.
68 Austen, *Sense and Sensibility*, 150. © Cambridge University Press 2006, reproduced with permission.

Austen shows that both women are 'certain' of their views of Edward's undivided attachment. Without physiognomic proof, Elinor contends that she will remain in a state of disbelief:

> 'Engaged to Mr. Edward Ferrars! – I confess myself so totally surprised at what you tell me, that really – I beg your pardon; but surely there must be some mistake of person or name. We cannot mean the same Mr. Ferrars.'[69]

The novelist dramatizes Elinor's conviction that she – not Miss Steele – is the recipient of Edward's authentic affections. The ambiguity of invisible appearances compels Lucy to show rather than tell her lover's identity. Elinor's hopes ultimately rest on the homophonic duplicity of proper names.

The narrative moves from the invisible Mr Edward Ferrars to a visible 'likeness' of him. Austen uses the miniature's entrance in the scene to inspire a change in the way in which Elinor regards Edward's affections. Inviting her surprised companion to 'look at' a representation of his face, Miss Steele weakens 'the possibility of a mistake':

> Then taking a small miniature from her pocket, she added, 'To prevent the possibility of a mistake, be so good as to look at this face. It does not do him justice to be sure, but yet I think you cannot be deceived as to the person it was drew for. – I have had it above these three years.'[70]

The miniature's visual impact serves a greater function than calling to mind the minutiae of Edward's appearance. While Lucy concedes that the miniature cannot 'do him justice', it weakens Elinor's hopes for the possibility of benevolent deception: she cannot be 'deceived' when her companion has 'possessed' his image – a physiognomic correlative for his person – for over three years.

Austen moves from the 'trustworthiness' of the miniature to the untrustworthiness of its owner. For a woman who professes to be long attached to the original, Lucy is ironically not possessive of this sentimental token of Edward's affections. Insisting that Elinor look at 'the face', Lucy relinquishes the miniature. Elinor's 'allergic' reaction to the sight and touch of the painting articulates what her silence cannot:

---

69 Austen, *Sense and Sensibility*, 150. © Cambridge University Press 2006, reproduced with permission.
70 Austen, *Sense and Sensibility*, 151. © Cambridge University Press 2006, reproduced with permission.

when Elinor saw the painting, whatever other doubts her fear of a too hasty decision, or her wish of detecting falsehood might suffer to linger in her mind, she could have none of its being Edward's face. She returned it almost instantly, acknowledging the likeness.[71]

Austen shows that Elinor refuses to 'have' the likeness remain in her hands because she cannot 'have' it be Edward's face. She will only 'have' the original for herself. Through visuality, the novelist fills in the blanks in the scene, or that which Tandon describes as the omissions between the sayable and the unsayable in her prose.[72]

While Lavater contends that 'yes the Physionomy [sic] is true and truth is incontestable',[73] Austen uses the 'likeness' of Edward's 'true' character to achieve an ironic outcome: the miniature draws attention to the precariousness of the couple's engagement. Seizing upon the gap between transmission and reception, the novelist uses visuality to show that representations have a tendency to lie. As she later writes in *Emma*, 'Seldom, very seldom, does complete truth belong to any human disclosure; seldom can it happen that something is not a little disguised or a little mistaken.'[74] Although Edward has provided Lucy with his image, she is incapable of reciprocating:

'I have never been able [...] to give him my picture in return, which I am very much vexed at, for he has been always so anxious to get it!'[75]

Lucy's claim about Edward's 'anxiety' over not possessing a copy of his lover's image exhibits the one-sidedness of their relationship. Despite the four years that they have been engaged, Lucy has not made much of an effort to sit for her portrait. Her romantic apathy and insincere 'determination' suggest her inability to satisfy Edward's desires, material and immaterial.

Austen emphasizes that not all tokens of sentimental attachment have the same value. The couple's 'long-distance' separation has strengthened the visual and emotional rift between them; they ' "hardly meet above twice a-year" '.[76] While Lucy has the 'comfort' of her lover's miniature, Edward

---

71 Austen, *Sense and Sensibility*, 151. © Cambridge University Press 2006, reproduced with permission.
72 See Tandon's *Jane Austen and the Morality of Conversation* (London: Anthem Press, 2003), which offers a comprehensive study of the relationship between voice and voicelessness in the novelist's fiction.
73 Lavater, *Essays on Physiognomy*, 2.1: 199.
74 Austen, *Emma*, 470. © Cambridge University Press 2005, reproduced with permission.
75 Austen, *Sense and Sensibility*, 151. © Cambridge University Press 2006, reproduced with permission.
76 Ibid., 312.

remains 'uneasy'. Lucy portrays her lover as devoted and miserable in her absence, but the novelist's visual technique encourages readers to suspect that his uneasiness about the engagement arises from more than regret. In his eyes, locks of hair are not 'equal to a picture':

> 'Yes, *I* have one other comfort, in his picture; but poor Edward has not even *that*. If he had but my picture, he says he should be easy. I gave him a lock of my hair set in a ring when he was at Longstaple last, and that was some comfort to him, he said, but not equal to a picture.'[77]

Austen uses Lucy's resistance to having her likeness taken to imply that she wishes to conceal something about her character. Miss Steele's much-discussed reluctance implies that she has experienced a change of heart since Edward's portrait first came into her hands.

In *Sense and Sensibility*, Lucy's reference to 'poor Edward' speaks on more than a superficial level. Despite its affiliation with affections, the ring is but a 'cheap' likeness of the woman whose character it represents.[78] Even if it contains a lock of Lucy's hair – an extension of her actual person – it lacks the communicative potential that Lavater ascribes to the well-painted portrait:

> Every well painted portrait […] brings us acquainted with the soul and character of a particular individual. In it we see him think, feel, reason. We discern in it the peculiar character of his propensities, of his affections, of his passions; in a word the good and the bad qualities of his heart and mind. And in this respect the portrait is even still more expressive than Nature, in which nothing is permanent, where every thing is only a rapid succession of movements infinitely varied; rarely does Nature present the human face in a light so advantageous as a skilful Painter can procure for it.[79]

As sentimental as the ring that Miss Steele has given Edward may appear to the reader, it conceals the 'peculiar character of [her] propensities, [her] affections, of [her] passions' that the 'skilful Painter's' scrutiny of her physiognomy would otherwise convey. According to Graeme Tytler's analysis of Lavater's physiognomic theories, the hair can inform the viewer about a person's 'temperament, energy, sensibility and mental capacity' but not his affections.[80] The

---

77 Austen, *Sense and Sensibility*, 154. © Cambridge University Press 2006, reproduced with permission; emphasis in original.
78 On changing fashions and the rise of sentimental jewellery, see Eve Bertero's *Mode du XVIIIème siècle* (Paris: Editions Falbalas, 2009), 69.
79 Lavater, *Essays on Physiognomy*, 2.2: 241.
80 Tytler, *Physiognomy in the European Novel* 213.

portrait's superior expressive quality lies in its ability for self-expression at a time when the strictures on the seen and the unseen, the said and the unsaid scripted women's lives in fiction and in actuality.

Austen uses the absence of Lucy's 'image' to turn Elinor's attention to her companion's appearance. Perplexed at 'so unnecessary a communication',[81] Elinor hopes to 'discover something in her countenance' that would negate Lucy's words.[82] A 'skilful Painter' of landscapes in her own right, Elinor's hand–eye connection has taught her how to see physiognomic relationships, even if a man's written hand still has the capacity to deceive her.[83] She observes that 'Lucy's countenance suffered no change'.[84] Despite Miss Steele's propensity for revealing herself aloud, her determined illegibility and habit of visual concealment endures, encouraging her companion to suspect the veracity of her words. Elinor allows herself to entertain the idea that the miniature 'might have been accidentally obtained'; it bears no visible proof of being intended for Miss Steele.[85] Only a recent letter addressed in her rival's name – a physiognomic autograph – would make the truth of a 'positive engagement' irreconcilably apparent.[86] As Hazel Jones reminds us, a correspondence between lovers could only legitimately subsist under an actual engagement.[87]

Just as the miniature is revelatory of Edward's character, so, too, is his handwriting. Austen again draws the reader's attention to Lucy's mannerisms, appearing more 'careless' than 'casual' as she removes a letter from Edward from her pocket. Austen's technique of using the visual correlative exposes the inadequacies of language, the social habit of concealment and the tension between male and female modes of looking. Lucy persistently exposes visual objects that test the appearance of Elinor's emotional stability:

> 'You know his hand, I dare say, a charming one it is; but that is not written so well as usual. – He was tired, I dare say, for he had just filled the sheet to me as full as possible.'[88]

---

81 Austen, *Sense and Sensibility*, 152.
82 Ibid.
83 Ibid., 20.
84 Ibid., 152.
85 Austen, *Sense and Sensibility*, 154. © Cambridge University Press 2006, reproduced with permission.
86 Ibid.
87 Hazel Jones, *Jane Austen and Marriage*, 49.
88 Austen, *Sense and Sensibility*, 154. © Cambridge University Press 2006, reproduced with permission.

By applying Lavater's theories, it is clear that Austen assigns Edward's handwriting physiognomic implications. Like the silhouette, penmanship exercises the expressive potential of line: 'By fixing [the gaze] on the exterior contours alone, it simplifies the observation, which becomes by that more easy and more accurate – I say the observation, and consequently the comparison.'[89] The weight of the line, the roundness of the forms, and the proportions and regularity of the spacing wordlessly convey that which even the words themselves do not. However, as Tytler also observes in his reading of the *Fragmente*, Lavater warns his readers not to place implicit trust in handwriting because it can be easily feigned, a theme that Austen, like Frances Burney, uses to great effect.[90]

For Elinor, who sees with an artist's sensitivity to physiognomic relationships, the sight of Edward's handwriting confirms the nature of his affections. Austen uses the appearance of the woman's reaction, together with free indirect discourse, to create a 'dual voice' effect that informs the reader of the sight's impact on the young lady's emotions: 'Elinor saw that it *was* his hand, and she could doubt no longer.'[91] To borrow John Keats's phrase, Elinor witnesses 'This living hand, now warm and capable'.[92] Though Elinor is 'almost overcome – her heart sunk within her, and she could hardly stand', she resists the urge to drop her mask: 'she struggled so resolutely against the oppression of her feelings, that her success was speedy, and for the time complete'.[93] At the same time, the physiognomic forces at play alter Miss Dashwood's view of Edward: ' "When I see him again [...] I shall see him the husband of Lucy." '[94] Ironically, it is Elinor, who, as John Hardy puts it, 'does not wear her heart on her sleeve',[95] who owns an invisible and more powerful place in Edward's regard. As Marianne observes at the beginning of the novel, ' "though he admires Elinor's drawings very much, it is not the admiration of a person who can understand their worth [...] He admires as a lover, not as a connoisseur." '[96] He, like the other characters in the novel, must learn to see 'true

---

89 Lavater, *Essays on Physiognomy*, 2.1: 178.
90 Tytler, *Physiognomy in the European Novel*, 218.
91 Austen, *Sense and Sensibility*, 154. © Cambridge University Press 2006, reproduced with permission; emphasis in original.
92 For a discussion on Keats's poem, presumably addressed to Fanny Brawne, see Brooke Hopkins's 'Keats and the Uncanny: "This Living Hand"', *Kenyon Review* 11, no. 4 (Autumn 1989): 28–40.
93 Austen, *Sense and Sensibility*, 315–16. © Cambridge University Press 2006, reproduced with permission.
94 Austen, *Sense and Sensibility*, 329. © Cambridge University Press 2006, reproduced with permission.
95 John Hardy, *Jane Austen's Heroines* (London: Routledge & Kegan Paul, 1984), 34–35.
96 Austen, *Sense and Sensibility*, 19. © Cambridge University Press 2006, reproduced with permission.

worth' in order to recognize the superiority of inner beauty. The novelist's aesthetic technique throughout the course of the plot conveys to the reader that the physiognomies of characters resistant to visible change often conceal that which their correlatives exteriorize.

In *Emma*, as in *Sense and Sensibility*, Austen shows that portraits and affections are the centre of much physiognomic scepticism and misinterpretation. Her later courtship plot opens with one wedding, finishes with three and integrates another in the middle. Through an overt reliance on free indirect discourse, the novelist informs the reader that the heroine's ambitions for 'improving' Harriet Smith's character are image oriented, asserting the linkage between the aesthetic vocabulary of physiognomy and reputation. Emma attempts to arouse Mr Elton's affections by relying on the system that William Robson outlines in his *Grammigraphia* (1799):

> A system of appearance, which, by easy rules, communicates its principles, and shews how it is to be presented by lines; distinguishing the real figure in nature from the appearance, or shewing the appearance by the reality; rendering visual observation more correct and interesting; and proposing the pleasure, and universality of the science.[97]

Emma's objective in attempting a portrait of Harriet is to dictate a 'visual observation' that promotes a 'more correct and interesting' rendition of the original. The heroine decides upon the 'universal' language of line to persuade the viewer to see 'the appearance by the reality'. The irony in the novelist's aesthetic technique is that only the reader sees the reality of the scene that she invents.

Austen's method of visuality shows that in contrast to Emma, who tends to see character in terms of surfaces, Mr Knightley's perceptions are more ideologically inclined. It is Mrs Weston's rhetorical questioning and insistent praise of the heroine's image that alters his perspective, evoking in him an interest in Emma beyond a concern for her moral character:

> 'Such an eye! – the true hazel eye – and so brilliant! Regular features, open countenance, with a complexion – oh, what a bloom of full health, and such a pretty height and size! […] One sometimes hears of a child being the picture of health; and Emma always gives one the idea of being the complete picture of growing health. She is loveliness itself, Mr. Knightley, is she not?'[98]

---

97 William Robson, *Grammigraphia* (London: W. Wilson, 1799).
98 Austen, *Emma*, 39. © Cambridge University Press 2005, reproduced with permission.

Mrs Weston's ecstasies over Emma's superior beauty are, as Tytler suggests, similar to Lavater's more prosaic assessments of portraits.[99] By linking Emma's 'health' to her 'loveliness', Mrs Weston convinces Mr Knightley to see the heroine's 'bloom' as a 'complete picture' that embodies a correspondence between the visible and invisible dimensions of her character.

Emma's 'true hazel eye', like Austen's own, endows her with an unusual gift for physiognomic observation and manipulation, which in turn enhances the reader's understanding of the scene.[100] In the second volume of his *Physiognomy*, Lavater claims that hazel eyes 'are the more usual indication of a mind masculine, vigorous, and profound, just as genius, properly so called, is almost always associated with eyes of a yellowish cast bordering on hazel'.[101] He explains that '*blue* eyes announce more weakness, a character softer and more effeminate than *hazel* or *black* eyes.'[102] Emma applies the 'genius' of her 'hazle eye' by redesigning Harriet's image, visible and metaphorical, to attract a suitor of a greater social standing than Mr Robert Martin.

In *Emma*'s portrait-sitting scene, Austen's visual technique directs attention to the connection between the 'silhouette', which clarifies sight and understanding, and the irony of aesthetic 'improvements' to character. To succeed in her courtship manoeuvre, the heroine must elevate Harriet's social physiognomy by 'drawing out' a part of the young lady's character that does not actually exist. David Selwyn agrees, saying, 'Emma is an artist, re-creating Harriet before ever she gets out her pencils and paints.'[103] By forcing her pupil to reject Mr Martin, Emma begins to work upon Harriet's self-perceptions: '"I am sure you must have been struck by his awkward look and abrupt manner."'[104] Harriet's refusal of the man marks her increasing detachment from her feelings; she places her self, literally and metaphorically, in the heroine's 'skilled' hands. Even before Emma puts pencil to paper, Mr Elton's praise for the artist and her art are intrinsically blurred:

> 'You have given Miss Smith all that she required,' said he; 'you have made her graceful and easy. She was a beautiful creature when she came to you, but, in my opinion, the attractions you have added are infinitely superior to what she received from nature.'[105]

---

99 Tytler, *Physiognomy in the European Novel*, 311.
100 Austen, *Emma*, 544. Richard Cronin and Dorothy McMillan point out that Anna Lefroy, Austen's niece, remembered that the novelist had 'bright hazel eyes'.
101 Lavater, *Essays on Physiognomy*, 2.2: 338.
102 Ibid.; emphasis in original.
103 Selwyn, *Jane Austen and Leisure*, 82.
104 Austen, *Emma*, 32. © Cambridge University Press 2005, reproduced with permission.
105 Jane Austen, *Emma*, 43. © Cambridge University Press 2005, reproduced with permission.

Mr Elton finds that the 'attractions' that Emma has added have provided Harriet with an 'artificial' image that compensates for the faults of her 'natural' image. His second-person allusions to Emma tellingly outnumber his references to Miss Smith, suggesting the novelist is implicitly taking the moral position that nature is always superior to art.

In *Emma*, Austen reveals that for a young lady possessing Lavater's definition of 'the true hazel eye', Emma is ironically short-sighted. The heroine's subjectivity and misdirected internal persuasion have thwarted her attempts to draw and perceive appearances as they actually are. Rather than seeing through Mr Elton's rhapsodic praises of her 'art', Emma overlooks the possibility of ulterior motives. She acknowledges her 'usefulness' but refuses to accept responsibility for Harriet's 'natural' attractions aloud:

> 'I am glad you think I have been useful to her; but Harriet only wanted drawing out, and receiving a few, very few hints. She had all the natural grace of sweetness of temper and artlessness in herself. I have done very little.'[106]

The novelist's oxymoronic pairing of 'drawing' and 'artlessness' hints at the growing disconnect between Harriet's true self and the image that Emma draws for her. According to Lavater, 'hazel eyes' imply a masculine strength, explaining the heroine's determination to force her companion's character into the silhouette that she imagines for her.[107] At the same time, Emma's obsessive control over others' images and artful manipulation of their feelings illuminate her detachment from her own authentic feelings and self-perceptions.

The narrative progresses from the 'drawing out' of Harriet's character to the drama of drawing from life. While Samuel Johnson complained that portrait painting was an 'improper' employment for women, claiming that '"staring in men's faces, is very indelicate in a female"',[108] Emma's attempt to depict a woman reads as socially acceptable. The heroine–portraitist's rhapsodic exclamations and longing to attempt a portrait of Harriet attract Mr Elton's attention:

---

106 Jane Austen, *Emma*, 43. © Cambridge University Press 2005, reproduced with permission.
107 Lavater, *Essays on Physiognomy*, 2.2: 338.
108 See Angela Rosenthal, 'She's Got the Look! Eighteenth-Century Female Portrait Painters and the Psychology of a Potentially "Dangerous Employment"', in *Portraiture: Facing the Subject*, ed. Joanna Woodall (Manchester: Manchester University Press, 1997), 147–66 (147).

'What an exquisite possession a good picture of her would be! I would give any money for it. I almost long to attempt her likeness myself. You do not know it I dare say, but two or three years ago I had a great passion for taking likenesses, and attempted several of my friends, and was thought to have a tolerable eye in general. But from one cause or another, I gave it up in disgust. But really, I could almost venture, if Harriet would sit to me. It would be such a delight to have her picture!'[109]

Austen makes the reader of the novel see that Emma is deluded. The obsequious praise that the heroine receives for the portrait has clouded her internal persuasion; she does not consult her own conscience. Austen's figurative drama of sight and blindness reflects her religious background as the daughter of a clergyman and echoes Johnson's sceptical supposition that all human actions and perceptions are beset by the moral myopia of original sin.

Unlike Elinor, whose steady hand speaks of the solidity of her inner character, Emma's insecurity, ironic for someone possessing the 'true hazel eye', shows in her art. Emma notes that she 'was thought to have a tolerable eye' but gives up her 'great passion' because she lacks the will to 'labour':[110]

She had always wanted to do everything, and had made more progress both in drawing and music than many might have done with so little labour as she would ever submit to. She played and sang; – and drew in almost every style; but steadiness had always been wanting [...] She was not much deceived as to her own skill either as an artist or a musician, but she was not unwilling to have others deceived, or sorry to know her reputation for accomplishment often higher than it deserved.[111]

Emma's desire to create an attachment between Mr Elton and Harriet conquers her 'disgust' of taking likenesses. While she is repeatedly not 'unwilling' for her art to 'deceive' others, for she is not 'deceived' at her aim for the 'improvement' of her reputation, she lacks the internal persuasion 'not' to deceive others. Whereas physiognomic readings of Edward's character accelerate romantic entanglements in *Sense and Sensibility*, in *Emma*, Austen reverses gender roles, using physiognomy to convey matter that the limits of language and propriety would have precluded. Here, the man becomes the physiognomic interpreter and the woman the subject of physiognomic scrutiny.

---

109 Austen, *Emma*, 44. © Cambridge University Press 2005, reproduced with permission.
110 Ibid.
111 Austen, *Emma*, 45–46. © Cambridge University Press 2005, reproduced with permission.

In the portrait-sitting scene, Austen shows that Emma's reflections are tinged with the symptoms of self-love. The heroine's impassioned exclamations and deliberate vacillation effectively woo Mr Elton's visible encouragement. He stresses that the possession of Harriet's likeness would be a 'delight':

> 'Let me entreat you,' cried Mr. Elton; 'it would indeed be a delight! Let me entreat you, Miss Woodhouse, to exercise so charming a talent in favour of your friend. I know what your drawings are. How could you suppose me ignorant? Is not this room rich in specimens of your landscapes and flowers; and has not Mrs. Weston some inimitable figure-pieces in her drawing-room, at Randalls?'[112]

The 'exercise' of Miss Woodhouse's charming talent excites Mr Elton's imagination and induces his hyperbolic flattery and persistent entreaties. In eyeing a woman of superior social standing, he courts the notion of 'improving' his own image through matrimony.

While Emma approves of Mr Elton's *artistic* encouragement because it would improve her reputation as an accomplished woman, Austen's shift to free indirect discourse reveals the heroine's struggle to use the 'masculine' strength of her 'hazle eye' to direct his wandering gaze and 'raptures' to Harriet's face:

> Yes, good man! – thought Emma – but what has all that to do with taking likenesses? You know nothing of drawing. Don't pretend to be in raptures about mine. Keep your raptures for Harriet's face. 'Well, if you give me such kind encouragement, Mr. Elton, I believe I shall try what I can do. Harriet's features are very delicate, which makes a likeness difficult; and yet there is a peculiarity in the shape of the eye and the lines about the mouth which one ought to catch.'[113]

Emma seeks to seduce Mr Elton for Harriet by dictating her companion's physiognomic attractiveness. In poeticizing the 'peculiarity in the shape of the eye and the lines about the mouth', Emma invites him to trace Harriet's physiognomic 'attractions' that 'one' – Mr Elton – 'ought to catch'. The man's aptitude for rhetoric and habit of recitation prompt him to repeat after her, '"The shape of the eye and the lines about the mouth."'[114] Although Tytler contends that nineteenth-century novelists 'rarely share Lavater's concern

---

112 Austen, *Emma*, 44–45. © Cambridge University Press 2005, reproduced with permission.
113 Austen, *Emma*, 45. © Cambridge University Press 2005, reproduced with permission.
114 Ibid.

with, say the angle, position, or contours of an eye, the complex geometrical proportions of a nose, or the particular arrangement of a set of teeth',[115] this episode suggests otherwise. Even if Austen does not specify the mathematical proportions of facial features, she draws upon Lavater's theory of the silhouette, which 'simplifies the observation' and allows for the communication of character, whether invented or actual.[116] While the silhouette clarifies the improved Harriet's appearance for each viewer, the perceptual clash that arises indicates the lack of a dialogic interchange between male and female aesthetic vocabularies.

Austen describes Emma as a woman who hesitates out of concern for her reputation as an artist. However, the reader sees the scene differently from those within the novel: the portrait brings Emma face-to-face with her love for praise and unwillingness to 'see' criticism of herself and others. The heroine's initial doubts about her inability 'after all her pains' to produce a 'very good likeness' in Mr Elton's eyes are ironically accurate, confirming that throughout the novel, men and women see and interpret the same sight differently. Emma's reference to her last commission, a portrait of Mr John Knightley, alerts the reader to the 'provocations' of portraiture and the frustrations of subjectivity:

> 'I could not help being provoked; for after all my pains, and when I had really made a very good likeness of it – (Mrs. Weston and I were quite agreed in thinking it very like) – only too handsome – too flattering – but that was a fault on the right side – after all this, came poor dear Isabella's cold approbation of – "Yes, it was a little like – but to be sure it did not do him justice."'[117]

Austen contrasts Emma's perspective of her impulse towards flattery with fragments of others' opinions of her art. The 'right-sidedness' of the heroine's fault suggests that she seeks to enhance appearances in order to please the eyes of the subject and the viewer. Whereas Mrs Weston and the heroine 'see' similarly, Jones points out that Isabella is the conduct book prototype for the unimaginative way in which a woman 'ought' to see.[118] Isabella's 'cold approbation' of Emma's enhancements to her husband's appearance impels the heroine to vow against taking another likeness if it were to be thus '"apologised over as an unfavourable likeness, to every morning visitor in

---

115 Tytler, *Physiognomy in the European Novel*, 208.
116 Lavater, *Essays on Physiognomy*, 2.2: 178.
117 Austen, *Emma*, 47. © Cambridge University Press 2005, reproduced with permission.
118 Hazel Jones, *Jane Austen and Marriage*, 122.

Brunswick-square"'.[119] For Emma, flattering the eye is more important to her courtship ambitions than is the 'likeness' of the likeness.

Austen leaves it up to the novel's audience to speculate which of the three women's physiognomic readings is closest to the truth. Austen subtly directs the reader by an indirect aesthetic means to guess whose view is the most accurate. According to Lavater, 'Sometimes the eye or the hand of the Painter is in fault; sometimes it lies with the person who sits to him; and sometimes both are to blame. The former sees not that which is, or is incapable of drawing what he sees; the latter is perpetually changing his situation'.[120] While Mrs Weston and Emma may have flattered themselves into deeming it an accurate likeness of Mr Knightley's brother, Isabella may have been deceiving her eyes, not wanting to see a dissimilar view of her husband. Since a 'correct' perspective of Harriet has yet to be drawn, Emma is convinced that she is pursuing a safe subject for depiction.

In *Emma*, Austen multiplies the probability of her characters' perceptual misinterpretation, emphasizing to the reader that not one but three women are on display. Emma encourages Mr Elton's attendance at the portrait sitting but continues to find it a 'labour' to control his gaze and subsequently his affections:

> But there was no doing anything, with Mr. Elton fidgetting behind her and watching every touch. She gave him credit for stationing himself where he might gaze and gaze again without offence; but was really obliged to put an end to it, and request him to place himself elsewhere. It then occurred to her to employ him in reading.[121]

The heroine views Mr Elton's attraction to her hand's 'every touch' – its physical contact with the paper – as particularly disconcerting. Even if he has instinctively 'stationed' himself at a polite viewing distance, the scopic penetration that she feels more than sees continues to offend her. Contrary to Elizabeth Eger and Lucy Peltz's theory that the 'learned female was still less of a threat if she could be admired almost like a work of art',[122] Emma is determined not to be viewed by Mr Elton as such. Only by employing his eyes in reading another text can she relieve herself of his unwanted attentions.

Austen's visual approach makes the true situation visible to the attentive reader, who is following Mr Elton's gaze better than Emma can. Emma's belief

---

119 Austen, *Emma*, 47. © Cambridge University Press 2005, reproduced with permission.
120 Lavater, *Essays on Physiognomy*, 2.2: 246.
121 Austen, *Emma*, 48. © Cambridge University Press 2005, reproduced with permission.
122 Eger and Peltz, *Brilliant Women*, 48–49.

that the more Mr Elton looks at Harriet – the woman and the portrait – the more the two physiognomies and characters will blend together is an optical delusion. 'By making the fairness of the body the sign of the mind's purity', the *Mirror of Graces* wrote, 'man is imperceptibly attracted to the object designed for him by heaven as the partner of his life, the future mother of his children, and the angel which is to accompany him into eternity'.[123] When Mr Elton observes a likeness of the 'fairness of the body' before one has been drawn, Emma believes that her technique of affecting his interest in Harriet is working. Ironically, Mr Elton sees the opposite of what Emma wishes him to see. He observes in the portrait more of Emma's 'skilful hand' than Harriet's face – a risk that Lavater discusses in his rankings of 'likenesses'.[124] As *Bowles's Drawing Book for Ladies* similarly warns, drawing 'represents things to us in such pleasant resemblances, that we are apt to imagine we see things which we really do not'.[125] From Emma's subjective viewpoint, she is persuaded to believe that 'there was no being displeased with such an encourager, for his admiration made him discern a likeness almost before it was possible'.[126] Her bigoted perspective prevents her from detecting from Mr Elton's gaze the actual object of his flattery.

The duality of the portrait that Austen exaggerates in *Emma* further calls to mind Richard Samuel's *Portraits in the Characters of the Muses in the Temple of Apollo (The Nine Living Muses of Great Britain)*. Samuel's tableau depicts Angelica Kauffmann as the artist at her easel, modelling as Urania, Muse of Astronomy, 'universal vision' and therefore courtship.[127] Even if Emma is not posing like Kauffmann, the scene humorously invokes a similar reading. As Richard Handler and Daniel Segal suggest, Austen's narrative skill in the episode lies in her construction of contrasting stories from multiple viewpoints 'that nonetheless must be told together'.[128] Their assertion about multiple views and voices is, as Tytler proposes, inherent in the post-Lavaterian portrait:

---

123 Anon., *The Mirror of Graces or The English Lady's Costume* (London: B. Crosby, 1811), 131.
124 Lavater, *Essays on Physiognomy*, 2.2: 248–49.
125 Quoted in Selwyn, *Jane Austen and Leisure*, 77.
126 Austen, *Emma*, 48. © Cambridge University Press 2005, reproduced with permission.
127 For a detailed discussion on Samuel's 1778 oil on canvas, see Eger and Peltz, *Brilliant Women*, 60–63. The profound similarity of the women's appearances makes them impossible to discern, even for the women that it depicted. As Elizabeth Carter complained, 'by the mere testimony of my eyes, I cannot very exactly tell which is you, and which is I, and which is anybody else' (61). Eger and Peltz observe that the tableau went unremarked at the exhibition in 1779. In contrast, the 1777 etching on which it was based proved more successful. Unlike the oil painting, the faces on the etching are clearly labelled (61–62).
128 Richard Handler and Daniel Segal, *Jane Austen and the Fiction of Culture* (Tucson: Arizona University Press, 1990), 134.

perhaps the most important development is the tendency to describe characters not from the viewpoint of a first- or third-person narrator alone, as is common in the novel before 1800, but from the double viewpoint of both narrator and an observing character, a procedure that undoubtedly lends the portrait a certain dramatic interest, especially if the narrator has already said that the observing character's attention has been aroused by the appearance of the person about to be describe.[129]

For Bray, the double viewpoint and 'the Addition of Character' recall the longstanding eighteenth-century debate over the trustworthiness of the likeness.[130] In enhancing Harriet's invisible and visible attractiveness, Emma is wrongly convinced of her ability to determine the internal persuasions of others.

Austen's physiognomic vocabulary of character confirms Emma's aim in reconciling the sitter's actual appearance with William Combe's 'Addition of Character'.[131] Physiognomic 'improvements' improve the impact that the impression theoretically makes in the viewer's eyes:

> There was no want of likeness, she had been fortunate in the attitude, and as she meant to throw in a little improvement to the figure, to give a little more height, and considerably more elegance, she had great confidence of its being in every way a pretty drawing at last, and of its filling its destined place with credit to them both – a standing memorial of the beauty of one, the skill of the other, and the friendship of both; with as many other agreeable associations as Mr. Elton's very promising attachment was likely to add.[132]

While the sitter of the full-length watercolour is recognizable, the shift to free indirect discourse reveals that changes had to be made, particularly with regards to Harriet's deficiency in 'elegance', in order for Emma to produce a portrait that was 'in every way a pretty drawing'.[133] Lavater claims that 'disproportion in the parts of the face has an influence on the physiological constitution of man; it decides concerning his moral and intellectual imperfections'.[134] For Austen, 'greatness' becomes the result of benevolent 'disproportion'. Emma's attempt to exhibit Harriet's 'prettiness' is ironically self-destructive,

---

129 Tytler, *Physiognomy in the European Novel*, 186.
130 Bray, '*Belinda, Emma*, and the "Likeness" of the Portrait', 7.
131 Ibid.
132 Austen, *Emma*, 48–49. © Cambridge University Press 2005, reproduced with permission.
133 Ibid., 48.
134 Lavater, *Essays on Physiognomy*, 3.2: 271.

for it displays the heroine's abuse of her superior artistic power. The portrait corrupts the sitter's self-perceptions by convincing her to have feelings that are not her own.

Just as Emma's portrait of her brother-in-law elicits subjective reactions, Harriet's likeness receives conflicting reviews from characters in the text. The bluntest criticism comes from Mr Knightley: '"You have made her too tall, Emma."'[135] Rather than echoing Mr Knightley's negative critique, Mr Elton chivalrously defends the accuracy of Harriet's physiognomic proportions:

> 'Oh, no! certainly not too tall; not in the least too tall. Consider, she is sitting down – which naturally presents a different – which in short gives exactly the idea – and the proportions must be preserved, you know. Proportions, fore-shortening. – Oh, no! it gives one exactly the idea of such a height as Miss Smith's. Exactly so indeed!'[136]

The man's stuttered self-corrections signal to Austen's readers that he does not mean what he says, despite his melodramatic tone. Sensing the absurdity of his words, Mr Elton makes another attempt at eloquent flattery, using '"proportions, fore-shortening"' as the physiognomic basis of his argument.[137] His antics exemplify Bray's theory that textual images 'often reflect on the characters of those who observe them'.[138] Through its exposé of perceptual differences, the novelist's visual technique presents Mr Knightley, more than Emma, as the moral centre of the novel. His perspective, though imperfect, comes closer to the truth than does any other character's, pointing to the novelist's position on aesthetic values and gender politics.

In *Emma*'s portrait-sitting scene, Austen continues to emphasize the subjectivity of visual interpretation and the lack of a dialogic interchange between male and female aesthetic vocabularies. Whereas Mr Elton asserts the mathematical accuracy of Harriet's portrait, Mrs Weston is drawn to the lifelike expressiveness of Harriet's face. As much as she and the heroine tend to see alike, only Emma interprets Mr Elton's motions as indicative of his growing attachment to Harriet:

> 'Miss Woodhouse has given her friend the only beauty she wanted', – observed Mrs. Weston to him – not in the least suspecting that she was addressing a lover. – 'The expression of the eye is most correct, but Miss

---

135 Austen, *Emma*, 49. © Cambridge University Press 2005, reproduced with permission.
136 Jane Austen, *Emma*, 49. © Cambridge University Press 2005, reproduced with permission.
137 Ibid.
138 Bray, '*Belinda, Emma* and the "Likeness" of the Portrait', 1.

Smith has not those eye-brows and eye-lashes. It is the fault of her face that she has them not.'[139]

Mrs Weston finds that while Emma has captured the essence of the character – the expression of Harriet's eye – she has beautified nature in order to compensate for physiognomic deficiencies. To borrow Lavater's definition, it is the '*ideal representation of the [wo]man*': 'Here all is flattery, embellishment, heightening. The painter has thought only of bringing forward the beauties of the original and has skimmed too lightly over its defects.'[140] Emma has sought to create a vision of Harriet that reflects her ambition to improve her own 'image' through her enhanced representation of her companion's appearance.

Austen does not, as Hardy claims, blind Emma with Mr Elton's preaching of her artistic perfection.[141] The novelist's heroine with the 'true hazel eye' perceives the symptoms of deceptive gallantry: ' "he does sigh and languish, and study for compliments rather more than I could endure as a principal" '.[142] Emma's sole consolation is that if ' "there may be a hundred different ways of being in love" ', there must be as many ways of appearing to be in love.[143] Mr Elton reassures her, exclaiming, ' "I cannot keep my eyes from it. I never saw such a likeness." '[144] The heroine's conviction that her 'pretty drawing' has mesmerized him blinds her, leading her to believe that the portrait will foster an attachment to the original. Austen dramatizes the irony of subjective gazes in the scene. Emma does not see that the 'pretty drawing' in her hand reads on more than one level. For Mr Elton, Harriet's likeness is an extension of Emma's self rather than a representation of her 'nobody' companion. Lavater's premise of disproportion ironically does not affect Harriet's 'greatness' in his eyes.

Whereas Austen uses portraits to complicate romantic entanglements in *Sense and Sensibility* and *Emma*, in *Pride and Prejudice*, they transform prejudices in a way that convinces the reader of the affectionate attachment between Elizabeth Bennet and Fitzwilliam Darcy. The novelist introduces the subject of 'likenesses' when the pair dance together at the Netherfield ball. Darcy's inability to express himself perpetuates their strained dialogue.[145] While John Richetti contends that 'the heights of emotional inexpressibility' defined

---

139 Austen, *Emma*, 49. © Cambridge University Press 2005, reproduced with permission.
140 Lavater, *Essays on Physiognomy*, 2.2: 247; emphasis in original.
141 Hardy, *Jane Austen's Heroines*, 85.
142 Austen, *Emma*, 51. © Cambridge University Press 2005, reproduced with permission.
143 Ibid.
144 Ibid., 50. © Cambridge University Press 2005, reproduced with permission.
145 Austen, *Pride and Prejudice*, 197.

the 'female moment',[146] Darcy attributes his 'arrogance' to his unflinching reserve: '"I certainly have not the talent"', he remarks, '"which some people possess of conversing easily with those I have never seen before."'[147] As Mrs Bennet had earlier remarked, ' "Mrs. Long told me last night that he sat close to [Lizzy] for half an hour without once opening his lips." '[148] The reader knows that Darcy has indeed 'seen' Elizabeth on a number of occasions between the Meryton and Netherfield balls and that he has yet to see her actual character.

Austen uses Darcy's inability to communicate and Elizabeth's determined misinterpretation of his character to define the tension that the plot must use the affective forces of physiognomic portraiture and places to resolve. The novelist's choreography of social interaction at the Netherfield ball shows that had it not been for Sir William's interruption, the peace between the pair might have been longer lived.[149] Elizabeth acknowledges the poor success of the subjects that they have attempted to discuss and contends that '"what we are to talk of next I cannot imagine"'.[150] Despite the couple's antagonistic chemistry and Elizabeth's desire to prolong the verbal strain that thwarts their mutual understanding, Austen emphasizes that the hero and heroine must continue their show of communication, for it would 'look odd' to gossip-hungry gazes if they did not:

> 'One must speak a little, you know. It would look odd to be entirely silent for half an hour together, and yet for the advantage of *some*, conversation ought to be so arranged as that they may have the trouble of saying as little as possible.'[151]

Austen's readers observe that pleasantries and metacommunication complicate the heroine's efforts to form a clear picture of her partner's character. As Elizabeth remarks, ' "No – I cannot talk of books in a ball-room; my head is always full of something else." '[152] That 'something else' to which she refers

---

146 John J. Richetti, 'Voice and Gender in Eighteenth-Century Fiction: Haywood to Burney', *Studies in the Novel* 19, no. 3, Women and Early Fiction (Fall 1987): 263–72 (269).
147 Austen, *Pride and Prejudice*, 197.
148 Austen, *Pride and Prejudice*, 20. © Cambridge University Press 2006, reproduced with permission.
149 Ibid., 104.
150 Austen, *Pride and Prejudice*, 104. © Cambridge University Press 2006, reproduced with permission.
151 Austen, *Pride and Prejudice*, 102. © Cambridge University Press 2006, reproduced with permission; emphasis in original.
152 Austen, *Pride and Prejudice*, 104. © Cambridge University Press 2006, reproduced with permission.

is the deciphering of Mr Darcy's character. '"It is particularly incumbent on those who never change their opinion"', Elizabeth warns him, '"to be secure of judging properly at first."'[153] Knowingly or unknowingly, Austen echoes Lavater, who proposes that 'An imperfect knowledge of a Man is the foundation for Intolerance. When we know why such a man thinks and acts as he does – that is to say, when we put ourselves in his place – or rather, when we know how to appropriate to ourselves, in idea, the structure of his body [...] do not all his actions more easily explain themselves?'[154] Only by putting herself in Darcy's place at Pemberley can Elizabeth accommodate her perception of his character to reflect her new understanding of his motives.

Unlike Emma Woodhouse, Elinor Dashwood and the novelist, Elizabeth does not see with an artist's eyes. When Lady Catherine de Bourgh enquires whether she draws, Elizabeth shocks her in replying, '"No, not at all."'[155] While she has not received artistic instruction, the heroine proves herself to be a Lavaterian student of character, drawing mental sketches and illustrations with words. For the reader of the novel, the heroine's intentions for drawing out Darcy's character appear more social than 'artistic'. After his pointed questioning of Elizabeth at the Netherfield ball, Austen allows the heroine to reveal the artistic motive behind her persistent dialogue: '"Merely to the illustration of *your* character [...] I am trying to make it out."'[156] In view of the contrasting accounts that she has heard of the man's character, he puzzles her eyes. He is as vague visually as he is verbally. Darcy beseeches her to postpone her efforts, arguing, '"I could wish, Miss Bennet, that you were not to sketch my character at the present moment, as there is reason to fear that the performance would reflect no credit on either."'[157] Nonetheless, Austen makes her heroine's urge to draw patently apparent to the reader: '"But if I do not take your likeness now, I may never have another opportunity."'[158] The immaterial likeness that Elizabeth aims to produce is unachievable because she has not learned to draw and, as Robson proposes, see.

Through a sequence of artistic allusions – 'illustration', 'sketch' and 'likeness' – Austen blurs the distinction between the visual and the verbal portrait

---

153 Austen, *Pride and Prejudice*, 105. © Cambridge University Press 2006, reproduced with permission.
154 Lavater, *Essays on Physiognomy*, 2.1: 47.
155 Austen, *Pride and Prejudice*, 105.
156 Austen, *Pride and Prejudice*, 105. © Cambridge University Press 2006, reproduced with permission; emphasis in original.
157 Austen, *Pride and Prejudice*, 105. © Cambridge University Press 2006, reproduced with permission.
158 Austen, *Pride and Prejudice*, 105. © Cambridge University Press 2006, reproduced with permission.

in *Pride and Prejudice*. Elizabeth tries to 'sketch' Mr Darcy, but, like the reader, is unable to do so. At the same time, Austen prevents the heroine, who is too close to her work, from judging her own 'performance'. Elizabeth's and Darcy's sole resemblance lies in the turn of their minds:

> 'for I have always seen a great similarity in the turn of our minds. – We are each of an unsocial, taciturn disposition, unwilling to speak, unless we expect to say something that will amaze the whole room, and be handed down to posterity with all the eclat of a proverb.'[159]

Austen shows that Darcy remains sceptical. He finds it difficult to see the picture of their mental similarity that she offers: ' "This is no very striking resemblance of your own character, I am sure [...] How near it may be to *mine*, I cannot pretend to say. – *You* think it a faithful portrait undoubtedly." '[160] Their mutual taciturnity foreshadows the function of visuality and 'faithful' portraiture in their transformation in vision and perception.

To convince the reader of Elizabeth's and Darcy's changing affections, Austen advances the subject of the likeness to visible portraiture. In *Pride and Prejudice*, the novelist's visual technique emphasizes that Darcy must learn to look at Elizabeth as the portrait yet-to-be-pictured at Pemberley in order to appreciate her character. Rather than following Charlotte Lucas's advice of ' "showing more affection than she feels" ',[161] Elizabeth's words and mannerisms exaggerate her distaste for the man. Darcy's prejudiced conviction that she lacks 'a good feature in her face' yields once his subjectivity allows him to observe the way in which nature has 'rendered' her physiognomy.[162] He views the heroine the same way in which she looks at his canvassed character:[163]

> Mr. Darcy had at first scarcely allowed her to be pretty; he had looked at her without admiration at the ball; and when they next met, he looked at her only to criticise. But no sooner had he made it clear to himself and his friends that she had hardly a good feature in her face, than he began to find it was rendered uncommonly intelligent by the beautiful expression of her dark eyes. To this discovery succeeded some others equally mortifying. Though he had detected with a critical eye more than one

---

159 Austen, *Pride and Prejudice*, 103. © Cambridge University Press 2006, reproduced with permission.
160 Austen, *Pride and Prejudice*, 103. © Cambridge University Press 2006, reproduced with permission; emphasis in original.
161 Ibid., 24.
162 Ibid., 26.
163 Ibid.

failure of perfect symmetry in her form, he was forced to acknowledge her figure to be light and pleasing; and in spite of his asserting that her manners were not those of the fashionable world, he was caught by their easy playfulness. Of this she was perfectly unaware; – to her he was only the man who made himself agreeable no where, and who had not thought her handsome enough to dance with.[164]

Darcy's words and haughty air allow his 'mortifying' discovery of Elizabeth's 'expressive dark eyes' to remain unsuspected by his friends. As Tytler observes, Lavater maintains that blue eyes bespeak weakness, femininity and a melancholy temperament.[165] In contrast, Elizabeth's dark eyes imply physical and moral virility and 'uncommon intelligence'.[166]

In *Pride and Prejudice*, Austen links the heroine's inner and outer character to existing theories on the picturesque by rendering Elizabeth's 'light and pleasing' figure asymmetrical. Although Lavater contends in his *Physiognomy* that 'without regularity there can be no such thing as organized beauty', he concedes that 'the highest degree of *correctness* does not, after all constitute *beauty*, or, rather, is not sufficient of itself to determine a form to be beautiful'.[167] In line with Lavater's concession, William Gilpin's *Observations Relating Chiefly to Picturesque Beauty* (1786) and Sir Uvedale Price's *Essay on the Picturesque* (1796) showed how irregular features, whether in people or places, possessed a certain charm that made them desirable subjects for painting. A decade later, Richard Payne Knight similarly asserted that 'irregularity of appearance is generally essential to picturesque beauty'.[168] Elizabeth, unlike the majority of Burney's heroines, is innately attractive. Elizabeth is irregular – unusual – in various ways: her wit, her daring, her forthrightness. The novelist's use of a physiognomic vocabulary of character implies that these qualities, like picturesque scenery, have more loveliness to the trained eye than symmetry and conformity.

Austen's visual technique emphasizes that in Darcy's view, the heroine's unladylike but affectionate cross-country walk to Netherfield had improved her figure's picturesque quality and intensified the expressiveness of her eyes. The novelist calls on Miss Bingley's subjective perspective to alert the reader to the way in which the '"adventure"' that had made Elizabeth's hair '"so untidy, so

---

164 Austen, *Pride and Prejudice*, 25–26. © Cambridge University Press 2006, reproduced with permission.
165 Tytler, *Physiognomy in the European Novel*, 212.
166 Ibid.
167 Lavater, *Essays on Physiognomy*, 3.1: 18.
168 Richard Payne Knight, *An Analytical Inquiry into the Principles of Taste* (London: [n.p.], 1805), 196.

JANE AUSTEN'S AESTHETIC VOCABULARY OF CHARACTER

blowsy" and soiled her petticoat had '"rather affected"' his '"admiration of her fine eyes"'.¹⁶⁹ The allusions to picturesque beauty inspire Miss Bingley to turn her satirical comments to portraiture:

> 'Oh! yes. – Do let the portraits of your uncle and aunt Philips be placed in the gallery at Pemberley. Put them next to your great uncle the judge. They are in the same profession, you know; only in different lines. As for your Elizabeth's picture, you must not attempt to have it taken, for what painter could do justice to those beautiful eyes?'¹⁷⁰

Though joining Darcy's 'line' becomes an actual prospect for the heroine, it does not take place during the course of the novel. Austen's pun on the word links genealogy and painting, showing the reader how art captures and places the figure within a silhouette. While Darcy admits that it would be difficult to '"catch"' the expression of Elizabeth's eyes, much in the way that Pemberley would be difficult to imitate, he maintains that '"their colour and shape, and the eye-lashes, so remarkably fine, might be copied"'.¹⁷¹ The novelist's aesthetic technique encourages the reader to wish for a convergence of the four 'lines' at play – aesthetic and biological, male and female.

Miss Bingley turns from her prediction that a portrait of Elizabeth Bennet will be placed in the picture gallery at Pemberley to exciting Darcy's eyes by framing Elizabeth as a living portrait. The manoeuvre shifts his 'inflexibly studious' gaze from reading books to reading Elizabeth's moving silhouette:

> 'Miss Eliza Bennet, let me persuade you to follow my example, and take a turn about the room. – I assure you it is very refreshing after sitting so long in one attitude.'
>
> Elizabeth was surprised, but agreed to it immediately. Miss Bingley succeeded no less in the real object of her civility; Mr. Darcy looked up. He was as much awake to the novelty of attention in that quarter as Elizabeth herself could be, and unconsciously closed his book.¹⁷²

Austen strengthens Miss Bingley's subtle allusion to a portrait sitting by showing that Elizabeth moves from sitting in 'one attitude' to turning about. The

---

169 Austen, *Pride and Prejudice*, 39.
170 Austen, *Pride and Prejudice*, 57. © Cambridge University Press 2006, reproduced with permission.
171 Austen, *Pride and Prejudice*, 57. © Cambridge University Press 2006, reproduced with permission.
172 Austen, *Pride and Prejudice*, 61. © Cambridge University Press 2006, reproduced with permission.

novelist contrasts Darcy's unconscious attraction to Elizabeth's figure with the women's conscious awareness that their '"figures appear to the greatest advantage in walking"'.[173] The Reverend Thomas Gisborne, whose *Enquiry into the Duties of the Female Sex* Austen had read and claimed to enjoy, emphasized the warm feelings that a woman reputedly experienced when a man first singled her out: 'She beholds him with general approbation: she is conscious that there is no other person whom she prefers to him [...] Yet it is very possible that she maybe unacquainted with the real state of her heart.'[174] Even if the reader of the novel sees that Elizabeth and Darcy are awake to 'the novelty of attention' in the room, visual stimulation does not elicit their understanding of affections, including their own.

Following Elizabeth's initial rejection of Mr Darcy's affections, she is reluctant to join the Gardiners on their spontaneous visit to Pemberley. Once assured of the owner's absence, however, the heroine feels at liberty to explore what might have been her domestic domain. Austen choreographs the tour of Pemberley's interior in a way that hints to the reader that its windings will lead Elizabeth somewhere, literally and metaphorically. The novelist's insistence that 'Elizabeth knew nothing of art' explains the heroine's reliance on other women's perspectives to direct her gaze to pictures worthy of attention.[175] Austen first leads the party to a miniature of a man of disreputable character:

> Her aunt now called her to look at a picture. She approached, and saw the likeness of Mr. Wickham suspended, amongst several other miniatures, over the mantle-piece. Her aunt asked her, smilingly, how she liked it. The housekeeper came forward, and told them it was the picture of a young gentleman, the son of her late master's steward, who had been brought up by him at his own expence. – 'He is now gone into the army,' she added, 'but I am afraid he has turned out very wild.'[176]

Not being acquainted with Elizabeth's Mr Wickham, Mrs Gardiner judges the young gentleman according to his physiognomic attractiveness and the miniature's privileged position over the mantelpiece. In concealing rather than exteriorizing the man's inner self, the miniature allows the heroine to perceive how her eyes had allowed her to miscalculate his character.

---

173 Austen, *Pride and Prejudice*, 62.
174 Thomas Gisborne, *An Enquiry into the Duties of the Female Sex*, 9th ed. ([1797] London: T. Cadell, 1813), 258–59.
175 Austen, *Pride and Prejudice*, 276.
176 Austen, *Pride and Prejudice*, 273. © Cambridge University Press 2006, reproduced with permission.

Austen uses the direction of Elizabeth's gaze to show the reader that she is drawn to portraits of familiar faces, regardless of their artistic merit. After borrowing Mrs Gardiner's naive perspective to communicate the dangers of first impressions, the novelist shifts the narrative voice to Mrs Reynolds, whose surname wittingly implies that she possesses the physiognomic eye of Joshua Reynolds and his equally talented younger sister, Frances Reynolds.[177] The housekeeper guides the party towards a man of contrasting superiority:

> 'And that,' said Mrs. Reynolds, pointing to another of the miniatures, 'is my master – and very like him. It was drawn at the same time as the other – about eight years ago.'
> 'I have heard much of your master's fine person,' said Mrs. Gardiner, looking at the picture; 'it is a handsome face. But, Lizzy, you can tell us whether it is like or not.'
> Mrs. Reynolds's respect for Elizabeth seemed to increase on this intimation of her knowing her master.[178]

Ironically, Elizabeth does not answer Mrs Gardiner's question; rather, she merely acknowledges that she knows Darcy 'a little' and thinks that he is 'very handsome'.[179] In specifying the age of the portrait, Austen highlights the consistency of Darcy's 'very handsome' visible and invisible character. For the heroine, Mrs Gardiner and Austen's readers, portraits invite the female gaze to deduce a man's moral worth from his redrawn physiognomy.

Contrary to Ashley Tauchert, who situates Elizabeth's 'transformation of consciousness'[180] in her reading of Darcy's letter, I would argue that Austen uses the physiognomic vocabulary of the miniature to reopen the heroine's eyes, and hence the reader's, to the 'attractiveness' of the man's authentic self. The heroine's quest for the '"finer, larger picture"'[181] to which Mrs Reynolds

---

177 Sir Joshua Reynolds's younger sister issued the following claim in her second section of *An Enquiry Concerning the Principles of Taste, and of the Origin of Our Ideas of Beauty, &c.* (1785): 'We discard every thing, that is not beauty, to compose beauty; but every thing that is not beauty is not therefore deformity. The wrong we see in each individual we do not call deformity: when it is so, it stands on the limit of the common circle, in opposition to beauty'. By extension, Frances Reynolds's theory highlights the shift that portraiture evokes in Elizabeth's view of Darcy.
178 Austen, *Pride and Prejudice*, 273. © Cambridge University Press 2006, reproduced with permission.
179 Ibid.
180 Ashley Tauchert, *Romancing Jane Austen: Narrative, Realism, and the Possibility of a Happy Ending* (Basingstoke: Palgrave Macmillan, 2005), 85.
181 Austen, *Pride and Prejudice*, 273.

refers confirms physiognomy's power to serve as the dialogic 'language of consciousness', to borrow Bray's phrase.[182] While Elizabeth shows little enthusiasm for the 'many good paintings' in her midst, she has a taste for the 'more interesting, and also more intelligible' drawings, including those of Miss Darcy, to which she can personally relate:[183]

> In the gallery there were many family portraits, but they could have little to fix the attention of a stranger. Elizabeth walked on in quest of the only face whose features would be known to her. At last it arrested her – and she beheld a striking resemblance of Mr. Darcy, with such a smile over the face, as she remembered to have sometimes seen, when he looked at her. She stood several minutes before the picture in earnest contemplation, and returned to it again before they quitted the gallery.[184]

Austen depicts the heroine's spatial and perceptual progress as a courtly 'quest'. Unlike Maria Edgeworth, who also advances from miniatures to large-scale likenesses in her novels, Austen reserves her visual strategy for transforming the heroine's prejudices. Only 'it' has the power to 'arrest' Elizabeth, whose disinterestedness in art ironically enables her to judge the portrait like a connoisseur of characters.[185] Not only does the 'striking' accuracy of the piece captivate her eyes but so does the expressiveness of the man's physiognomy that it frames. The artist has unknowingly reproduced the ambiguous smile that had appeared on Darcy's face when the couple were debating 'likenesses' at the Netherfield ball: 'He smiled, and assured her that whatever she wished him to say should be said'.[186] The agreement between the man's visible and audible self-expression presages the psycho-physiological role that his portrait plays in transforming Elizabeth's perception of his inner character.

In *Pride and Prejudice*, Austen's method of physiognomic visuality shows that, while the miniature of Mr Darcy opens Elizabeth's eyes to the man's handsome appearance, the large-scale likeness stimulates the greatest emotional

---

182 Bray, *The Epistolary Novel*, 81.
183 Austen, *Pride and Prejudice*, 276–77.
184 Austen, *Pride and Prejudice*, 277. © Cambridge University Press 2006, reproduced with permission.
185 For a discussion on connoisseurship, see Jonathan Richardson, *The Works of Jonathan Richardson* (Strawberry Hill: [n.p.], 1792), 201. Also quoted in Ann Bermingham's 'The Aesthetics of Ignorance: The Accomplished Woman in the Culture of Connoisseurship', *Oxford Art Journal* 16, no. 2 (1993): 3–20 (14).
186 Austen, *Pride and Prejudice*, 102. © Cambridge University Press 2006, reproduced with permission.

watershed that occurs in the 'height of their acquaintance'.[187] The views of the artist and Mrs Reynolds shift the heroine's perspective and bring her to her senses:

> What praise is more valuable than the praise of an intelligent servant? As a brother, a landlord, a master, she considered how many people's happiness were in his guardianship! – How much of pleasure or pain it was in his power to bestow! – How much of good or evil must be done by him! Every idea that had been brought forward by the housekeeper was favourable to his character, and as she stood before the canvas, on which he was represented, and fixed his eyes upon herself, she thought of his regard with a deeper sentiment of gratitude than it had ever raised before; she remembered its warmth, and softened its impropriety of expression.[188]

Elizabeth's thoughts reveal the self-questioning that her first impression of the portrait has occasioned. For Tauchert, Austen's treatment of free indirect discourse is to 'narrative realism' what 'perspective is to visual realism'.[189] However, I would argue that the convergence of free indirect discourse and visuality is fundamental to Austen's 'narrative realism', creating a 'dual voice' effect through narrated and self-confessed perspectives. The physiognomic force that draws the heroine back to the portrait before she quits the picture gallery informs the reader of the shifts taking place within her. By fixing his eyes upon her self, Elizabeth attempts to 'fix' Mr Darcy's prejudice with a 'striking' expression of her gratitude.

In Elizabeth's eyes and subsequently the reader's, Darcy's portrait and actual person are essentially interchangeable. The visual impact of the portrait adheres to the definition that Lavater assigns to a 'striking likeness':

> No. 20. A most striking likeness, most astonishingly exact! It lives, it breathes! It is not a portrait; it is Nature! It is the Original itself. Drawing, form, proportion, situation, attitude, colouring, light and shade, all is truth, every thing transports. What boldness, yet what precision! What accuracy, yet what ease! In the whole combined, it is Nature; in the detail, it is still Nature. View it near, or at a distance; directly in front, or on one side, and still you find nothing but Nature. It presents the happiest

---

187 Austen, *Pride and Prejudice*, 102. © Cambridge University Press 2006, reproduced with permission.
188 Austen, *Pride and Prejudice*, 277. © Cambridge University Press 2006, reproduced with permission.
189 Tauchert, *Romancing Jane Austen*, 124.

and the most individual disposition of mind. At all times, and in every place this resemblance must strike. The more one is a Connoisseur, the more he will value it: but Connoisseur or not, every one will admire it. Nothing here recalls the idea of a picture. It is the face itself viewed in a Mirror. You feel yourself inclined to speak to it, and it seems ready to answer. It fixes us, more than we fix it; we run to meet it, we embrace it. We forget ourselves; and, scarcely recovered from our error, we fall into it again.[190]

The physiognomic force of the painting 'fixes' Elizabeth's interpretation of the man's character by inviting her to stare at a representation that 'simplifies the observation' and in turn the interpretation.[191] The resemblance to what the heroine has seen of his person 'strikes' her in a way that speaks to her more clearly than his stunted dialogue. The novel's reader observes that the heroine is alerted to a memory of him viewing her 'with such a smile over the face'. Austen shows that there is a tacit conversation in the scene between the absent figure and the present one. The memory and acknowledgement of the reaction that she elicits in him is vital to Elizabeth's changing vision. The reader observes that she, like Emma, begins to understand how she is seen. The heroine can gaze at will – like a man – and in doing so is alerted to the sexual aspect of Darcy's all-embracing smile 'over' the face rather than 'on' the face.

The Power of Place in Constructing Attachments in *Pride and Prejudice*, *Mansfield Park* and *Emma*

While Austen relies on portraiture to inform the reader of Elizabeth's changed view of Darcy in *Pride and Prejudice*, she uses architectural identification – the second of her visual strategies – to transform the heroine's emotions. Architecture conveys to the reader the man's moral and aesthetic values. Relationships between characters become visible through spatial relationships and hierarchies of power that would be difficult to signal through any other language. Hazel Jones explains that 'the law of primogeniture disadvantaged many spinsters and widows – Mrs. Dashwood loses Norland to her stepson, Mrs. Bennet will lose Longbourne to Mr. Collins [...] Somewhere in the narrative, there is always a description of the properties they will inhabit'.[192] Although references to architecture and landscape appear

---

190 Lavater, *Essays on Physiognomy*, 2.2: 249.
191 Ibid., 2.1: 178.
192 Hazel Jones, *Jane Austen and Marriage*, 179. Used by permission of Bloomsbury Publishing Plc.

in all of Austen's novels, in *Pride and Prejudice*, *Emma* and *Mansfield Park*, they are dominant forces. A. R. Humphreys proposes that the correlation between aesthetic ideals and ethical ideologies is particularly entrenched in the sister arts of architecture and gardening: 'Better than anywhere else, society saw its ideals of enlightenment, amenity, progress, classical discipline, and "polite imagination" expressed in its architecture, and of serene pastoralism realized in its parks.'[193] For Austen, however, portraiture and architecture work together to transform perceptions and affections. To borrow Tony Tanner's words, 'Man, and woman, need to be *both* an experiencer *and* a reasoner [...] Both experience and reason depend upon impressions.'[194]

Austen's recurring references to the debate surrounding 'improvements' imbue her physiognomic allusions with ethics-based connotations. As William Cowper writes in 'The Garden', 'improvement' was the 'idol of the age', and the most loved and hated illusionist of 'improvements' was Humphry Repton.[195] In his *Plans, Sketches, and Hints for the Improvement of Ferne-Hall in the Countie of Salop* (1789), Repton details his process of creating 'nature' from Nature:

> The removal of the hedge C will alone almost let in the views of this Scene, but it may be effectually done by paring off a little of the ridge on which the hedge stands. I am sure that I am not deceiv'd in my expectations from this spot, because by bending aside a few boughs & breaking off twigs, I got a clear line of sight with the help of a telescope which I use for such purposes. This opening must be made to appear accidental, & not a hole cut thro' the wood on purpose.[196]

For Austen and Edmund Burke, such 'improvements' detracted from the beauty inherent in the landscape. Lavater similarly claims that 'it is impossible for me to imagine [...] that a Painter should ever be able to produce forms more beautiful than Nature. For his happiest ideas he is not always indebted (exclusively) to the rules of Art.'[197] Society's absorption of Lavater's prejudice

---

193 Quoted in Ann Banfield's 'The Moral Landscape of Mansfield Park', *Nineteenth-Century Fiction* 26, no. 1 (June 1971): 1–24 (1).
194 Tony Tanner, introduction to *Pride and Prejudice* ([1813] New York: Penguin, 1972), 13; emphasis in original
195 For a discussion of Cowper's *The Task* and Humphry Repton, see Alistair M. Duckworth's essay 'Mansfield Park and Estate Improvements: Jane Austen's Grounds of Being', *Nineteenth-Century Fiction* 26, no. 1 (June 1971): 29–35.
196 Quoted in Wenner, *Prospect and Refuge in the Landscape of Jane Austen*, 78.
197 Lavater, *Essays on Physiognomy*, 3.1: 19.

for unaltered nature made Repton 'the scapegoat for the sins of [a] flock of fashionable "improvers" '.[198]

In *Pride and Prejudice*, Austen combines the affective forces of physiognomic portraiture and architecture to signal changes in Elizabeth's impression of Darcy. Only by penetrating Pemberley's facade can the heroine fall out of prejudice and into acknowledged love, first with the place and then with its owner. In order to make her method seem natural to the reader, Austen positions the initial phase of the 'Pemberley effect' in Elizabeth's mind. The structure's frequently discussed superiority fascinates the heroine, inspiring her and the reader to speculate about the visual reciprocity of estate and owner: 'It was impossible for her to see the word without thinking of Pemberley and its owner.'[199] Pemberley and its proprietor become physiognomically synonymous in the heroine's mind. For the reader, they are two complements of a single living being. As Roger Sales and Wenner similarly conclude, 'Pemberley basically *is* Darcy'.[200]

Austen uses Elizabeth's mental picture of Pemberley–Darcy to communicate the heroine's fear of her own visibility. Elizabeth imagines how unseemly her visit as a tourist to Pemberley would appear to Darcy: her belonging to Pemberley (and therefore Pemberley's belonging to her) was what he had desired. Whereas an impromptu visit to his residence would allow Elizabeth to consider him in his 'natural' habitat, she would appear out of place. Although Austen exposes Elizabeth's reasons for hesitation to the reader, her misgivings perplex the Gardiners. The heroine can only say that 'she was tired of great houses; she really had no pleasure in fine carpets or satin curtains'.[201] In actuality, Elizabeth is attuned to Pemberley's allure: she knows that the structure must be in a class of its own for it to receive consistent praise from those of all social classes. Like Ben Jonson's Penshurst,[202] Darcy's residence is a paragon for literal and moral emulation. Its imitation, as Mr Bingley contends, would be unattainable: ' "I would think it more possible to get Pemberley by purchase than by imitation." '[203] The singularity of the heroine's expressive dark eyes

---

198 For a discussion on the controversy surrounding Reptonian improvements, see Donald Pilcher's *The Regency Style* (London: B. T. Batsford, 1947), 17–46.
199 Austen, *Pride and Prejudice*, 265. © Cambridge University Press 2006, reproduced with permission.
200 Wenner, *Prospect and Refuge in the Landscape of Jane Austen*, 57; emphasis in original.
201 Austen, *Pride and Prejudice*, 267. © Cambridge University Press 2006, reproduced with permission.
202 See Ben Jonson, 'To Penshurst', in *The Complete Poems of Ben Jonson* (Harmondsworth: Penguin, 1975). Jonson concludes with a poignant refrain extolling well-proportioned edifices, which, unlike 'proud, ambitious heaps', enable their residents to 'dwell'. (2.99–102)
203 Austen, *Pride and Prejudice*, 42. © Cambridge University Press 2006, reproduced with permission.

and the architectural correlative for Darcy's character frame the suitability of the match in the reader's imagination.

Austen uses the heroine's first glimpses of Pemberley to prompt an emotional response in her that is articulated through a language other than straightforward speech. The novelist's use of visuality informs the reader of Elizabeth's changing view of Darcy through her encounter with Pemberley. Although the heroine's 'mind was too full for conversation', the narrative emphasizes that 'she saw and admired every remarkable spot and point of view'.[204] The unity of Pemberley–Darcy allows the sights that Elizabeth encounters at Pemberley to alter her perception of its proprietor. The scene reads as a rite of passage from Elizabeth's first and final impressions of the man that she ultimately accepts for a husband. As the novelist leads her and the Gardiners upward to a promontory, the aesthetic marvel that is Pemberley House appears. It instantly catches the eye in a way that encourages the party to penetrate further into the metaphorical heart of the property:

> They gradually ascended for half a mile, and then found themselves at the top of a considerable eminence, where the wood ceased, and the eye was instantly caught by Pemberley House, situated on the opposite side of a valley, into which the road with some abruptness wound.[205]

The edifice redefines elegance as a combination of form and function; it is the golden mean between use and grandeur, nature and design: 'It was a large, handsome, stone building, standing well on rising ground, and backed by a ridge of high woody hills; – and in front, a stream of some natural importance was swelled into greater, but without any artificial appearance. Its banks were neither formal, nor falsely adorned.'[206] Austen presents Pemberley as the visual antithesis of Lady Catherine de Bourgh's Rosings, with its ostentatious ornaments and 800-pound chimney piece that had, by contrast, produced Mr Collins's raptures.[207]

Austen's treatment of landscape design informs the reader of Elizabeth's changing feelings for Mr Darcy as she winds through Pemberley's grounds. Through the heroine's shifting viewpoints, the reader observes the tasteful

---

204 Austen, *Pride and Prejudice*, 271. © Cambridge University Press 2006, reproduced with permission.
205 Austen, *Pride and Prejudice*, 271. © Cambridge University Press 2006, reproduced with permission.
206 Austen, *Pride and Prejudice*, 271. © Cambridge University Press 2006, reproduced with permission.
207 Ibid., 84.

and unpretentious character of the place: 'She had never seen a place for which nature had done more, or where natural beauty had been so little counteracted by an awkward taste.'[208] In contrast to the Reptonian octagon, where some views are superior to others, Pemberley's every vantage point, inside and out, high and low, bespeaks the harmonious collaboration between gardener and nature.[209] From the house's windows, Elizabeth witnesses that 'every disposition of the ground was good',[210] which calls to mind Duckworth's point about the relationship between 'character' and 'disposition' in Austen's fiction. He contends that 'even without Cowper and Knight, it is likely that Jane Austen's own experience would have led her to a dislike of the drastic alterations to landscape which frequently attended Brownian or Reptonian improvements.'[211] Elizabeth's perception of Pemberley's grounds of being corresponds with Gilpin's remark in his *Observations* that relates 'the whole disposition of a landscape' to the positioning of a scene's individual features, or physiognomic traits.[212] In the heroine's eyes, Pemberley's superlative degree of 'natural beauty' manifests itself from every point of view, signalling to the reader the opening of her eyes and mind to Darcy's disposition and natural tastes.

In the Pemberley outing in *Pride and Prejudice*, Austen's visual technique turns the reader to Elizabeth's awareness of the character of Pemberley's interior. Having impressed the heroine with Pemberley's grounds, Austen invites her to explore the equivalent show of modesty within the structure's walls. The visual harmony across exteriors and interiors suggests that a penetration of Darcy's façade would reveal an analogous glimpse of 'natural beauty'. From the size of the rooms to their furnishings, Austen's depiction shows that every architectural feature is in proportion to Darcy's neoclassical values: 'The rooms were lofty and handsome, and their furniture suitable to the fortune of their proprietor; but Elizabeth saw, with admiration of his taste, that it was neither gaudy nor uselessly fine.'[213] Even if the high ceilings are in keeping with the man's wealth, Austen's conjunction insists to the reader that the rooms are

---

208 Austen, *Pride and Prejudice*, 271. © Cambridge University Press 2006, reproduced with permission.
209 On Repton's model, see Wenner, 46–47. Drawn as an octagon inscribed in a circle, it bore the label 'Mr. Repton's Opinion of Aspects'. It rates north, south, east and west views from a house as 'good', 'not bad', 'bad' and 'worst'.
210 Austen, *Pride and Prejudice*, 272. © Cambridge University Press 2006, reproduced with permission.
211 Duckworth, *The Improvement of the Estate*, 44.
212 Gilpin, *Observations on the River Wye*, 1: 23.
213 Austen, *Pride and Prejudice*, 272. © Cambridge University Press 2006, reproduced with permission.

'handsomely fitted up' rather than ostentatious.[214] The connection that the novelist draws between sight and admiration highlights Pemberley's ability to reconstruct the heroine's perceptions through the relationship between its physiognomic features and likeable aura.

During the Pemberley outing, Elizabeth repeatedly consults windows to view and review the entire composition – architecture and landscape design – within alternate frames of reference. Austen uses windows to signal her opening up to new outlooks on Mr Darcy through the character of the place. Elizabeth's interpretation of what she sees reveals to the reader that the place appears more living than stationary: 'As they passed into other rooms, these objects were taking different positions; but from every window there were beauties to be seen', pointing to the transparent attractiveness of interiors and exteriors.[215] From picture frames to prospects suspended within windowpanes, the novelist's treatment of perspective confirms that at Pemberley, all views lead to the same judgement of the place's attractive character. Rosemarie Bodenheimer offers a similar conclusion on the novelist's dialogic manipulation of voices and viewpoints:

> The multiplicity of views, all fine, contributes to the general strategy of piling up positive impressions, and of superseding the earlier rigid and partial assessment of Darcy.[216]

Innumerable 'fine' views have the potential to override one-sided character assessments, reorienting the viewer's moral compass of internal persuasion. Austen's strategy shows the reader that Pemberley is more than a collage of positive impressions: the place is a being and a state of being that encourages Elizabeth to see Darcy with a physiognomic eye and feel with a changed heart.

In *Pride and Prejudice*, Austen uses Pemberley's aesthetic values to indicate the shift in the way that Elizabeth views her relationship with Darcy. The novelist's visual technique shows that the heroine becomes consciously aware of her attachment to Pemberley and its proprietor:

> and at that moment she felt, that to be mistress of Pemberley might be something!'[217]

---

214 Ibid.
215 Austen, *Pride and Prejudice*, 272. © Cambridge University Press 2006, reproduced with permission.
216 Bodenheimer, 'Looking at the Landscape in Jane Austen', 610.
217 Austen, *Pride and Prejudice*, 271. © Cambridge University Press 2006, reproduced with permission.

The heroine's physical penetration of the place inspires her to imagine how she would have experienced the place differently if she had accepted Darcy's proposal. Her mind transforms the space into a theatre in which she plays the role of the would-have-been mistress of the place. Here, the word 'mistress' points to the sexual aspect of Elizabeth's changing vision and perceptions. She begins to imagine a power relationship that would allow the 'lines' of her own desiring gaze and Darcy's to meet by roaming freely in a landscape where natural wildness and man's governance exist in peaceful harmony. Within Pemberley's walls, the heroine's introspection and retrospection continue: '"Instead of viewing [these rooms] as a stranger, I might have rejoiced in them as my own."'[218] Elizabeth ironically views her socio-economic inferiority in a positive light. Her recollection that the Gardiners' Gracechurch Street address would have prevented them from being guests 'saved her from something like regret'.[219]

In *Pride and Prejudice*, Austen creates an epiphany for the reader through Pemberley–Darcy's physiognomy. Pemberley's aesthetic vocabulary communicates that the heroine sees and describes the place as a metaphorical reflection and concrete projection of the owner's exemplary values. Darcy's selflessness in improving the house according to his sister's desires strengthens the moral attractiveness of the portrait of the man evolving in Elizabeth's mind.[220] The house's aesthetics and Mrs Reynolds's narrated tour invite the reader of the novel to witness the heroine's mental reconstruction of the owner of the place. Austen's use of visuality shows that when the tour concludes and Elizabeth and the Gardiners take their leave, more than spatial and perceptual progress have come to pass: as the heroine gazes back at Pemberley House, Darcy's figure suddenly 'comes forward from the road'.[221] His emergence from within the landscape exhibits his physical and ideological connection to it. Darcy's materialization in his proper place, though 'unexpected', renders his appearance 'so little dignified' and subsequently natural to the novel's readers:

> She blushed again and again over the perverseness of the meeting. Never in her life had she seen his manners so little dignified, never had he spoken with such gentleness as on this unexpected meeting. What a contrast did it offer to his last address in Rosing's Park, when he put his letter into her hand! She knew not what to think, nor how to account for it.[222]

---

218 Ibid., 272.
219 Ibid., 273.
220 Ibid., 296.
221 Ibid., 278.
222 Austen, *Pride and Prejudice*, 279. © Cambridge University Press 2006, reproduced with permission.

The heroine's repeated blushes in the scene permit Darcy to witness her self-consciousness of the 'perverseness' of their encounter. Darcy's visibly contrasting mannerisms strengthen the heroine's newfound view of his actual character. After succumbing to the physiognomic persuasion of Elizabeth's experience at Pemberley, the reader needs no further evidence of the heroine's prejudice for Darcy's natural self.

As Bodenheimer observes, Austen experiments with changes in elevation to alert the reader to this dramatic change of heart:

> Her party enters Pemberley Woods 'in one of its lowest points', and makes a gradual ascent to a hill from which 'the eye was instantly caught by Pemberley House,' perfectly set in the landscape.[223]

The place appears to the reader to have provided Elizabeth with the most direct means of reaching Darcy's genuine self. While the 'gradual ascent' brings Elizabeth to a new emotional peak, her progress through the woods has broadened her view of the proprietor's true nature. Elizabeth ultimately observes to Jane that it was not the man but his domain that had corrected her prejudice and allowed them to be ' "the happiest couple in the world" ': ' "It (love) has been coming on so gradually, that I hardly know when it began. But I believe I must date it from my first seeing his beautiful grounds at Pemberley." '[224] For Charlotte Lucas, ' "Happiness in marriage is entirely a matter of chance." '[225] In the scene at Pemberley, Austen reminds the reader that had the party been 'only ten minutes sooner' in departing, they would have been 'beyond the reach of his discrimination'.[226] Timing and physiognomy work together to convince the reader of the possibility of a companionate marriage between characters, whose views of each other had long been diametrically opposed.

Austen's preoccupation with the physiognomic relationship between characters continues to represent a dominant theme in *Mansfield Park*. As in *Northanger Abbey* and *Sanditon*, a structure rather than character traits provides the novel's title. Fanny's ultimate attachment to Edmund underscores the importance of *feeling* in one's right physical and social place – a harmony that is more visual than verbal. While Elizabeth has no difficulty in seeing the physiognomic harmony

---

223 Bodenheimer, 'Looking at the Landscape in Jane Austen', 610.
224 Austen, *Pride and Prejudice*, 414. © Cambridge University Press 2006, reproduced with permission.
225 Austen, *Pride and Prejudice*, 25. © Cambridge University Press 2006, reproduced with permission.
226 Ibid., 279.

between Pemberley and Darcy, in her later novel, Austen's treatment of aesthetics becomes more sophisticated, for it directs attention to the way in which the heroine is seen rather than sees in a particular place.

Not all of the novel's characters display the same sensitivity to the singularity of Mansfield's physiognomic attributes. Lady Bertram, for instance, carelessly remarks, '"It can make very little difference to you, whether you are in one house or in the other."'[227] In contrast, Fanny is intimately attuned to her natural and domestic environs. One residence is not interchangeable with another, for she *feels* like she is a different person in a different place. Upon relocating to Mansfield Park, she acknowledges her instant affinity with the house and its contents: '"I love this house and everything in it."'[228] Shortly thereafter, Fanny makes her feelings known to Edmund – the other individual who empathizes with her anti-Reptonian views:

> 'If I could suppose my aunt really to care for me, it would be delightful to feel myself of consequence to any body! – *Here*, I know I am of none, and yet I love the place so well.'[229]

Even if Fanny does not 'feel' important to any 'body', as she is 'of none', she has a right to love 'the place'. No 'body' can prevent her from owning her own feelings. While Douglas Murray's claim that Fanny 'aestheticizes' her observations holds true in some contexts, her love for Mansfield, like Emma's attachment to Donwell, does not depend on detail.[230] The heroine's silent observation confirms Hudson's theory that Austen forms marriages 'between individuals based on a hierarchy of moral qualities'[231] rather than sexual attraction. Here, the affectionate union between woman and house anticipates the love between man and wife.

As Lamont agrees, the organization of a structure's interior compensates for the lack of interior description in the novel.[232] Mary Crawford's initial scrutiny of Mansfield merely leads her to describe the place as 'a park, a real park five miles round, a spacious modern-built house, so well placed and well screened as to deserve to be in any collection of engravings of gentlemen's seats in the kingdom'.[233] Unlike Walter Scott's *Waverley*, with its scenic

---

227 Austen, *Mansfield Park*, 28.
228 Ibid., 29.
229 Ibid., 31; emphasis in original.
230 See Douglas Murray's 'Spectatorship in Mansfield Park: Looking and Overlooking', *Nineteenth Century Literature* 52, no. 1 (June 1997): 1–26.
231 Hudson, *Sibling Love and Incest in Jane Austen's Fiction*, 107.
232 Lamont, 'Domestic Architecture', 229.
233 Austen, *Mansfield Park*, 55. © Cambridge University Press 2005, reproduced with permission.

precision, Austen persistently demonstrates her preference for using a single telling line to empower the reader to see the way in which spaces affect characters and shift their vision. Drawing from Alexander Pope's *An Essay on Criticism*, where everything and everyone must be ' "but proportion'd to their light or place" ',[234] the novelist instead engages with the physiognomy of the picturesque to gauge inner worth.

Mansfield Park's interior design makes the heroine's progress from neglect to notice visible in the reader's mind. Fanny Price, like Elizabeth Bennet, endures the self-consciousness of social inferiority. At first, she is forced into the cramped confines of the white attic, the only place fit for Fanny to occupy. Mrs Norris remarks, ' "Indeed, I do not see that you could possibly place her any where else." '[235] The heroine's physical position within the structure corresponds with her liminal position in the social sphere. While Doody claims that Fanny is more of an inaudible spectre than a living spectacle,[236] Austen draws attention to the heroine's fear of her own of visibility and her habit of 'shrinking from notice'.[237] When Mary Crawford first sets her eyes on Fanny, she cannot make her out: ' "Pray, is she out, or is she not? – I am puzzled. – She dined at the parsonage, with the rest of you, which seemed like being *out*; and yet she says so little, that I can hardly suppose she *is*." '[238] Edmund echoes Mary's incertitude, stating, ' "She has the age and sense of a woman, but the outs and not outs are beyond me." '[239] Neither subjective perspective can determine the heroine's place in society because she straddles both interiors and exteriors. According to Wenner, 'Fanny's position as simultaneous insider and outsider, as curative and inflexible, fits well with the geographical description of limen as outsider.'[240] It is the heroine's liminal status that permits her to 'cure' Mansfield of the faults that lie within its residents' perceptions.

Austen uses Fanny's position on the threshold to negotiate her increasing visibility and social acceptance at Mansfield Park. When Edmund encounters Fanny in her most concealed position – on the back stairs – and when she is most emotionally exposed, he begins to see Fanny as worthy of *feeling* part of the house and

---

234 Quoted in Banfield, 'The Moral Landscape of Mansfield Park', 2.
235 Austen, *Mansfield Park*, 11. © Cambridge University Press 2005, reproduced with permission.
236 See Murray, 'Spectatorship in Mansfield Park: Looking and Overlooking', 14.
237 Austen, *Mansfield Park*, 13.
238 Austen, *Mansfield Park*, 56. © Cambridge University Press 2005, reproduced with permission; emphasis in original.
239 Austen, *Mansfield Park*, 56. © Cambridge University Press 2005, reproduced with permission.
240 Wenner, *Prospect and Refuge in the Landscape of Jane Austen*, 70.

the household.[241] Edmund's benevolent penetration presages her gradual movement from the white attic to the East Room – her 'nest of comforts'[242] – and the drawing room, where she enters the public eye. Hart aptly observes that the East Room is the most detailed room in the novel because of the heroine's particular attachment to its aesthetic meaning:

> One recalls the scenes as inseparable from their places, almost as one does the scenes of Thackeray. The drawing room is never described, yet from the many intensely felt interpersonal events that happen there, we gradually acquire a feeling of its size arrangement, atmosphere. Fanny's attic is too small and remote to appear, but the East Room acquires effective force as her private place, especially since it is the place where she can be caught.[243]

The East Room's sparse furnishings reflect the physiognomic attributes of Fanny's character. Her acquisition of a new private space within Mansfield serves as a metaphor for her progress towards social acceptance.

Austen relies on the themes of visual presence and absence to communicate Fanny's attachment to Mansfield – the place and its inheritor. Aesthetic contrasts teach the heroine and the reader to see that Mansfield's values are diametrically opposed to those at Portsmouth, with its crowded, agitating interior:

> Every thing where we now were was in full contrast to it (Mansfield). The elegance, propriety, regularity, harmony – and perhaps, above all, the peace and tranquillity of Mansfield, were brought to her remembrance every hour of the day, by the prevalence of every thing opposite to them here [...] At Mansfield, no sounds of contention, no raised voices, no abrupt bursts, no tread of violence was heard; all proceeded in a regular course of cheerful orderliness; every body had their due importance; every body's feelings were consulted. If tenderness could be ever supposed wanting, good sense and good breeding supplies its place.[244]

As a paragon country house, Mansfield Park embodies the combination of elegance, propriety, regularity and orderliness that Lavater praises: 'Without

---

241 For an architectural analysis of public and private spaces in English country houses, see Mark Girouard's *Life in the English Country House* (New Haven, CT: Yale University Press, 1978), 276–79.
242 Austen, *Mansfield Park*, 179.
243 Hart, 'The Spaces of Privacy: Jane Austen', 326.
244 Austen, *Mansfield Park*, 453. © Cambridge University Press 2005, reproduced with permission.

regularity there can be no such thing as organized beauty; or, at least, this beauty, if it could exist, never would produce, at the first instant, those happy effects which result from an agreeable symmetry, and exactness of proportion.'[245] Whereas Elizabeth's raptures over Pemberley's physiognomic display highlight the place's picturesque irregularity, here, Austen defers to the presentation of organized beauty and agreeable symmetry, implying her own changed view of landscape design.

Austen's visual technique convinces the reader that when others view Fanny as an insider, Mansfield feels like 'home' to her. The heroine's acknowledgement of Mansfield Park's newfound status again takes place in the far-removed context of her former 'home', Portsmouth:

> When she had been coming to Portsmouth, she had loved to call it her home, had been fond of saying that she was going home; the word had been very dear to her; and so it still was, but it must be applied to Mansfield. That was now the home. Portsmouth was Portsmouth; Mansfield was home.[246]

The aesthetic comparison that Austen draws between the two houses points to Fanny's changing relationship with the residents of both structures. Following her three-month absence, the heroine returns to Mansfield as an insider: she replaces Maria to become 'indeed the daughter that he (Sir Thomas) wanted' and the woman whom Edmund has always loved.[247] The ineffable happiness that ends the novel highlights the role of physiognomic visuality in the plot: 'But there was happiness elsewhere which no description can reach. Let no one presume to give the feelings of a young woman on receiving the assurance of that affection of which she has scarcely allowed herself to entertain a hope.'[248] As Tauchert acknowledges, the unspeakable 'finds an indirect register in the Edenic scenery of the Park that meets her return'.[249] Through seeing and experiencing physiognomic contrasts, Fanny ends up exactly where and with whom she wants to be. The novelist's aesthetic technique signals the way in which other characters' changing perspectives of the heroine's position enable her to be recognized as an insider.

---

245 Lavater, *Essays on Physiognomy*, 3.1: 18.
246 Austen, *Mansfield Park*, 499. © Cambridge University Press 2005, reproduced with permission.
247 Austen, *Mansfield Park*, 546. © Cambridge University Press 2005, reproduced with permission.
248 Austen, *Mansfield Park*, 545. © Cambridge University Press 2005, reproduced with permission.
249 Tauchert, *Romancing Jane Austen: Narrative, Realism, and the Possibility of a Happy Ending*, 102. Reproduced with permission of Palgrave Macmillan.

While Austen does not cite her home in Chawton as a source of architectural inspiration, it was the Mansfield Park of her personal life and the place where she wrote or revised most of her novels:[250]

> 'Our Chawton home, how much we find
> Already in it, to our mind;
> And how convinced, that when complete
> It will all other Houses beat
> That ever have been made or mended
> With rooms concise, or rooms distended'.[251]

Austen's rhyming couplets echo the balance that the house embodies. Like Mansfield Park and the Austens' Chawton cottage, Fanny internalizes Pope's delineation of the 'golden mean' in her physical appearance. Her inner and outer beauty adheres to Lavater's correlation between the appearance of organized beauty and its essence. Fanny is not tall and striking like Julia and Maria or lively and witty like Mary.[252] However, when studied with a physiognomic eye, her superior natural beauty catches the gaze in a way that does not draw attention to the details of her appearance. Henry Crawford tells his sister that '"she is quite a different creature from what she was in the autumn. She was then merely a quiet, modest, not plain-looking girl, but she is now absolutely pretty [...] And then – her air, her manner, her tout ensemble is so indescribably improved!"'[253] Fanny, like Mansfield, is a natural beauty; nature 'improves' her looks and enables her to mature.

In *Emma*, Austen uses physiognomic places to reveal the attachment between Emma and Mr Knightley. As Mrs Oliphant famously writes of the novel's convincing setting, '"It is impossible to conceive a more perfect piece of village geography [...] a scene more absolutely real [...] We know it as well as if we had lived there all our lives and visited Miss Bates every other day."'[254] Todd's critique of *Emma* rightly asserts the connection between the novel's fully developed type of heroine and the plot's 'minutely realised' setting:

> Emma is Austen's most fully developed heroine, and the large village or small town to which she belongs, Highbury, is of all Austen's places the

---

250 See Claire Tomalin's *Jane Austen: A Life* (London: Penguin, 2000), 246.
251 Quoted in David Cecil's *A Portrait of Jane Austen* (London: Penguin, 2000), 128.
252 For a discussion on the visual relationship that Austen creates, see Banfield, 'The Moral Landscape of Mansfield Park', 18.
253 Austen, *Mansfield Park*, 267–68. © Cambridge University Press 2005, reproduced with permission.
254 Cited in Janet Todd's introduction to *Emma* ([1815] Cambridge: Cambridge University Press, 2005), xxi–lxxiv (lxvi); Margaret Oliphant, 'Miss Austen and Miss Mitford', *Blackwood's Edinburgh Magazine* 107 (March 1870): 290–313 (304).

most minutely realised. The implication is clear. Austen's focus in *Emma*, as in all her novels, is on the accommodation that the individual must make with the society in which she lives, the successful accomplishment of which is celebrated as a marriage, but in no other novel is that act of accommodation so intricately depicted.[255]

In this vein, Emma, more than Austen's other heroines, is as much a product of Highbury as she is a shaper of it: she is simultaneously the shaping eye and the shaping hand, an architect of idealistic 'prospects' and a character 'improved' by the 'accommodation' that she makes in the place where she sees herself happiest. As Tauchert similarly finds, *Emma*'s happy ending is the effect of a force beyond that of 'her own work', for she learns to incorporate Mr Knightley's subjectivity.[256]

Whereas Austen uses portraiture in the novel to alert Emma to the impossibility of controlling others' subjectivities and forces of internal persuasion, physiognomic associations of landscape clarify her self-perceptions. The novelist's visual technique continues to resolve omissions between the politely sayable and the unsayable through the 'dual voice' effect that visuality and free indirect discourse engender. The reader observes how the heroine's 'imaginist' bias prevents her 'true hazel eye' from seeing truly: she refrains from reading texts because she cannot read characters, whether in print or *in propria persona*.[257] Emma's status as a woman with a selfish, often naive perspective shows the reader that she is divided between the dullness of modest female experience and the perils of the imagination, an extreme that Austen personifies in the character of *Northanger Abbey*'s Catherine Morland, who is deluded by expectations gleaned from Radcliffe's *The Romance of the Forest*. Emma's character 'type' is more sophisticated, analytical and, in some respects, 'masculine' than the Gothic 'type' of heroine. As LeRoy W. Smith points out, 'In trying to distance herself from the common plight of single women, Emma attempts to join the ranks of their oppressors.'[258] Visuality informs the reader that in leading Harriet's ambitions astray, Emma's eyes

---

255 Todd, introduction to *Emma*, lxxiv. © Cambridge University Press 2005, reproduced with permission.
256 Tauchert, *Romancing Jane Austen*, 131.
257 Austen, *Emma*, 314. Emma's thoughts read, 'How much more must an imaginist, like herself, be on fire with speculation and foresight! – especially with such a ground-work of anticipation as her mind had already made.' © Cambridge University Press 2005, reproduced with permission.
258 LeRoy W. Smith, *The Drama of Woman*, 138. Reproduced with permission of Palgrave Macmillan.

have distanced their focus from the place – literal and metaphorical – to which they belong.

In contrast to Austen's treatment of Elizabeth Bennet and Fanny Price, Emma's return to her proper senses begins in the metaphorical landscape of the mind's eye. According to Bodenheimer's reading of both novels, Austen 'draws on the metaphorical possibilities in the rather technical relationship between "the eye", on the one hand, and "the prospect", on the other'.[259] While waiting 'in great terror' for Harriet to identify Mr Knightley as her imaginary lover, Emma sees the misdirection of her attempts at self-determination with 'blessed' clearness:

> She saw it all with a clearness which had never blessed her before. How improperly had she been acting by Harriet! How inconsiderate, how indelicate, how irrational, how unfeeling had been her conduct! What blindness what madness, had led her on! It struck her with dreadful force, and she was ready to give it every bad name in the world.[260]

Austen repeatedly uses Harriet to model Emma's 'unfeeling' self-delusions. Joseph Litvak points out that the two women are, at times, interchangeable: 'As characters in a novel, Harriet and Emma fall short of uniqueness and unity because, substituting for each other, they "mean" something other than themselves.'[261] In this manner, Emma has redrawn Harriet's character, which now 'acts' as improperly as the eye and hand that have shaped it. The women's ironic reciprocity inspires the heroine to see her feelings for Donwell and its owner. Emma is, as John Hardy suggests, 'struck [...] with dreadful force' by her former conduct and self-sacrifice but feels sorrier for herself than for Harriet.[262]

Austen strengthens the apparent bond between Harriet's and Emma's vision by making their matrimonial 'prospects' somewhat similar. By contriving the circumstances necessary for the heroine to acknowledge the 'blindness of her own head and heart', the novelist gives her reason to deplore her situation, '"Oh God! That I had never seen her!"'[263] No place within or beyond Hartfield allows Emma to escape from the knowledge of her self-deceptions, even if she cannot 'understand' them:

---

259 Bodenheimer, 'Looking at the Landscape in Jane Austen', 613.
260 Austen, *Emma*, 444. © Cambridge University Press 2005, reproduced with permission.
261 Joseph Litvak, 'Reading Characters: Self, Society, and Text in *Emma*', *PMLA* 100, no. 5 (October 1985): 763–73 (769).
262 Hardy, *Jane Austen's Heroines*, 99.
263 Austen, *Emma*, 448. © Cambridge University Press 2005, reproduced with permission.

How to understand it all! How to understand the deceptions she had been thus practising on herself, and living under! – The blunders, the blindness of her own head and heart! – she sat still, she walked about, she tried her own room, she tried the shrubbery – in every place, every posture, she perceived that she had acted most weakly; that she had been imposed on by others in a most mortifying degree; that she had been imposing on herself in a degree yet more mortifying; that she was wretched, and should probably find this day but the beginning of wretchedness.[264]

Emma 'tries' to blind herself to her past 'blunders' and their cause: the 'blindness of her own head and heart'. Having 'seen' Harriet acting as 'Emma', she cannot undo her 'perception' that she 'had acted most weakly'. Through symmetry, exclamation and persistent alliteration, Austen's visual technique stages for the reader the dramatic shift in the heroine's vision and perceptions.

In *Emma*, Austen uses the spectre of Mrs Harriet Knightley to sensitize the heroine to her surroundings. Emma initially wishes for life in Highbury to remain the same, save for the matrimonial attachments that she seeks to engineer. Her necessary 'wish' to prolong the 'precious intercourse of friendship and confidence' between Donwell and Hartfield rests on the condition of Mr Knightley's similar refusal to marry:

Wish it she must, for his sake – be the consequence nothing to herself, but his remaining single all his life. Could she be secure of that, indeed of his never marrying at all, she believed she should be perfectly satisfied. – Let him but continue the same Mr. Knightley to her and her father, the same Mr. Knightley to all the world; let Donwell and Hartfield lose none of their precious intercourse of friendship and confidence, and her peace would be fully secured. – Marriage, in fact, would not do for her. It would be incompatible with what she owed to her father, and with what she felt for him. Nothing should separate her from her father. She would not marry, even if she were asked by Mr. Knightley.[265]

Austen's architectural metaphor for Emma's self-security attests to the heroine's perceptual confusion between selfishness and selflessness. The heroine deceives herself in 'wishing' her wish to be for Mr Knightley's sake. In depicting Donwell and Hartfield as physiognomic correlatives of hero and heroine, the novelist's aesthetic vocabulary intimates that Emma has yet to perceive

---

264 Austen, *Emma*, 448. © Cambridge University Press 2005, reproduced with permission.
265 Austen, *Emma*, 453. © Cambridge University Press 2005, reproduced with permission.

that her attraction to the place has taken on a sexual dimension, even if marriage 'would not do for her'. LeRoy W. Smith acknowledges that, 'although she rejects the woman's role handed to her, she is not free, apparently, to be whatever it is within her nature to be'.[266] In wishing their 'intercourse' to remain as friends, the novelist indicates the heroine's unnaturally childish way of seeing her attachment to both places.

Austen reveals that Emma's sole rationale for marrying is vision based. Mr Knightley remarks, '"I should like to see Emma in love [...] But there is nobody hereabouts to attach her"'.[267] In having 'no view' of whom Emma ought to marry, Mr Knightley asserts his similar obliviousness to his feelings. The heroine's enduring blindness, together with Highbury's limited choice of suitors, prevents the threat of her separation from Mr Woodhouse:

> 'I must see somebody very superior to any one I have seen yet, to be tempted [...] and I do not wish to see any such person. I would rather not be tempted. I cannot really change for the better. If I were to marry, I must expect to repent it.'[268]

Emma's wish to be blind to 'any such person' points to her deluded view that she 'cannot' improve. Litvak proposes that 'like every one else in this world, she is always "making a figure" in one message or another because she is always being reinvented, or reread, both by herself and by other selves'.[269] In Highbury's world of perpetual reinvention and revision, Austen shows that absolute moral vision is an optical illusion where subjectivity must inevitably reign.

Austen introduces the threat of loss, first of Donwell and then of its owner, to signal to the reader that Emma begins to see that her happiness depends on being '*first*' in Mr Knightley's mind and affections. Early in the novel, Emma remarks to Harriet, '"I believe few married women are half as much mistress of their husband's house, as I am of Hartfield; and never, never could I expect to be so truly beloved and important; so always first and always right in any man's eyes as I am in my father's."'[270] Since Emma is already adored in a 'man's eyes', she is not disposed to changing the existing intercourse between

---

266 LeRoy W. Smith, *The Drama of Woman*, 132. Reproduced with permission of Palgrave Macmillan.
267 Austen, *Emma*, 41. © Cambridge University Press 2005, reproduced with permission.
268 Austen, *Emma*, 90. © Cambridge University Press 2005, reproduced with permission.
269 Litvak, 'Reading Characters: Self, Society, and Text in *Emma*', 770.
270 Austen, *Emma*, 90–91. © Cambridge University Press 2005, reproduced with permission.

Donwell and Hartfield. Only the prospect of a separation of the estates forces her to reflect on her own view of 'happiness':

> Till now that she was threatened with its loss, Emma had never known how much of her happiness depended on being *first* with Mr. Knightley, first in interest and affection.[271]

Austen stresses the significance of the word 'first' in the passage to highlight that the heroine assigns greater importance to the way in which Mr Knightley views her than her father. At first, Emma is presumptuous of her place in Mr Knightley's regard and 'had enjoyed it without reflection'.[272] Her habit of not 'reflecting' on her 'place' signals the analogous way in which she neglects her feelings. Emma's dread of being supplanted by the woman acting as her exceeds her fear of being 'transplanted'. Mrs Elton sees a woman's ideal place differently, remarking, ' "Whenever you are transplanted [...] you will understand how very delightful it is to meet with any thing at all like what one has left behind. I always say this is quite one of the evils of matrimony." '[273] The threat of Donwell's loss compels Emma to 'perceive' that should Harriet and Mr Knightley marry, she would be 'transplanted' to a worse degree of wretchedness by remaining within Hartfield's walls. Whereas Elizabeth Bennet and Fanny Price seek to become 'insiders', Emma wishes to remain one.

Through free indirect discourse, Austen reveals the influence that the hypothetical loss of Donwell–Knightley has on Emma's self-perceptions. The heroine's inability to endure the prospect of an end to Mr Knightley's voluntary movement between the two homes, all 'for Harriet's sake', transforms her view of her 'closeness' to him:

> Mr. Knightley to be no longer coming there for his evening comfort! – No longer walking in at all hours, as if ever willing to change his own home for their's! – How was it to be endured? And if he were to be lost to them for Harriet's sake; if he were to be the chosen, the first, the dearest, the friend, the wife to whom he looked for all the best blessings of existence; what could be increasing Emma's wretchedness but the reflection never far distant from her mind, that it had been all her own work?[274]

---

271 Austen, *Emma*, 452. © Cambridge University Press 2005, reproduced with permission; emphasis in original.
272 Ibid.
273 Austen, *Emma*, 294. © Cambridge University Press 2005, reproduced with permission.
274 Austen, *Emma*, 460. © Cambridge University Press 2005, reproduced with permission.

Austen uses Emma's dismal conjectures to exhibit the growing clarity of the heroine's reflections and self-perceptions. Emma had been too close to her work to see the way in which she had ironically been inflicting self-harm. While Austen also uses the reflection model to compel Elizabeth to see her sexual attraction to a place and its owner, Wiltshire posits a critical difference between Pemberley and Donwell, arguing that Emma never thinks, '"To be mistress of Donwell might be something!"'[275] In Emma's mind's eye, however, being mistress of Donwell would indeed be something.

Unlike the boxwood at Box Hill that softens the hill's precipitous sides, Austen reserves the restrictive shrubbery at Hartfield to clarify the reader's view of the ultimate union between hero and heroine. Seizing upon its ability to guide eyes and filter views, Austen stages Emma's fortuitous encounter with Mr Knightley:

> There, with spirits freshened, and thoughts a little relieved, she had taken a few turns, when she saw Mr. Knightley passing through the garden door, and coming towards her. – It was the first intimation of his being returned from London. She had been thinking of him the moment before, as unquestionably sixteen miles distant. – There was time only for the quickest arrangement of mind.[276]

Emma's mental picture of Mr Knightley 'as unquestionably sixteen miles distant' anticipates his sudden appearance. Whereas the heroine has moved outdoors, the hero has passed 'through the garden door'. Similar to the Pemberley 'outing' in *Pride and Prejudice*, the hero appears from within the landscape. Mr Knightley pursues Emma into the shrubbery, 'wholly unsuspicious of his own influence', an influence that forces her to rearrange her thoughts.[277]

During the shrubbery episode at Hartfield, Austen shows that Emma and Mr Knightley meet with the changed self-perceptions necessary for mutual understanding. Bodenheimer's theory that landscape design, when read dramatically, provides 'a clever imitation of the indirect process through which a clear picture of reality is finally achieved' holds true in the novelist's way of uniting characters with redesigned subjectivities.[278] While Emma recognizes that she has never loved Frank Churchill, Mr Knightley realizes that in escaping to London, he had gone to the 'wrong place' to forget Emma: 'Isabella

---

275 John Wiltshire, '*Mansfield Park, Emma, Persuasion*', in *The Cambridge Companion to Jane Austen*, ed. Edward Copeland and Juliet McMaster (Cambridge: Cambridge University Press, 1995), 58–83 (74).
276 Austen, *Emma*, 462. © Cambridge University Press 2005, reproduced with permission.
277 Ibid., 470.
278 Bodenheimer, 'Looking at the Landscape in Jane Austen', 612.

was too much like Emma – differing only in those striking inferiorities, which always brought the other in brilliancy before him'.[279] Even if the sisters' physiognomies are 'too much like', Austen's method of comparison shows that Isabella's 'striking inferiorities' enhance the attractiveness of the woman who is physically absent from view. In specifying that Mr Knightley has 'no selfish view, no view at all', and therefore no ulterior motive, Austen shows that he passes through the garden door with open eyes and an open mind.[280] To borrow Tauchert's phrase, 'Emma and Mr. Knightley quite literally come to a shared and open "understanding" over half an hour in the shrubbery: their eyes are "open" to each other'.[281] The shrubbery supplies them with a 'certain' view of each other that communicates their 'precious certainty of being beloved'.[282]

As this discussion has illustrated, the companionate marriages that Austen's novels produce owe much of their success to the novelist's use of physiognomic correlatives of character to elevate shared views and values over the isolated attractions of money in marriage. Her cunning visual technique, which operates alongside free indirect discourse, allows for gender equality, inviting the heroine's gaze to study a man, albeit indirectly. Through the understood correspondence between physiognomy and ethics, visuality serves as a coded method that guides her strong-willed heroines from self-deception to self-determination in the marriage market. Even if Austen's heroines and heroes read their affections differently and the implicit attractiveness of socio-economic compatibility persists, the reader sees that her fictional protagonists are subject to the same essential truth: they, like all people, are influenced by the aesthetic values and characteristics that impressions extenuate.

---

[279] Austen, *Emma*, 471. © Cambridge University Press 2005, reproduced with permission.
[280] Ibid.
[281] Tauchert, *Romancing Jane Austen: Narrative, Realism, and the Possibility of a Happy Ending*, 130. Reproduced with permission of Palgrave Macmillan.
[282] Austen, *Emma*, 473.

Chapter 2

ANN RADCLIFFE'S GOTHIC RECONSTRUCTIONS OF FEMALE IDENTITY AND EXPERIENCE

Moving on from Austen's visual treatment of self-projection and introspection, this chapter illuminates how Ann Radcliffe uses visuality in her fiction to explore sexual, religious and social forms of female subjection. Her work, unlike Austen's, is not concerned with the formation of companionate couples. Instead, the Gothic novel's preoccupation with terror and the undefined allows her to dramatize real power structures in ways that torment the eyes and minds of her heroines. By removing her plots to extreme situations that are foreign in time and place, the novelist is at liberty to subvert existing presentations of women's perceptions and experiences. Radcliffe borrows from the work of male artists and philosophers to interrelate the natural and the supernatural, the ordinary and the extraordinary. Her narrators move freely between the eye of the body and the eye of the mind, destroying conventional boundaries between interiority and exteriority, private and public.

After positioning Radcliffe's treatment of Gothic sublimity in relation to recent scholarship, the chapter investigates the five concentric visual realms that she uses to depict the inescapability of female persecution. The analysis focuses on *A Sicilian Romance* (1790), *The Mysteries of Udolpho* (1794) and *The Italian* (1797) in order to underscore Radcliffe's reliance on visuality as an effective yet liminal means of negotiating the psychological conditions imposed on the female sex. The chapter uses an edition of *A Sicilian Romance* that is based on the 1821 version of the text – the last to appear in her lifetime – to confirm that her deployment of visuality does not significantly alter over time.[1] The study orders the novels' visual frames according to scale, moving from man-made and natural thresholds to that which is supernatural.

---

1 This chapter uses texts that are based on the first editions of *The Mysteries of Udolpho* and *The Italian*.

The first section considers Radcliffe's treatment of portraiture – textual, ekphrastic and spectral. It exposes the ways in which women who are trapped in two dimensions convey ekphrastic messages of terror to female spectators within the plot. Radcliffe's portraits are as much signifiers of live burial and double imprisonment as they are representations of *natures mortes*. The portrait as an analogue for double imprisonment advances the discussion to architecture, the second man-made frame of patriarchal power. Radcliffe's references to castles and convents are conventional in form but unconventionally psychological in function: she correlates malevolent facades with those that are duplicitously benign. Whereas the menacing exteriors of castles project the terrors contained within, convents are not the sanctuaries that they appear to be.

The third visual frame concentrates on the veil. Radcliffe reinterprets the religious veil as a mobile prison that moves the heroine between man-made and natural frames of subjection. The spatial progress from interior to exterior leads to the fourth visual frontier in the novelist's fiction: sublime panoramas that are inhabited by invisible predatory males. The section engages with Elizabeth Bohls's critique of Radcliffe's aesthetics of self-division and patriarchal power.[2] The novelist's mimetic representations of seventeenth-century landscape painting affect her fictional women's appearances and temperaments. In *A Sicilian Romance*, men prey on the wrong women and are blind to the visual power of women who unknowingly look alike. While literary criticism tends to disparage Radcliffe's penchant for repetition, Claudia Johnson contends that such repetition illustrates the unavoidability of persecution.[3] Shifting from the natural to the supernatural, the chapter's fifth and final section explores how Radcliffe's fictional women are still 'framed' within that which cannot be defined. To explain the novelist's visual technique, the section refers to Alexander Cozens's ink-blot method of watercolour painting. In Radcliffe's novels, the obscure compels fictional women to see that which does not, in fact, exist. By shifting the responsibility for interpreting sights onto the reader, Radcliffe's narratives encourage the vicarious viewer to picture the same inconceivable horrors that haunt her heroines' imaginations.

Even if Radcliffe's overarching preoccupation with 'sublime' experience and the limits of language dominates scholarship, a thorough analysis of her use of visuality for psychological effect has yet to be conducted. Up until the

---

2 Elizabeth Bohls, *Women Travel Writers and the Language of Aesthetics, 1716–1818* (Cambridge: Cambridge University Press, 2010). Her study sheds light on female self-division in Radcliffe's novels as it relates to the aesthetic categorizations in her narratives.

3 Claudia Johnson, *Equivocal Beings: Politics, Gender and Sentimentality in the 1790s: Wollstonecraft, Radcliffe, Burney, Austen* (Chicago: University of Chicago Press, 1995), 113.

propagation of Freudian psychology in the twentieth century, eighteenth- and nineteenth-century readers were most interested in the unprecedented degree of suspense found in Radcliffe's oeuvre.[4] In her review of Radcliffe's *The Italian*, Mary Wollstonecraft wrote:

> We are made to wonder, only to wonder; but the spell, by which we are led, again and again, round the same magic circle, is the spell of genius.[5]

Wollstonecraft was not the only one to be left spellbound by Radcliffe's extraordinary manipulation of Gothic sublimity. Samuel Taylor Coleridge similarly observed the novelist's dexterity in drawing the reader into the terror continuum of the plot.[6]

In 1819, the *Monthly Magazine* issued a protofeminist review of Radcliffe's treatment of sublime terror. The anonymous author praises the novelist as the 'greatest sorceress in *the terrific* that has ever appeared',[7] lauding her vivid portraits of female experience against the backdrop of the patriarchal sublime:

> [She has] dared to lay open the arteries of *male* dereliction from the oracles of the heart to the marrow in the bones. She has penetrated beyond the metaphysics of her sex, and exposed the criminality peculiar to ours.[8]

Though the critique does not examine the means through which Radcliffe illustrates '*male* dereliction', it attests to her exposure of the corruption of society.

By the end of the nineteenth century, critics of Radcliffe's novels, including George Saintsbury and Sir Walter Raleigh, claimed that her technique of the explained supernatural had lost its psychological potency. In 1891, George Saintsbury emphasized the role that novelty played in shaping the reader's perceptions of Radcliffe's imagery:

---

4 Robert Miles, *Ann Radcliffe: The Great Enchantress* (Manchester and New York: Manchester University Press, 1995), 11.
5 [Mary Wollstonecraft?], 'Review of *The Italian*', *Analytical Review*, 25 (1797): 516–20 (516). Also quoted in Deborah D. Rogers's *Ann Radcliffe: A Bio-Bibliography* (Westport, CT, and London: Greenwood Press, 1996), 46.
6 For a discussion on Coleridge's reading of Radcliffe's narrative technique, see Miles, *Ann Radcliffe: The Great Enchantress*, 51.
7 [Anon.] 'Estimate of the Literary Character of Mrs. Ann Ratcliffe [sic]', *Monthly Magazine*, 47 (1819): 125–26 (125). Also published in Rogers's *Ann Radcliffe: A Bio-Bibliography*, 57; emphasis in original.
8 'Estimate of the Literary Character of Mrs. Ann Ratcliffe [*sic*]', 126; emphasis in original.

But the whole secret of the success was that the imagination of that day was not *blasé*, that the thing was quite new to readers, that the more ingenuous had no idea but that 'something very horrid' might happen at any moment, while even the more experienced found the titillation of terror rather agreeable.[9]

Like Saintsbury, Raleigh explored how Radcliffe exploited her contemporary society's aesthetic tastes. He, however, recognized that verbal art provides an emotional index: 'Her landscapes might be named after the particular emotions they are built to house – terror, regret, security, or melancholy – and they would be perfect in keeping'.[10] By that point, Radcliffe's use of visual typologies had become intuitively perceptible to a readership with changed expectations of visuality.[11]

A number of twentieth-century critics reassert the relationship between power and aesthetics in Radcliffe's Gothic novels. Clara Frances McIntyre's *Ann Radcliffe in Relation to Her Time* (1920) and Alida Alberdina Sibbelina Wieten's *Mrs Radcliffe in Relation to Romanticism* (1926) attempt to decipher the relationship between what the novelist saw and her art of literary suspense.[12] Unlike their biographically focused studies, Samuel H. Monk's *The Sublime: A Study of Critical Theories in XVIII-Century England* (1935) represents a landmark in the scholarly debate on the Gothic genre, for it proposes that the sublime has multiple definitions that 'usually implied a strong emotional effect, which in the latter years of the century, frequently turned on terror'.[13] He theorizes that as an aesthetic force that resists neoclassical boundaries, the sublime is entrenched in pre-Romantic perceptions of gender and power. In *The Romantic Novel in England* (1972), Robert Kiely also considers the visual structure of the sublime but posits the relationship between space, consciousness and character:

> Believable relationships – sexual or otherwise – are impossible, not because the state is tottering with corruption, but because the essence

---

9 George Saintsbury, introduction, *Tales of Mystery*, ed. George Saintsbury (New York: Macmillan, 1891), xiv–xvii (xvi); emphasis in original.
10 Sir Walter Raleigh, *The English Novel* (New York: Charles Scribner's Sons, 1894), 227–33 (233).
11 Refer to my Introduction for a discussion on Crary's *The Techniques of the Observer* and technology's influence on perceptual expectations.
12 See Clara Frances McIntyre, *Ann Radcliffe in Relation to Her Time* (New Haven, CT: Yale University Press, 1920) and Alida Alberdina Sibbellina Wieten, *Mrs Radcliffe in Relation to Romanticism* (Amsterdam: H. J. Paris, 1926).
13 Samuel H. Monk, *The Sublime: A Study of Critical Theories in XVIII-Century England* (Ann Arbor: University of Michigan University Press, 1935; 1960), 233.

of individual identity has been dislodged from its human centres and diffused in an architectural construct which seems to have more life than the characters who inhabit it.[14]

While his concept of the 'dislodgement of human centres'[15] sparked the explosion of interest in Gothic literature in the 1970s and 1980s, Kiely does not address an element that this chapter makes explicit: architecture is, more specifically, Radcliffe's means of giving 'life' to the male abuse that is central to her plots.

Post-Kiely critics advance the scholarly debate and examine patriarchal power from historicist, aesthetic and psychological approaches. Robert Miles departs from Emma Clery's and Fred Botting's preoccupation with the relationship between supernatural fiction and literary consumption.[16] His study draws upon Pierre Arnaud's 1976 analysis of Radcliffe's heavy use of visual doubles and dualistic forces.[17] In *Gothic Writing 1750–1820: A Genealogy* (1993), Miles links the problematization of gender relations to what Michel Foucault describes as 'an especially dense transfer point for relations of power'.[18] In *Ann Radcliffe: The Great Enchantress* (1995), Miles re-examines the transfer of power from an artistic vantage point. He situates the aesthetic satisfaction of Radcliffe's novels in how 'they make power visible in unexpected ways' and give rise to a new 'topography of the self':

> Unlike the pre-Romantic one, the Romantic encounter is not between an observing self and a stimulating nature, between two discrete entities or realms which meet and separate. On the contrary, the observing self is shown to be constituted in and through nature. To be more precise, self and nature are revealed as sharing the same constituent terms, the same metaphors, turns of phrase, figures of speech. In short, they are constituted by the same shaping rhetoric [...] In setting out to constitute itself through the rhetoric of nature the Romantic self discovers itself grounded in the nature of rhetoric.[19]

---

14 Robert Kiely, *The Romantic Novel in England* (Cambridge, MA: Harvard University Press, 1972), 40.
15 Ibid. According to Kiely, space plays a more important role than consciousness in forming perceptions.
16 See Emma Clery's discussion of consumption in *The Rise of Supernatural Fiction: 1762–1800* (Cambridge: Cambridge University Press, 1995); for Fred Botting's critiques of the hybridization of conventions in Radcliffe's novels, see *Gothic* (London and New York: Routledge, 1996–1997) and *Gothic Romanced: Consumption, Gender and Technology in Contemporary Fictions* (London and New York: Routledge, 2008).
17 See Pierre Arnaud, *Ann Radcliffe et le fantastique* (Paris: Aubier Montaigne, 1976).
18 Robert Miles, *Gothic Writing 1750–1820: A Genealogy* (Manchester: Manchester University Press, 1993; 2002), 20 and 27.
19 Miles, *Ann Radcliffe: The Great Enchantress*, 12.

Miles's critique offers valuable insight into the Romantic reciprocity between the self and the rhetoric that dominates Radcliffe's novels. While the first section of this chapter draws on Miles's interpretation of the rhythms of Gothic fiction and the self as a 'figure of speech', it discards his view of the universal relationship between the self and nature. Even if Radcliffe's fictional men and women are 'figures of speech', their gender conditions their susceptibility to all-encompassing psychological effect.

In line with Eve Kosofsky Sedgwick's theorization of the 'dissolution of the self',[20] Kamilla Elliott's *Portraiture and British Gothic Fiction: The Rise of Picture Identification, 1764–1835* (2012) analyses Radcliffe's treatment of figures of speech and visual identity. In particular, she underscores the role of ekphrasis and the subjectivity of perception. Elliott's reading of matriarchal picture identification sheds light on the textual portraits that this chapter's opening section examines in greater depth:

> Matriarchal picture identification in Gothic fiction, then, draws on the dead and the living, the animate and the inanimate, the religious and the secular, the natural and the artifactual, interiority and exteriority, aesthetics and science, the supernatural and the empirical, as well as on ruptures and contradictions in all of these binarisms.[21]

While Elliott appropriately differentiates matriarchal picture identification from its patriarchal counterpart, she does not fully consider the importance of novelistic context. This chapter posits that a linkage of portraiture with external visual realms of man-made, natural and supernatural subjection is simultaneously fundamental and inherent.

As well as evaluating the portrait on textual, ekphrastic and spectral levels, Elliott discusses how Radcliffe's fiction constructs and then violates the boundaries between past and present, memory and fancy, interiors and exteriors. In Elliott's view, the tension between *iconophilia* (the love of pictures) and *iconophobia* (the fear of pictures) generates the mental climate upon which psychological torment depends.[22] Essential to her argument is the coexistence of presence and absence:

---

20 Eve Kosofsky Sedgwick, *The Coherence of Gothic Conventions* (New York: Arno Press, 1980), 12. Sedgwick considers the spatialization of the self and how Radcliffe's characters are literally and metaphorically blocked from themselves.
21 Kamilla Elliott, *Portraiture and British Gothic Fiction: The Rise of Picture Identification, 1764–1835* (Baltimore: Johns Hopkins University Press, 2012), 136–37. © 2012 The Johns Hopkins University Press. Reprinted with permission of Johns Hopkins University Press.
22 Ibid., 260–84.

Inverting and joining *absent presence*, authors inscribe narratives of *present absence* that promise future usurpation. The past is absent, but its presence as absence proclaims that, just as what is past is absent now, so too, what is now present will be absent in future.[23]

As Elliott concludes, portraits, by definition, should preserve imaged afterlives. When art decays like bodies, 'negative iconophobia' – the fear of the unidentifiable – transforms sublime terror into uncanny horror.[24] Though Elliott restricts her analysis to portraiture, her argument is fundamental to my study's consideration of other visual frames of patriarchal abuse.

Recent scholarship frequently discusses Radcliffe's use of the sublime but does not see it as a component in the novelist's concentric visual frames of patriarchal abuse. According to Edmund Burke's *A Philosophical Inquiry into the Origin of Our Ideas of the Sublime and Beautiful* (1757), the sublime and the beautiful are mutually exclusive.[25] Burke posits terror – the fear of pain or death – as the basis of a sublime that does not threaten the viewer.[26] Alison Milbank decorously observes that 'the Burkean sublime has become both a means of dramatizing human, and particularly female subjection, and a catalyst to its overcoming'.[27] Nonetheless, as Bohls points out, the Radcliffean sublime finds the Burkean prototype deficient. In *Women Travel Writers and the Language of Aesthetics, 1716–1818*, Bohls distinguishes between aesthetic frames of gender and their psychological conditions:

> The picturesque and the Burkean sublime preside over contrasting realities and contrasting models of female selfhood. Radcliffe uses the language of aesthetics to register the unstable division of the middle-class female subject in a society where her class privilege coexists uneasily with her gendered oppression.[28]

In particular, Radcliffe rejects Burke's unconditional ultimatum: 'Terror is in all cases whatsoever, either more openly or latently the ruling principle of the sublime.'[29] Instead of divorcing love from the 'sublime' equation, Radcliffe

---

23 Elliott, *Portraiture and British Gothic Fiction: The Rise of Picture Identification, 1764–1835*, 5. © 2012 The Johns Hopkins University Press. Reprinted with permission of Johns Hopkins University Press; emphasis in original.
24 Ibid., 276.
25 Edmund Burke, *A Philosophical Enquiry into the Origin of our Ideas of the Sublime and Beautiful*, ed. James T. Boulton ([1757] New York: Oxford University Press, 1958; 1987), 58.
26 Ibid.
27 Alison Milbank, introduction, *A Sicilian Romance* ([1790] Oxford: Oxford University Press, 1993; 2008), ix–xxix (xix). Reproduced by permission of Oxford University Press.
28 Bohls, *Women Travel Writers and the Language of Aesthetics, 1716–1818*, 218. © Cambridge University Press 1995, reproduced with permission.
29 Burke, *A Philosophical Enquiry into the Origin of Our Ideas of the Sublime and the Beautiful*, 58.

suggests the interpenetration of love and terror as fundamental to a conception of sublimity that victimizes women.

The psychological tension between love and terror reaches back to what Radcliffe's childhood acquaintance Anna Laetitia Aikin (later Mrs Barbauld) refers to in her essay 'On the Pleasure Derived from Objects of Terror' (1773) as the 'paradox of the heart': 'the apparent delight with which we dwell upon objects of pure terror'.[30] The present chapter revisits Patricia Yaeger's theory of the 'failed sublime' in order to analyse the relation between women's inability to express their oppression and ekphrasis.[31] More than inspiring the fear of physical death, Radcliffe's images – textual, ekphrastic and spectral – terrorize her heroines with the prospect of something more obscure: the metaphorical death that arises from psychological trauma.

Radcliffe's preoccupation with landscape dominates much of the critical discussion of her Gothic aesthetic. A number of her contemporaries found direct references to seventeenth-century landscape painting in her imagery. As Radcliffe writes of her 1805 visit to Belvedere House,

> In a shaded corner, near the chimney [was] a most exquisite Claude, an evening view, perhaps over the Campagna of Rome. The sight of this picture imparted much of the luxurious repose and satisfaction, which we derive from contemplating the finest scenes of Nature. Here was the poet, as well as the painter, touching the imagination, and making you see more than the picture contained. You saw the real light of the sun.[32]

The novelist's assertion of the convergence of the visual and the verbal imagination resurfaces later in the nineteenth century. Margaret Oliphant was one of the many to have unearthed in Radcliffe's fiction 'the learned Poussin' infused with a 'light not unworthy of Claude'.[33] These painters are also mentioned by Charles Buck in one of the few surviving memoirs of Radcliffe in person:

> Her conversation was delightful! She sung *Adeste Fideles* with a voice mellow and melodious, but somewhat tremulous. Her countenance indicated

---

30 John Aikin and Anna Laetitia Barbauld, *Miscellaneous Pieces, in Prose*, 3rd ed. (London: J. Johnson, 1773), 120.
31 See Patricia Yaegar, 'Toward a Female Sublime', in *Gender and Theory: Dialogues on Feminist Criticism*, ed. Linda Kauffman (Oxford: Oxford University Press, 1989), 191–212.
32 Ann Radcliffe, *The Posthumous Works of Ann Radcliffe, comprising Gaston de Blondeville, A Romance; St Alban's Abbey, A Metrical Tale, with Various Poetical Pieces*, 4 vols. (London: Henry Colburn, 1833), 1: 65.
33 See Jayne Elizabeth Lewis, '"No Colour of Language": Radcliffe's Aesthetic Unbound', *Eighteenth-Century Studies* 39, no. 3 (Spring 2006): 377–90 (379).

melancholy. She had been, doubtless, in her youth beautiful. She was a great admirer of Schiller's Robbers. Her favourite tragedy was Macbeth. Her favourite painters were, Salvator, Claude and Gasper Poussin; her favourite poets, after Shakespeare, Tasso, Spenser, and Milton.[34]

Buck's inventory of the novelist's particularities suggests that the 'touches' of Claude Lorrain and Nicolas Poussin in her depictions of landscape are more than optical illusions. He merges her sources of artistic and literary inspiration into an aesthetic continuum. What she reveals about herself fits her appearance. Her melancholy countenance corresponds with the look of sublime–picturesque tableaux. It is telling that Radcliffe mentions her favourite tragedy but neglects to say whether any comedies struck her as forcefully as *Macbeth*, even though her references to *A Midsummer Night's Dream* in *The Romance of the Forest* (1791) indicate her familiarity with Shakespearean drama.[35] For Buck, Radcliffe's 'delightful' conversation was predicated on tragedy and terror.

Radcliffe did not venture abroad until after the publication of *Udolpho* in 1794.[36] She visited Holland, western Germany and the Rhine but never Southern Europe – the settings for her novels.[37] She relied on artists and travel literature to 'see' places that she could otherwise only imagine. Radcliffe copied male-authored landscapes, trusting in their accuracy, but redrew them through female eyes. As Miles writes,

> Her verbal depictions re-enforced their visual ones. This meant that her readers often had visual references to draw on. More subtly, Radcliffe's working assumption was that Rosa and Claude were faithful copyists of their seventeenth century Mediterranean world. Her art validated theirs; but so, by the same token, did theirs hers.[38]

Miles's analysis proposes a synergy between the visual art that Radcliffe alludes to and the verbal art that directs her Gothic fiction. By translating landscape painting into textual tableaux, the novelist makes the artistic 'original' and her verbal facsimile interchangeable. Though Miles confirms the exchange between the visual and the verbal in Radcliffe's prose, he overlooks the lexical power of suggestion: the novelist's verbal pictures convey messages that could not be articulated through images alone. Since terror and hysteria exceed that

---

34 Rogers, *Ann Radcliffe: A Bio-Bibliography*, 10.
35 For further discussion, see Peter Sabor and Paul Yachnin, eds., *Shakespeare and the Eighteenth Century* (Aldershot: Hampshire, 2008), 11.
36 For an introduction to Radcliffe's life, see Rogers, *Ann Radcliffe: A Bio-Bibliography*, 9.
37 Ibid.
38 Miles, *Ann Radcliffe: The Great Enchantress*, 122.

which words can communicate and art can depict, Radcliffe sees ekphrasis as a viable mode of illustrating the threats that complicated late eighteenth- and early nineteenth-century women's lives.

Rather than attempting to verbalize the 'voicelessness' of the female sex, Radcliffe allows portraits and metaphorical likenesses to communicate. Her use of visuality is aesthetically satisfying and psychologically disturbing. While Miles neglects to emphasize the role of ekphrasis, he correctly discerns the juxtaposition of presence and absence, maternal and patriarchal in her plots: 'These rhythms are reproduced through spectralization, through the pulsations of plot, through the text's self-reflexive meditations on the origins of romance, and through landscape representation'.[39] Radcliffe's inclusion of portraiture is nothing new. However, her motives differ from Austen's in one major respect: portraits are destined to haunt rather than merely 'arrest' the eyes and minds of female viewers.

Despite the critiques of Radcliffe's manipulation of Gothic sublimity that Miles and other scholars, including Sue Chaplin, provide, much of how she depicts women's physical and emotional powerlessness remains underexplored. To make the 'rhythms of the female Gothic' visible, the novelist encrypts her portraits with messages of distress. Rather than using portraits to speak of future reunions, as Burney does in *Evelina*, Radcliffe shows that in Gothic replications of patriarchal domination, even art imprisons women. Fictional women appear as trapped in two dimensions as they are in actuality.

First Visual Realm of Power: Portraiture

In *The Mysteries of Udolpho*, Radcliffe's references to portraiture invoke traumatic memories that become visible projections of tormented women. She saturates her textual, ekphrastic and spectral illustrations with the tenets of associationism, or the mind's inclination to link memories based on their contiguity.[40] According to Miles, associationism relies on John Locke's understanding of the mind as a blank tablet that is continuously moulded by subjective experience.[41] While David Hume's *A Treatise of Human Nature* (1739–40) asserts the relationship between memory and the imagination, it states that

---

39 Ibid., 127.
40 Ibid., 138. For a detailed discussion on the 'arts' of memory construction, refer to Aleida Assmann's *Cultural Memory and Western Civilisation: Functions, Media, Archives* (Cambridge: Cambridge University Press, 2011).
41 Ibid., 49. See also John Locke, *An Essay Concerning Human Understanding*, ed. Roger Woolhouse ([1689] London: Penguin, 1997).

remembered images are more powerful than invented ones.⁴² Locke's *An Essay Concerning Human Understanding* (1689) better relates to Radcliffe's treatment of impressionability because it allows for the accumulation of impressions – actual and imagined – but not their eradication. The irreversibility of such scars, Miles contends, forms the channels along which memory flows:

> The residue of these 'etches' aggregate in the mind along three possible associative paths: similarity, contrariety and contiguity. That is to say, one thing will remind us of another because it is similar, or because it is different, or because the residues are adjacent to each other in the memory.⁴³

Through visual associationism, Radcliffe links women who are trapped in dissimilar frames, thereby showing female distress as communal and transhistorical. As Elliott points out, 'Painted facial affect works not only to identify characters; it goes further to create identification *with* characters.'⁴⁴ Radcliffe's disconcerting illustrations suggest the impossibility of escape that torments the female mind. By transforming Burkean terror into her view of 'horror', she leaves her fictional women's bodies as paralysed as their minds.⁴⁵

Whereas the portrait is a subject of curiosity early on in *The Mysteries of Udolpho*, Radcliffe delays its disclosure. By deferring Emily's visual gratification, the novelist activates the heroine's and the reader's imagination. Elliott suggests that *iconism*, or 'the pictorial properties of verbal language', dominated the visual culture of the eighteenth and nineteenth centuries.⁴⁶ Radcliffe intensifies the psychological anxiety in the scene by protracting Emily's journey

---

42 See bk. 1, pt. 1, sec. 3 of David Hume's *A Treatise of Human Nature: Being an Attempt to Introduce the Experimental Method of Reasoning into Moral Subjects*, ed. Ernest C. Mossner ([1739–40] London: Penguin, 1985).
43 Miles, *Ann Radcliffe: The Great Enchantress*, 49. Miles notes that during the period in which Radcliffe was writing, the single most influential work on associationism was David Hartley's *Observations on Man* (1749).
44 Elliott, *Portraiture and British Gothic Fiction: The Rise of Picture Identification, 1764–1835*, 209. © 2012 The Johns Hopkins University Press. Reprinted with permission of Johns Hopkins University Press.
45 See Radcliffe, 'On the Supernatural in Poetry', *New Monthly Magazine* 16, no. 1 (1826): 145–52. Radcliffe contrasts her depiction of 'sublime' horror with that found in Lewis's *The Monk*: 'Terror and horror are so far opposite, that the first expands the soul, and awakens the faculties to a high degree of life; the other contracts, freezes and nearly annihilates them […] and where lies the great difference between horror and terror but in the uncertainty and obscurity, that accompany the first, respecting the dreaded evils?' (149–50).
46 Elliott, *Portraiture and British Gothic Fiction*, 203.

to where the portrait and its sitter lie, trapped in time and in space. As if emblematic of the heroine's attachment to the Marchioness, it is Emily who unlocks the chamber of secrets and Dorothée whose colourful memory brings the stillness to 'life':

> 'This saloon, ma'amselle, was in my lady's time the finest apartment in the chateau, and it was fitted up according to her own taste. All this grand furniture, but you can now hardly see what it is for the dust, and our light is none of the best – ah! How I have seen this room lighted up in my lady's time! – all this grand furniture came from Paris, and was made after the fashion of some in the Louvre there, except those large glasses, and they came from some outlandish place, and that rich tapestry. How the colours are faded already! – since I saw it last!'[47]

Dorothée contrasts the room's former decadence with its present state of dusty decay. Even if 20 years have passed since she last set eyes on the Marchioness, the impression has not faded. Her familiarity with invisible qualities of the 'ruins' on view influences Emily's perceptions, first of the place and then of the portrait.

Radcliffe's juxtaposition of past and present, visible and remembered, serves a psychological purpose. It allows the authority of Dorothée's backward-looking gaze to torment the eyes of her forward-looking companion:

> 'there is her very self! Just as she looked when she came first to the chateau. You see, madam, she was all blooming like you, then – and so soon to be cut off!'[48]

Dorothée's reference to the Marchioness's 'very self' speaks more of the supernatural than of a work of art, insinuating the sameness between life and portraiture. Dorothée's breathless exclamations communicate a critical, even if unarticulated, message. By alluding to a *nature morte* and 'her very self', Dorothée posits a mimetic resemblance between that which is visible and that which memory allows her to picture. Even if the Marchioness had once appeared in full bloom, a painter's hand has reduced her life to a body on two dimensions.

Only after Dorothée influences Emily's perceptions does Radcliffe allow the heroine to encounter the *nature morte* for herself. Unlike Dorothée, whose

---

47 Ann Radcliffe, *The Mysteries of Udolpho* (London: Oxford University Press, 1966), 532. Reproduced by permission of Oxford University Press.
48 Radcliffe, *The Mysteries of Udolpho*, 533. Reproduced by permission of Oxford University Press.

eyes have yielded to the effects of the sublime, Emily has yet to learn to see the spectral. The Marchioness's expression fixes her attention, reminding her mind's eye of an evocative miniature. Rather than leading the heroine to discover a physiognomic similarity, Radcliffe overwhelms Emily's eyes with a pathognomic resemblance. Nevertheless, she does not destabilize the heroine's rationality: 'she thought she perceived something of that pensive melancholy in the portrait, which so strongly characterised the miniature'.[49] In *The Mysteries of Udolpho*, resemblances between portraits produce knowledge. Though the novelist allows Emily to identify the 'very same self', she again postpones recognition in order to haunt the heroine's mind: 'she could not now recollect who this was'.[50] Since the context has changed, the heroine cannot 'place' the face.

In *The Mysteries of Udolpho*, Radcliffe continues to emphasize the psychological relationship between pictured and invisible forms of social subjection. From attracting the heroine's gaze to what lies within the portrait, the novelist shifts her focus to the article that is tellingly absent. As if instinctively, Emily seeks out the long black veil missing from the composition.[51] Like a maturing oil painting, the material cracks with age.[52] The narrative's transition from the unveiled face in the portrait to the material veil allows the novelist to project the Marchioness's 'very self' onto the canvas of actuality. The process intimates that there is more to the portrait than what the naked eye can detect. By casting the veil outside of the portrait, Radcliffe suggests a masculine artistic tendency to conceal the abuse of women. When Dorothée persuades her companion to stand alongside the likeness, the image of the young woman and the stilled life converge: ' "I thought [...] how like you would look to my dear mistress in that veil; – may your life, ma'amselle, be a happier one than hers!" '[53] Instead of remaining a visually distinct individual, Emily becomes what Elliott refers to as a *tableau vivant*, which allows Radcliffe to transfer 'the power of representation from the past and the inanimate to the present and living'.[54] Through resemblance, Radcliffe warns of an obscure threat to Emily's future, a threat that continues to indicate the presence of an invisible despotism.

---

49 Radcliffe, *The Mysteries of Udolpho*, 533. Reproduced by permission of Oxford University Press.
50 Radcliffe, *The Mysteries of Udolpho*, 533. Reproduced by permission of Oxford University Press.
51 Ibid., 534.
52 Ibid.
53 Radcliffe, *The Mysteries of Udolpho*, 534. Reproduced by permission of Oxford University Press.
54 Elliott, *Portraiture and British Gothic Fiction*, 77.

Whereas the heroine perceives only a veil, the older woman sees through the translucent surface. The impression resurrects the image of the dying Marchioness from the depths of her memory. As a sufferer of psychological trauma, Dorothée unintentionally perpetuates it:

> 'How well I remember her look at the time – death was in it! – I can almost fancy I see her now. – There she lay, ma'amselle – her face was upon the pillow there! This black counterpane was not upon the bed then; it was laid on, after her death, and she was laid out upon it.'[55]

Radcliffe uses Dorothée's unnerving recollection, this time of the look of death, to prompt Emily's imagination, compelling her to see that which does not exist in the natural world. The novelist's visual technique corresponds with the theories on memory that Gregor Von Feinaigle would publish nearly two decades later: 'Sensible objects have a powerful effect in recalling to the mind the ideas with which it was occupied when those ideas were presented'.[56] The 'powerful effect' to which he alludes serves a psychological function, correlating rational and irrational, natural and supernatural. For Radcliffe, almost seeing becomes a mode of believing. By converting fancy into fact and fact into fancy, Emily's ability to distinguish between material and imaginary worlds becomes increasingly eroded.

After the vision of the Marchioness's deathbed, Radcliffe continues to intensify hysteria by projecting an after-image of the Marchioness's portrait into the visible world. On the dark curtains, 'where she almost expected to have seen a human face', Dorothée's anticipation leads the heroine to invent that which does not, in fact, exist.[57] The spectre that Dorothée conjures elicits Emily's recollection of the 'look' of the dying Madame Montoni. The heroine, like her companion, capitulates to the sway of resurrected horrors:

> suddenly remembering the horror she had suffered upon discovering the dying Madame Montoni in the turret-chamber of Udolpho, her spirits fainted, and she was turning from the bed, when Dorothée, who

---

55 Radcliffe, *The Mysteries of Udolpho*, 535. Reproduced by permission of Oxford University Press.
56 Gregor Von Feinaigle, *The New Art of Memory: Founded upon the Principles Taught by M. Gregor Von Feinaigle to Which Is Prefixed Some Account of the Principal Systems of Artificial Memory, from the Earliest Period to the Present Time* (London: Sherwood, Neely and Jones, 1812), 242.
57 Radcliffe, *The Mysteries of Udolpho*, 532.

had now reached it, exclaimed 'Holy Virgin! Methinks I see my lady stretched upon that pall – as when last I saw her!'[58]

Emily's susceptibility to traumatic after-images induces hysteria. Rather than suggesting internal pain, the narrative makes anguish outwardly manifest. The heroine's distress is visible in her tears, which relieve her agony by occluding clear sight.

In *The Italian*, portraiture acquires a new dynamic. Radcliffe inverts the power of artistic representation in *The Mysteries of Udolpho*, allowing the villain's misidentification of a likeness to preserve the heroine's life. The novelist abandons female portraiture for a male miniature. On a metaphorical level, the visual stratagem temporarily allows the heroine to 'possess' the man that it features. When Schedoni steals into the sleeping Ellena's chamber, Radcliffe exposes the heroine in her most vulnerable state:

> As the light passed over her face, he perceived that the smile had vanished – the visions of her sleep were changed, for tears stole from beneath her eyelids, and her features suffered a slight convulsion. She spoke![59]

By not condemning Ellena to silence or rendering her speechless, the passage presages her survival. Seizing his opportunity, the assassin draws back the fabric draped across her heart, only to find a self-encounter:

> vengeance nerved his arm, and drawing aside the awn from her bosom, he once more raised it to strike; when, after gazing for an instant, some new cause of horror seemed to seize all his frame, and he stood for some moments aghast and motionless like a statue [...] When he recovered, he stooped to examine again the miniature, which had occasioned this revolution.[60]

Radcliffe empowers Ellena with a passive and irrefutably modest means of self-defence. Catching his eye, the man's miniature shields the heroine's heart from penetration by mirroring the assailant himself. Overcome with emotion and streaked with tears, The Confessor confesses what Radcliffe convinces him to see as his relationship to the young woman: '"Unhappy child! – behold your more unhappy father!"'[61] Even if the novelist's use of visuality intercepts assassination, the attempted murder suggests that women's fears were not far-fetched.

---

58 Radcliffe, *The Mysteries of Udolpho*, 532–33. Reproduced by permission of Oxford University Press.
59 Ann Radcliffe, *The Italian*, ed. Frederick Garber (Oxford: Oxford University Press, 1968), 534. Reproduced by permission of Oxford University Press.
60 Radcliffe, *The Italian*, 234–35. Reproduced by permission of Oxford University Press.
61 Radcliffe, *The Italian*, 236. Reproduced by permission of Oxford University Press.

In the assassination scene, Radcliffe enables Ellena to see through the villain's appearance; the heroine of *The Italian* is more of a reader of visible faces than a seer of invisible ones. As an artist by nature and by upbringing, Ellena has an eye for ocular evidence. By retracing the contours of both men's countenances, Radcliffe invites the heroine to find them as different in character as they are in years:

> He looked as if he had never smiled since the portrait was drawn; and it seemed as if the painter, prophetic of Schedoni's future disposition, had arrested and embodied that smile, to prove hereafter that cheerfulness had once played upon his features.[62]

Ellena's manner of discerning identity and character proves accurate. Even in the 'shade of the trees', Radcliffe invites her to see the word 'assassin' ekphrastically inscribed in his visage.[63] Whereas the artist had 'arrested' Schedoni's final smile, Radcliffe arrests Ellena's eyes with the man's look of malevolence. The novelist uses Olivia's perspective to provide a second reading of the miniature. In contrast to Ellena, who examines what is present before her, Olivia's gaze is influenced by the past. She beholds the haughty mask of pride characteristic of her second husband. From one visual conclusion, Olivia deduces another: she is the young woman's mother, and Schedoni is a masquerading pretender.[64] While their initial rencontre had led Olivia to detect in Ellena's features 'a slight resemblance' to the late Count di Bruno, Olivia had *feared* to trust her eyes.[65] Radcliffe's method of conjoining perspectives transforms the miniature in Ellena's possession into a material extension of her persecutor, converting a feminist 'weapon' into a patriarchal curse. *The Italian* is, by extension, less progressive than a number of critics, including Elizabeth P. Broadwell, Frederick Garber and Cannon Schmitt, have supposed.[66]

Earlier in *A Sicilian Romance*, Radcliffe uses portraiture to juxtapose the themes of live burial and double imprisonment. The novelist again introduces the likeness early on, this time in a physical portrait. In the eyes of Julia,

---

62 Radcliffe, *The Italian*, 237. Reproduced by permission of Oxford University Press.
63 Ibid., 250.
64 Ibid., 380–81.
65 Ibid.
66 See the following works that are representative of the views of *The Italian*'s stylistic shift: Elizabeth P. Broadwell's 'The Veil Image in Ann Radcliffe's *The Italian*', *South Atlantic Bulletin* 40, no. 4 (November 1975): 76–87; Frederick Garber's introduction to *The Italian* ([1797] Oxford: Oxford University Press, 1968), vii–xv; Cannon Schmitt's 'Techniques of Terror, Technologies of Nationality: Ann Radcliffe's *The Italian*', *ELH* 61, no. 4 (Winter 1994): 853–76.

whose 'extreme sensibility subjected her to frequent uneasiness',[67] the woman trapped in the miniature almost appears to come to life: 'She almost fancied that the portrait breathed, and that the eyes were fixed on hers with a look of penetrating softness'.[68] Through the conflation of actual and fanciful perceptions, the narrative allows the sitter's gaze to speak of metaphorical and literal unrest and what Daly calls ' "an invisible tyranny" '.[69]

Radcliffe's oxymoronic conjunction of 'penetrating' and 'softness' reads as appropriate for a likeness that, unlike the Marchioness's portrait, appears to breathe. More than a still life or stilled-life, the portrait is eerily animate. Instead of depicting a 'speaking body' that, as Daniel Cottom claims, is the result of the 'conflict between the desire for expression and the fear of impropriety',[70] Radcliffe uses the motif to voice women's fears of male abuse. By assigning the woman's gaze an active role, the novelist allows the miniature's look of supplication to affect Julia's perceptions. Moved beyond words, the heroine's tears articulate her sorrow. As Miles correctly suggests, the value of the miniature 'is not just that it is a valuable object for them; in their mother's absence, it is, in an obscure but definite way, an aspect of their identity'.[71] For the novelist, portraiture's significance lies in its capacity to serve as a visible intermediary between literal and metaphorical manifestations of female oppression.

Seizing upon the subjectivity of female vision and experience, Radcliffe brings the woman-as-tormented-subject to life. For Madame de Menon, the portrait stands as a material souvenir of Louisa de Bernini. Whereas Julia's imagination fills in the gaps in her memory, Madame de Menon's gaze favours the colours of the past. The sight of the miniature inspires her to look backwards and 'retrace' scenes from her past that she had tried to suppress: ' "Our pleasures and our tastes were the same; and a similarity of misfortunes might, perhaps, contribute to cement our early friendship" '.[72] Radcliffe's transition to the first-person plural suggests the similarity of women's experiences in a patriarchal society.

As in her other novels, Radcliffe's heroine must embrace her past and hear of men's malevolence in order to understand how she, too, inherits female oppression. Julia's journey to 'enlightenment' moves from portraits to subterranean wombs. As Luce Irigaray contends, the architectural *ventre*, or womb, that the

---

67 Ann Radcliffe, *A Sicilian Romance*, ed. Alison Milbank ([1821] Oxford: Oxford University Press, 1993; 2008), 4.
68 Radcliffe, *A Sicilian Romance*, 27. Reproduced by permission of Oxford University Press.
69 Quoted in LeRoy W. Smith, *Jane Austen and the Drama of Woman*, 23.
70 Daniel Cottom, *The Civilized Imagination: A Study of Ann Radcliffe, Jane Austen, and Sir Walter Scott* (Cambridge: Cambridge University Press, 1985), 53.
71 Miles, *Ann Radcliffe: The Great Enchantress*, 99.
72 Radcliffe, *A Sicilian Romance*, 28–29. Reproduced by permission of Oxford University Press.

heroine reaches offers a space in which 'children may learn to "imagine" their mothering, and to establish a maternal genealogy which patriarchy obscures'.[73] Radcliffe suggests that even if Julia's mother is free from the frame of portraiture, she still remains an object-on-view. The impossibility of verbal communication plagues her existence in art and in life. Though the portrait captures the appearance of life, what life is possible when the sitter is concealed in a subterranean dungeon? The torture that Julia's mother had experienced imprisons her mind in 'sacred horrors':

> 'Once when midnight increased the darkness of my prison, and seemed to render silence even more awful, touched by the sacred horrors of the hour, I poured forth my distress in loud lamentation [...] I remembered the dreadful vengeance which the marquis had sworn to execute upon me, if I ever, by any means, endeavoured to make known the place of my concealment; and though life had long been a burden to me, I dared not to incur the certainty of being murdered [...] and the marquis, you know, has not only power to imprison, but also the right of life and death in his own domains.'[74]

Radcliffe's pair of aural antitheses – 'silence' and 'loud lamentation' – captures Louisa's struggle between self-preservation and self-determination. Even if the Marquis's threat of physical death does not come to pass, imprisonment reads as visually synonymous with live burial. While Radcliffe allows Louisa to view her children, the castle of Mazzini had barred communication with the world beyond its walls: ' "Alas! You knew not the wretched fate of your mother, who then gazed upon you!" '[75] Rather than representing one form of female oppression, portraiture carries three distinct functions in Radcliffe's novels. As a metaphor for *natures mortes*, *tableaux vivants* and double incarceration, portraiture supplies a vivid exhibition of female oppression.

Second Visual Realm of Power: Architecture

The theme of double imprisonment introduces architecture as the second visual frame of subjection in Radcliffe's novels. After inviting Julia and Madame de Menon to resurrect Louisa de Bernini in the mind's eye, Radcliffe

---

73 Milbank, Introduction to Radcliffe's *A Sicilian Romance*, xxiii. For further discussion, see the following texts: Luce Irigary's *Speculum of the Other Woman*, trans. Gillian C. Gill (Ithaca, NY: Cornell University Press, 1985), 214–26; Bohls's *Women Travel Writers and the Language of Aesthetics 1716–1818*.
74 Radcliffe, *A Sicilian Romance*, 180. Reproduced by permission of Oxford University Press.
75 Radcliffe, *A Sicilian Romance*, 180. Reproduced by permission of Oxford University Press.

brings the 'framed' woman of *A Sicilian Romance* to life within another visual realm of oppression. The novelist moves from portraiture to architecture, much in the way that Austen does, leading Julia's contemplations from the two-dimensional figure to an in-person encounter with the woman whom the miniature depicts: her mother.[76] In the opening of the novel, the heroine's intuition allows her to see that which has yet to become visible:

> Julia observed that her chamber, which opened beyond madame's, formed a part of the southern building, with which, however, there appeared no means of communication. The late mysterious circumstances relating to this part of the fabric, now arose to her imagination, and conjured up a terror which reason could not subdue.[77]

By 'conjuring' a visual impression based on 'mysterious circumstances', Radcliffe generates the dark 'fabric' upon which Julia's imagination feeds. The heroine's awareness of the secrets that architecture conceals produces paranoia, allowing sublime terror to transform into 'horror'.

In *A Sicilian Romance*, the castle's facade communicates the unutterable evils that exist within walls that the female gaze cannot penetrate. The interplay between the surfaces of nature and architecture creates a masculine gloom that terrorizes the heroine's mind. Julia's first glimpse of the castle of Mazzini renders her eyes and mind powerless; she cannot help but surrender her thoughts to the powers of darkness:

> Julia trembled as she entered; and her emotion was heightened, when she perceived at some distance, through the long perspective of the trees, a large ruinous mansion. The gloom of the surrounding shades partly concealed it from her view; but, as she drew near, each forlorn and decaying feature of the fabric was gradually disclosed, and struck upon her heart a horror such as she had never before experienced. The broken battlements, enwreathed with ivy, proclaimed the fallen grandeur of the place, while the shattered vacant window-frames exhibited its desolation, and the high grass that overgrew the threshold seemed to say how long it was since mortal foot had entered. The place appeared fit only for the purposes of violence and destruction: and the unfortunate captives, when they stopped at its gates, felt the full force of its horrors.[78]

---

76 See Chapter 1.
77 Radcliffe, *A Sicilian Romance*, 27. Reproduced by permission of Oxford University Press.
78 Radcliffe, *A Sicilian Romance*, 111. Reproduced by permission of Oxford University Press.

Julia's reading of the castle begins in the active voice – 'she perceived' – implying that she has control over her eyes and mind. Radcliffe transforms the heroine's manner of looking by pointing her to ekphrastic messages of 'decaying features' and the 'partly concealed'. The castle, like the portrait, possesses anthropomorphic qualities but in a way that contrasts with Austen's treatment of architecture;[79] its exterior 'seemed to say' that it has not allowed anyone to leave alive.[80] The impression 'strikes upon her heart' the *idea* of oppression.[81] As well as absorbing 'the surrounding shades' in her mind's eye, Julia's body language – 'she trembled' – exteriorizes the control that the sight has over her, physically and emotionally. Only when she nears the gates does she feel 'the full force of its horrors'.[82] Radcliffe's imagery intensifies the correlation between visual and verbal communication, perception and feeling. While Julia comprehends the stronghold's visual warning, she becomes one of 'the unfortunate captives' of the Radcliffean sublime before she passes the gates: the structure becomes a metaphor for abusive men in her aesthetically sensitive eyes.

In *The Mysteries of Udolpho*, Emily's impressions of Udolpho inspire her to picture her own escape. Radcliffe shows that the imagination is free even when the heroine is physically confined. By re-envisioning and retracing the scene before her, Emily's hand–eye connection controls the wandering of her thoughts while sketching. Her physical movement reads as an act of defiance: when she picks up her drawing instruments to engage in a mindless activity, she raises her hand against the man-made oppression in which she is contained. The heroine 'dismisses' the thought of architecture's terrors by drawing a vista of fictitious optimism:

> She, however, checked her propensity to anticipate evil; and, determined to enjoy this respite from actual misfortune, tried to dismiss thought, took her instruments for drawing, and placed herself at a window, to select into a landscape some features of the scenery without.
>
> As she was thus employed, she saw, walking on the rampart below, the men, who had so lately arrived at the castle. The sight of strangers surprised her, but still more, of strangers such as these. There was a singularity in their dress, and a certain fierceness in their air, that fixed all her attention. She withdrew from the casement, while they passed, but soon returned to observe them further. Their figures seemed so well suited to

---

79 See Chapter 1.
80 Radcliffe, *A Sicilian Romance*, 111.
81 See Elliott, *Portraiture and British Gothic Fiction*, 5.
82 Radcliffe, *A Sicilian Romance*, 111.

the wildness of the surrounding objects, that, as they stood surveying the castle, she sketched them for banditti, amid the mountain-view of her picture, when she had finished which, she was surprised to observe the spirit of her group. But she had copied from nature.[83]

Radcliffe's portrait of the landscape artist at work calls attention to Emily's constant realization of her status as a viewer and an object on view, even when she is indoors. Rather than passively condoning fear inspired by men, Emily attempts to take the scene into her own hands. By changing the manner in which she perceives, she literally gains the upper hand. Though Emily observes the 'fierceness' in their countenances, she appropriates the 'strangers' as fortuitous models for her banditti. Radcliffe warns her that she must not lose sight of actuality: Emily cannot escape her identity as an object on view. As Bohls suggests, 'Emily's sessions at her window are the moments when the novel insists most strongly on its schizophrenic division into picturesque dream and sublime nightmare'.[84] The novelist insinuates that, above all, the heroine must avoid drawing attention to herself. Emily – like Radcliffe's other heroines – must not be seen, particularly when attempting to escape from the frame of female subjection.

In *The Italian*, architecture acquires another form of female escapism: the novel scripts the heroine's self-decay, or what Sedgwick describes as the 'dissolution of the self'.[85] When Ellena is carried off from the sanctuary of San Sebastiano to Spalatro's ancient and peculiar abode, her helplessness becomes the fragmentation of the self. Though she, like Julia and Emily, allows exteriors to shape her perceptions of interiors, she internalizes images of subjection. By making the murderous character of the edifice and its owner visible, Radcliffe enables Ellena to perceive that the Marchesa di Vivaldi has ordered her there for a graver purpose than imprisonment. The heroine cannot rid herself of foreboding; even sleep does not provide a means of escape. When she awakens the following morning, Ellena's muddled view of her surrounding prison reflects her psychological torment:

when starting from her mattress, she looked around her with surprise and dismay, as imperfect recollections of the past began to gather on her

---

83 Radcliffe, *The Mysteries of Udolpho*, 276. Reproduced by permission of Oxford University Press.
84 Bohls, *Women Travel Writers and the Language of Aesthetics, 1716–1818*, 226. © Cambridge University Press 1995, reproduced with permission.
85 Sedgwick, *The Coherence of Gothic Conventions*, 12.

mind. She distinguished the undrawing of iron bars, and then the countenance of Spalatro at her door, before she had a clear remembrance of her situation – that she was a prisoner in a house on a lonely shore, and that this man was her jailor.[86]

Radcliffe's reference to the 'undrawing of iron bars' is highly nuanced. The image suggests that men have the power to affect and 'bar' women's self-perceptions. As Sedgwick contends, Radcliffe's heroines are literally and metaphorically blocked from themselves.[87] Spalatro's act of 'undrawing' allows Ellena to remember that she is more than a 'prisoner': she is a castaway, stranded on a lonely shore. In labelling Ellena's jailer as 'this man', the novelist universalizes the heroine's situation, identifying it within the broader genre of female oppression. Paradoxically, her isolation as an imprisoned wanderer is not unique; she is one of the many women who see and are seen behind bars, literal and metaphorical.

To strengthen the imbalance of power between masculine architecture and Ellena's self-perceptions, Radcliffe gradually replaces the heroine's first-person viewpoint with that of 'the miserable wanderer', thereby reflecting and projecting Ellena's estrangement from her personal history:

> 'Alas! [...] I have no longer a home, a circle to smile welcomes upon me! I have no longer even one friend to support, to rescue me! I – a miserable wanderer on a distant shore! Tracked, perhaps, by the footsteps of the assassin, who at this instant eyes his victim with silent watchfulness, and awaits the moment of opportunity to sacrifice her!'[88]

Ellena's use of 'I' in the passage is short-lived. In changing patterns of self-expression from first to third person, she sees herself as hunted from the outside; she fears being cut off from the community to which she belongs. Like Julia in Burney's later work, *The Wanderer* (1814), Ellena loses herself in the fragmented identity of a woman who, though lost, remains the object of the hunt – a hunt that commences with the penetrating male gaze.[89]

Not only does Radcliffe illustrate Ellena as lost in reality, she also depicts her as lost in thought. As Emily Jane Cohen explains, 'Contemplation is "attentive consideration," whereas reverie is the "abstracted musing" of one lost in

---

86 Radcliffe, *The Italian*, 215. Reproduced by permission of Oxford University Press.
87 Sedgwick, *The Coherence of Gothic Conventions*, 12.
88 Radcliffe, *The Italian*, 220. Reproduced by permission of Oxford University Press.
89 See Laura Mulvey, 'Visual Pleasure and Narrative Cinema', *Screen* 16, no. 3 (Autumn 1975): 6–18.

thought'.[90] The heroine's contemplation of her identity crisis reaches its visible climax as her body, mind and spirit 'lean' against the man-made structure in which she is contained:

> All day Ellena either leaned against the bars of her window, lost in reverie, while her unconscious eyes were fixed upon the ocean, whose murmurs she no longer heard; or she listened for some sound from within the house, that might assist her conjectures, as to the number of persons below, or what might be passing there.[91]

The passage calls to mind a scene in Edgeworth's *Belinda* (1801), where Lady Delacour appears framed in a glass-world of female domesticity. In Radcliffe's novel, the terms and forms of imprisonment are different. Instead of being trapped in a female safe haven, Ellena awakens to the realization that she is imprisoned in a structure of patriarchal power. As Kiely has argued, Radcliffe makes space more critical than consciousness in forming perceptions.[92] Her method illustrates the heroine's Lockean self-decay, for she becomes as senseless as she is self-less. Radcliffe draws attention to the window in order to reinforce the impossibility of escape. Rather than inviting the reader to look in on Ellena, the narrative aligns the reader with the heroine in the act of looking out.

As well as using castles to imprison women in times of terror, Radcliffe uses convents to illustrate how the ancien régime of male power 'shelters' oppression, especially within sanctified walls. In Radcliffe's Gothic plots, idealized architectural forms appear to female viewers as zones of refuge. Only after moving behind convent walls do fictional women see the structures for what they are: prisons in disguise. In *A Sicilian Romance*, Radcliffe uses the convent to negate the heroine's implied belief in the moral reciprocity between aesthetics and ethical ideologies. The novelist plants the image of the convent in Madame de Menon's mind when the Marchioness discovers that her affair has been 'seen'.[93] Madame's realization of her precarious situation as a witness changes her perceptions of 'the scenes and occupations for which long habit had formed claims upon her heart'.[94] Even if Madame's circumstances have transformed her view of castle life, they have not ruptured her faith in the

---

90 Emily Jane Cohen, 'Museums of the Mind: The Gothic Art of Memory', *ELH* 62, no. 4 (Winter 1995): 883–905 (898). © 1995 The Johns Hopkins University Press. Reprinted with permission of Johns Hopkins University Press.
91 Radcliffe, *The Italian*, 217. Reproduced by permission of Oxford University Press.
92 Kiely, *The Romantic Novel in England*, 40.
93 Radcliffe, *A Sicilian Romance*, 102.
94 Ibid., 105.

comparative benevolence of religion. She imparts her belief to Julia, who is also in flight:

> Madame [...] earnestly advised her to quit her present situation, and to accompany her in disguise to the monastery of St Augustin, where she would find a secure retreat; because, even if her place of refuge should be discovered, the superior authority of the church would protect her. Julia accepted the proposal with much joy.[95]

The passage's 'earnest' tone invites the reader to sympathize with the exiles. Through the older woman's perspective, Radcliffe implies the certainty of the view that the monastery would offer a 'secure retreat', even if their male persecutors see their whereabouts. The image of the divine's unconditional protection has power, for though invisible, it fills the heroine with joy, an emotional state that rarely enters Radcliffe's Gothic plots. The novelist's emphasis on the women's 'blind faith' in superior forms of patriarchal power dramatizes their transformed perceptions of the church as an unfeeling institution.

In contrast to Madame de Menon, who envisions convent life as preferable to the menaces behind castle walls, Julia ultimately perceives St Augustin as a place where religious and secular abuses collide. Instead of sheltering Julia from patriarchal persecution, Radcliffe surrounds her heroine with the inescapable threat of attack, making her as vulnerable to secular power inside the convent as outside. Unlike the castle of Mazzini, which manifests evil on its surface, St Augustin conceals its sins. Even if the structure initially appears to them as a visual metaphor for divine protection, the novelist forces them to see a 'truth' that would have been evident to her contemporary Anglican readership: its walls stand for hypocritical values. The novelist heightens her visual irony as she illuminates to the heroine that the Abate is as oppressive as her father. Instead of showing compassion, he contemplates the sin of denying sanctuary to the woman and returning her to her persecutor. Embracing a Protestant prejudice, Radcliffe exploits the patriarchal power of the Catholic Church to invert right and wrong. Ironically, the Abate 'sees' in Julia the duplicity that he embodies:

> 'Your duplicity [...] is not the least of your offences. Had you relied upon our generosity for forgiveness and protection, an indulgence might have been granted; – but under the disguise of virtue you concealed your crimes, and your necessities were hid beneath the mask of devotion.'[96]

---

95 Radcliffe, *A Sicilian Romance*, 105. Reproduced by permission of Oxford University Press.
96 Radcliffe, *A Sicilian Romance*, 132. Reproduced by permission of Oxford University Press.

Radcliffe's insistent references to 'invisible' hypocrisy – 'duplicity', 'disguise of virtue' and 'mask of devotion' – reveal how the heroine's perceptions have altered. Her recognition of duplicity shows that her perceptions have changed to Radcliffe's own. The episode epitomizes the way in which the novelist uses architecture as a visual means of questioning the moral reciprocity between architectural form and architectural function, estate and owner. Structures are not, as Kiely proposes, characters; rather, they are analogues for the immortality of patriarchal abuse.[97] In Radcliffe's novels, whereas some structures exteriorize evil and others internalize it, architecture consistently serves as a visual metaphor for the plight of womanhood instead of a means of 'sighting' companionate couples.

Third Visual Realm of Power: Veils

Radcliffe's third analogue for patriarchal abuse treats the veil as a prison that moves between man-made and natural frames of female oppression. In *The Italian*, the novelist reintroduces the motif of double imprisonment, this time focusing on the power relationship between the convent and the veil. In its religious context, the veil projects a degree of visual anonymity that exhibits men's power over women's appearances. Rather than preserving Ellena's identity through forced concealment, the fabric thwarts Vivaldi's attempts to identify his lover. His timely arrival on the morning of what the Prior calls '"our *lady's* day"' (the occasion where women receive the veil, whether willingly or unwillingly) amplifies the image of impending doom in the reader's imagination.[98] By making Ellena's identity opaque, Radcliffe denies her rescuer of the power of clear sight:

> With what anxious solicitude did Vivaldi endeavour to look through the veils of the several nuns in search of Ellena, whom he believed the barbarous policy of his mother might already have devoted to the cloister! With a solicitude still stronger, he tried to catch a glimpse of the features of the novices, but their faces were shaded by hoods, and their white veils, though thrown half back, were disposed in such artful folds that they concealed them from observation, as effectually as did the pendant lawn the features of the nuns.[99]

Here, Radcliffe turns the penetrating male gaze into a selectively chivalric trait. Vivaldi has to see through veils in order to save the heroine from an

---

97 Kiely, *The Romantic Novel in England*, 40.
98 Radcliffe, *The Italian*, 118; emphasis in original.
99 Radcliffe, *The Italian*, 118. Reproduced by permission of Oxford University Press.

obscure destiny. The novelist uses three visual impediments – hoods, veils and folds – to complicate his frantic attempts to make out the novices' features. As well as intensifying visual confusion through variation, Radcliffe manipulates chiaroscuro, juxtaposing fabrics of white and shade. The other women have a hand in warding against penetration: not trusting to material alone, they had 'artfully' folded the fabric to add depth to their anonymity.

Having imbued the scene with visual tension, Radcliffe enables Vivaldi's *manner* of looking to overcome the Catholic Church's customary fashioning of women. As he sees with his heart as well as his eyes, Vivaldi's love conquers his fears of failure. Radcliffe delays his identification of the woman approaching the altar of self-sacrifice in order to drive the suspense to its psychological climax. Through the architectural prison of the convent, Radcliffe reveals how Ellena has become 'our lady of tears' in human form:

> The priest was beginning the customary exhortation, when she lifted her half-veil, and, shewing a countenance where meek sorrow was mingled with heavenly sweetness, raised her blue eyes, all bathed in tears, and waved her hand as if she would have spoken.[100]

Only by lifting the heroine's half-veil can the novelist expose Ellena's emotion. Even when expressed, her sorrow appears self-consciously 'meek'.

In *The Italian*'s scene of resisted sacrifice, Radcliffe imbues her anti-Catholic perspective with the theme of verbal inexpressibility. Ellena makes three attempts to raise her voice before managing to translate her ekphrastic messages into audible speech. By lifting her hand to remove her veil, she communicates her desire to speak out. Through visuality, Radcliffe communicates that the heroine is simultaneously on the cusp of speech and the threshold of invisibility. Ellena appears to find it as difficult to raise her voice as it had been to lift her veil. As Elliott writes, 'even as these passages undermine the representational capacities of words, they do so paradoxically *through* words'.[101] Only after waving her hand does Ellena generate the strength that she requires to translate her visual language into verbal speech:

> 'I protest in the presence of this congregation […] that I am brought hither to pronounce vows which my heart disclaims.'[102]

---

100 Radcliffe, *The Italian*, 119. Reproduced by permission of Oxford University Press.
101 Elliott, *Portraiture and British Gothic Fiction: The Rise of Picture Identification, 1764–1835*, 207. © 2012 The Johns Hopkins University Press. Reprinted with permission of Johns Hopkins University Press; emphasis in original.
102 Radcliffe, *The Italian*, 119. Reproduced by permission of Oxford University Press.

Radcliffe's scripting of female protest shows that Ellena's words and gestures are synonymous. The heroine's body and voice speak the same language. For Radcliffe's fictional women, ekphrastic messages serve as verbatim substitutes for verbal expression. In a man-made structure sanctifying patriarchal power, Ellena's actions and words may be seen as 'blasphemous'. With the hypocritical Abate's vision as the convent's guide, the structure has 'progressed' to the Dark Ages, subjecting the women that it possesses to tears of ekphrastic sorrow rather than proclamations of effable joy.

In *The Italian*, the religious veil acts as a mobile prison, attracting patriarchal abuse beyond architectural confines. It fastens the convent's malediction on women who quit its walls, tricking them into seeing the material as a means of visual protection. In order to escape, Ellena must appear as someone she is not, even amongst her own sex. Mistaking the fabric for a benediction, Olivia gives the heroine a nun's veil as a weapon of disguise: '"but my veil, though thin, has hitherto protected you, and we must hope it may still assist your purpose"'.[103] Her 'hope' identifies the veil as a manifestation of the paranoia of being seen. Even if it thwarts male penetration, the novelist suggests that the nuns' eyes are accustomed to identifying a woman from her veil. Fearing that the article would be 'insufficient protection', Ellena is haunted by 'the terror of instant discovery'.[104] As Sedgwick proposes, 'It is in the insistence of this constitutive struggle, and the attenuated versions involving the veil and the habit rather than the countenance itself, that the Gothic novel makes its most radical contribution to the development of character in fiction.'[105] In order to escape from patriarchal power, the novelist informs the reader that, ironically, the heroine must trick the eyes of other women.

Despite the veil's thinness, Radcliffe allows its selective transparency to assist the heroine's flight from the convent. Rather than projecting visual anonymity, Ellena's religious veil – in this 'foreign' context – labels her as a runaway. By altering the heroine's surroundings, Radcliffe changes the manner in which the heroine's veil becomes seen. Instead of serving as a cloak of invisibility, the article makes Ellena dangerously conspicuous, even if it shields her face from view. The narrative reveals that those whose eyes are accustomed to seeing the veil become visually desensitized. Through metaphor, the novelist extends the motif's influence to both sexes' perceptions. Outside the convent, Ellena loses her awareness of her veil's religious connotation:

---

103 Radcliffe, *The Italian*, 133. Reproduced by permission of Oxford University Press.
104 Ibid., 129.
105 Eve Kosofsky Sedgwick, 'The Character in the Veil: Imagery of the Surface in the Gothic Novel', *PMLA* 96, no. 2 (March 1981): 255–70 (263).

> During this interval, her mind had been too entirely occupied by cares and apprehension to allow her once to notice, that the veil she wore was other than her usual one; but it had been too well observed by some of the Ursaline sisters.[106]

Her eyes grow used to the world as it appears through its surface. Vivaldi's vision is selectively blind: he fails to see the inappropriateness of his lover's attire, for he 'observed, for the first time, that Ellena was shrouded in a nun's veil'.[107] Only when the Inquisition accuses him of stealing a nun from her convent does Radcliffe open his eyes to the plight of visibility that women face.

As well as provoking her heroine's innermost fears, Radcliffe uses visuality to shift the interpretation of sights onto the reader. Not long after Annette warns Emily of Signora Laurentini's wandering spirit, the heroine seeks out the curiously veiled picture frame that everyone fears. The visual tension between that which is pictured – Emily becoming the living image of death – and that which cannot be ascertained haunts the reader's imagination:

> Emily passed with faltering steps, and having paused a moment at the door, before she attempted to open it, she then hastily entered the chamber, and went towards the picture, which appeared to be enclosed in a frame of uncommon size, that hung in a dark part of the room. She paused again, and then, with a timid hand, lifted the veil; but instantly let it fall – perceiving that what it had concealed was no picture, and, before she could leave the chamber, she dropped senseless on the floor.[108]

By leaving her illustration disturbingly unfinished, Radcliffe makes the sight as curious for the reader as Annette had made it for Emily. Referring to *The Mysteries of Udolpho*, Coleridge writes, 'This art of escaping the guesses of the reader has been improved and brought to perfection along with the reader's sagacity.'[109] The process to which Coleridge alludes is what Elliott understands as 'negative iconophobias', or 'phobias of the *absence* of imaged identity'.[110] As she explains, 'The horror is that an image turns out to be an original – that a representation turns out to be what is represented.'[111] Instead of bringing

---

106 Radcliffe, *The Italian*, 188. Reproduced by permission of Oxford University Press.
107 Ibid.
108 Radcliffe, *The Mysteries of Udolpho*, 248–49. Reproduced by permission of Oxford University Press.
109 Quoted in Miles, *Ann Radcliffe: The Great Enchantress*, 133.
110 Elliott, *Portraiture and British Gothic Fiction*, 276; emphasis in original.
111 Elliott, *Portraiture and British Gothic Fiction: The Rise of Picture Identification, 1764–1835*, 268. © 2012 The Johns Hopkins University Press. Reprinted with permission of Johns Hopkins University Press.

clarity, the narrator allows the dark matter to appear darker, inviting the reader to picture an unthinkable evil.

Sedgwick offers a different interpretation of the scene. She claims that Emily's seeing a decaying body 'proves deluded, since the figure in the pall behind the veil is *really* made of wax, an old 'monkish' memento mori, and is no way related to the rest of the story'.[112] Only in the novel's penultimate chapter does Radcliffe unravel the dark secrets of the traumatizing spectacle: 'Had she dared to look again, her delusion and her fears would have vanished together, and she would have perceived, that the figure before her was not human, but formed of wax.'[113] By cementing the connection between fear, sight and delusions, Radcliffe allows the reader to partake in the psychological consequences of that which is literally or metaphorically veiled: the self from its own penetration. In her Gothic novels, the veil in literal and metaphorical, visible and invisible forms illuminates that the heroines' fears are as much before their eyes as they are within their minds.

Fourth Visual Realm of Male Power: Natural Panoramas

Radcliffe continues to use visuality to depict patriarchal power's omnipotence in natural landscapes. Her heroines remain under threat wherever they find themselves, for predatory males lurk unseen in sublime panoramas. As Cohen argues, the novelist's visual technique reflects the *Ad Herennium*'s classical teachings.[114] The text, commonly attributed to Marcus Tullius Cicero, suggests a reason for the sharp sense of menace that Radcliffe's landscapes evoke to women:

> It will be more advantageous to obtain backgrounds in a deserted than in a populous region, because the crowding and passing to and fro of people confuse and weaken the impress of the images, while solitude keeps their outlines sharp.[115]

Radcliffe seeks an analogous approach to aesthetics for psychological effect. The deserted landscapes that she depicts draw attention to the outline of the female body. With her fluid transitions between concentric visual realms,

---

112 Sedgwick, 'The Character in the Veil', 258.
113 Radcliffe, *The Mysteries of Udolpho*, 662. Reproduced by permission of Oxford University Press.
114 Emily Jane Cohen, 'Museums of the Mind', 885–86.
115 [M. Tulli Cicero?], *Rhetorica Ad. Herennium*, trans. Harry Caplan (Cambridge, MA: Harvard University Press, 1954; 1981), 3.19: 31.

Radcliffe's depictions of male power turn her fictional women's lives into endlessly enfolded nightmares from which they can never awake.

To transform natural scenery into a psychological medium, Radcliffe turns to landscape painting. She seizes upon its ability to communicate ineffable horrors through ekphrasis. According to Cottom, Radcliffe's landscapes have a 'talismanic importance':

> Characters often seem nothing but reflections of those landscapes, over which their various psychological states may be displayed on a larger scale [...] Landscape comes to appear as a the central character of her novels, or her individual characters as fragments of a general human nature that cannot be fully revealed unless one makes a tour of the variety of nature, discovering character through cartography.[116]

While Cottom rightly posits a reflective relationship between character and landscape, he does not observe nature's greater function in Radcliffe's Gothic fiction. Rather than representing the 'central character of her novels', as Cottom suggests, the antagonistic landscapes that Radcliffe draws act as zones of psychological osmosis, or interchange, between mood and atmosphere. The relationship implies the homeostasis that exists between characters' temperaments and the appearances of landscapes.

Radcliffe's use of chiaroscuro helps illustrate women's susceptibility to visual impressions. The mood of landscapes colours her heroines' perceptions, imbuing them with the emotional depth and thematic meaning that a sequence of unequivocal contrasts produces. In the process, the novelist ensures that similar landscapes will always be seen through different eyes. To make her message about patriarchal power visible, she alternates between the wild obscurities of Salvator Rosa's *Landscape with Hermits* (1664) and the soft luminosity of Claude Lorrain's *The Enchanted Castle* (1664). Even if her panoramas are often very similar, visually attuned women respond to nature and the tension between the individual and society in a variety of ways.

Sir Walter Scott's account of Radcliffe's landscape technique includes a simple illustration. He explains that were six artists to transpose her imagery onto the canvas, their work would attest to the diverse views that her imagery has the potential to conjure:

> As her story is usually enveloped in mystery, so there is, as it were, a haze over her landscapes, softening indeed the whole, adding an interest and

---

116 Cottom, *The Civilized Imagination: A study of Ann Radcliffe, Jane Austen, and Sir Walter Scott*, 35. © Cambridge University Press 1985, reproduced with permission.

dignity to particular parts, and thereby producing every effect which the author desired, but without communicating any absolutely precise or individual image to the reader.[117]

As Scott suggests, Radcliffe's artistic genius lies in her balancing of revealed and concealed details. Even if her penchant for vivid adjectives seems indicative of an 'absolutely precise' message, specificity is an optical illusion.

In addition to creating visual depth through opposing layers of description, Radcliffe manipulates chiaroscuro for another effect. Jayne Lewis concedes that even if other Gothic novelists, including Horace Walpole and Matthew Gregory Lewis, drew their scenes from the same tableaux, the quality that sets Radcliffe's novels apart is their preoccupation with colour. She concludes that as 'in effect, a "language", colour emerges as a mode of mediation that possesses considerable potential as an autocritical rhetorical form'.[118] The aesthetic tension between the coloured and the colourless becomes a language of moral disjunction.

As much as critics applaud Radcliffe's word-painted landscapes, many disparage their repetitive quality. In a letter to John Hamilton Reynolds, John Keats satirizes Radcliffe's prosaic tendency:

I am going among Scenery whence I intend to tip you the Damosel Radcliffe – I'll cavern you, and grotto you, and waterfall you, and wood you, and water you, and immense-rock you, and tremendous-sound you, and solitude you.[119]

The poet's assessment of Radcliffe's technique mocks its formulaic presentations of landscapes. His account also points to the novelist's habit of appending visible motifs with invisible sounds and emotions. Overlooking the multisensory depth of her landscapes, Keats exaggerates the novelist's repetitive depictions. The *British Critic* issues a similar complaint, proclaiming, 'We have somewhat too much of evening and morning or woods, and hills, and vales, and streams.' The *Gentleman's Magazine* also laments a 'too great frequency of landscape-painting, which, though it shews the extensiveness of her observation and invention, wearies the reader with repetitions'.[120] Radcliffe's obsession with hyperbole and repetition breeds 'sameness', but 'sameness' functions as an unerring recreation of post-traumatic shock.

---

117 See Lewis, '"No Colour of Language"', 383.
118 Ibid., 385.
119 John Keats, Letter to John Hamilton Reynolds, 14 March 1818, *Letters of John Keats*, ed. Frederick Page (London: Oxford University Press, 1954), 90. Reprinted by permission of Oxford University Press.
120 *British Critic*, 4 (August 1794), 110; *Gentleman's Magazine*, 64 (September 1794), 834.

Radcliffe suggests a more complex function for repetition in *A Journey through Holland, &c. made in the summer of 1794*, where she vindicates her stylization of nature:

> It is difficult to spread varied pictures of such scenes before the imagination. A repetition of the same images of rock, wood and water, and the same epithets of grand, vast and sublime, which necessarily occur, must appear tautologous, on paper, though their archetypes in nature, ever varying in outline, or arrangement, exhibit new visions to the eye, and produce new shades of effect upon the mind.[121]

Radcliffe informs the reader that she creates 'new visions' of landscapes out of codified models. The redundancy that 'desensitizes' the reader ironically sensitizes her fictional women; their vantage points are perpetually on the move, physically and metaphorically. As much as the mind colours landscapes, landscapes have the potential to colour the mind. By 'tormenting' her various young heroines' eyes and imaginations with the same vistas, the novelist endows her landscapes with a psychological subtext. Instead of sparking terror through the foreign, the 'uncanny' is recognizable and inescapable.[122] Without repetition, it would fail to function.

In *A Sicilian Romance*, landscape initially appears to shelter the female sex. As Bohls contends, it is important to distinguish between the sublime scenery that Radcliffe's heroines experience during their travels and the Burkean sublime of man-made structures.[123] The novelist leads her heroines in flight to horizons that offer them the appearance of emotional relief. Rather than using free indirect discourse, she relies on a third-person narrator to trace how nature hypnotizes Madame de Menon:

> The rich colouring of evening glowed through the dark foliage, which spreading a pensive gloom around, offered a scene congenial to the present temper of her mind, and she entered the shades. Her thoughts, affected by the surrounding objects, gradually sunk into a pleasing and complacent melancholy, and she was insensibly led on. She still followed the course of the stream to where the deep shades retired, and the scene again opening to day, yielded to her a view so various and sublime, that she paused in thrilling and delightful wonder. A group of wild and

---

121 For an insightful analysis of this passage, refer to Cottom, *The Civilized Imagination*, 35.
122 See David B. Morris, 'Gothic Sublimity', *New Literary History* 16, no. 2, The Sublime and the Beautiful: Reconsiderations (Winter 1985): 299–319 (307).
123 Bohls, *Women Travel Writers and the Language of Aesthetics, 1716–1818*, 216.

grotesque rocks rose in a semicircular form, and their fantastic shapes exhibited Nature in her most sublime and striking attitudes. Here her vast magnificence elevated the mind of the beholder to enthusiasm.[124]

The scene's vivid incorporation of chiaroscuro corresponds with a gradation of morals. Madame de Menon's 'insensible' state prevents her from seeing the 'rich glow of evening' for what it is: the manifestation of the patriarchal 'divine'. Architectural imprisonment has left the woman's perspective untrained to see through nature's illusion of transparent congeniality.

In correlating the 'pensive gloom' of the evening with the 'temper' of the woman's mind, Radcliffe asserts the interdependency between woman-as-beholder and vista-on-view. Cottom suggests that Madame de Menon is simultaneously included and excluded from 'worldly darkness':

Melancholy at once preserves and transcends worldly darkness and oppression. It captures better than any other feeling the boundary that Radcliffe's art must draw between observed and inhabited nature, for it includes the problems of social life and yet excludes them by assigning them to memory and using this memory as a launching pad for futurity.[125]

While Cottom alludes to the powers of 'melancholy', he does not analyse their connection to Radcliffe's concentric realms of female powerlessness. By projecting 'melancholy' into the visible landscape, Radcliffe metaphorically absorbs Madame de Menon into her surroundings. In suspending the woman's mind from the trials of the physical world, the novelist invites her to enter into communion with the sublime of the Christian God.

In *A Sicilian Romance*, Radcliffe also exploits landscape's deceptive promise to her fictional women that they can remain 'overshadowed' by natural backgrounds. At first, the heroine succeeds, becoming only a voice:

Madame looked around in search of the sweet warbler, and observed at some distance a peasant girl seated on a small projection of the rock, overshadowed by drooping sycamores.[126]

Unlike man-made thresholds of patriarchal power, nature does not deliberately deprive women of their voices. Convinced that she is alone, the peasant

---

124 Radcliffe, *A Sicilian Romance*, 104. Reproduced by permission of Oxford University Press.
125 Cottom, *The Civilized Imagination: A Study of Ann Radcliffe, Jane Austen, and Sir Walter Scott*, 49–50. © Cambridge University Press 1985, reproduced with permission.
126 Radcliffe, *A Sicilian Romance*, 105. Reproduced by permission of Oxford University Press.

girl feels at liberty to express herself in a natural manner. The novelist emphasizes that it is the heroine's distinctly human tone of voice that gives her away. Sight becomes the effect of sound: Madame de Menon's eyes suddenly find within the rocky landscape a 'distinct' physiognomy. The narrative traces the transformation from invisibility and visual anonymity to full recognition. Through selective visibility, the novelist reveals to Madame de Menon that the 'warbler' is not the 'peasant girl' that her appearance suggests: 'Language cannot paint the sensation of Madame, when, in the disguise of a peasant girl, she distinguished the features of Julia, whose eyes lighted up with sudden recollection, and who sunk into her arms overcome with joy.'[127] Only when Julia's eyes show sudden knowledge does Radcliffe invite the heroine to appear as herself rather than as a wandering songster.

In other episodes, Radcliffe uses sublime scenery to shock fictional women out of their reveries. The 'innumerable roseate tints' initially soothe Julia into 'a temporary forgetfulness of her sorrows', only to give way to the terrors of the earth.[128] Overwhelming the heroine's eyes with the spectres of her pursuers, Radcliffe renders the feminine picturesque an optical delusion:

> She observed a party of horsemen winding down the side of a hill behind her. Their uncommon speed alarmed her, and she pushed her horse into a gallop. On looking back Madame de Menon clearly perceived they were in pursuit. Soon after the men suddenly appeared from behind a dark grove within a small distance of them; and, upon their nearer approach, Julia, overcome with fatigue and fear, sunk breathless from her horse.[129]

Through visual repetition, Radcliffe informs the reader that in sublime landscapes, men usurp women's traditional powers of blending in. Here, it is the sudden emergence of the men from the 'dark grove' that terrorizes the fictional women, affecting their perceptions of what they see. The figures appear to rise out of the landscape, even if they are 'winding down' the hill, bringing the panorama nightmarishly to life. In the scene, the villains are insiders rather than outsiders; they appear as much at home in nature as they do within their imposing abodes. Though Julia and Madame de Menon attempt to 'preserve' themselves, the psychological potency of the sight overcomes their bodies. Instead of spurring them to flight, the women's emotions immobilize their efforts. The image of Julia sinking into the hands of the Duke's men articulates

---

127 Radcliffe, *A Sicilian Romance*, 105. Reproduced by permission of Oxford University Press.
128 Ibid., 125.
129 Radcliffe, *A Sicilian Romance*, 110. Reproduced by permission of Oxford University Press.

what the rest of the scene only suggests: men's power over women operates like gravity. 'Natural law' is ultimately inescapable.

In *A Sicilian Romance*, Radcliffe's fictional women who look alike are more likely to survive. As the hunt begins with the gaze, similar appearances lead to visual confusion that, unlike disguise, is unintended but useful. The novelist makes men's lust for power visible through two all-too-similar episodes. The Marquis becomes Radcliffe's first victim, for his passions distort his vision:

> But his attention was quickly called from the beauties of inanimate nature, to objects more interesting; for he observed two persons, whom he instantly recollected to be the same that he had formerly pursued over the plain [...] In the lady the duke saw the very air and shape of Julia, and his heart bounded at the sight. They were seated with their backs to the cliffs upon which the duke stood, and he therefore surveyed them unobserved. They were now almost within his power, but the difficulty was how to descend the rocks, whose stupendous heights and craggy steeps seemed to render them impassable.[130]

As Miles and Milbank also contend when analysing the scene, Radcliffe makes patriarchal power visible to fictional women and to the reader.[131] Even if the Duke remains 'unobserved', his bird's-eye perspective yields nothing more concrete than the woman's 'air' and 'shape'. His physical strength appears to compensate for his perceptual impairment; he overcomes natural obstacles with 'supernatural' rapidity. Whereas Julia and Madame de Menon accurately identify other landscape-bound women, visual assumptions taint Julia's pursuers' perceptions. The conceited Duke only sees who he wants to see, exclaiming, '"Wretched girl! I have at last secured you!"'[132] Only after he seizes his prey does Radcliffe invite the reader to observe that the male gaze is not always infallible, even if it is inescapable. Instead of catching Julia, he secures her visual double, who – unlike Julia – is fleeing from the 'live burial' of convent existence.

Radcliffe continues to illustrate that self-preservation is a joint endeavour in the subsequent hunt scene. She shifts the reader's attention to the cavalier's view of the woman in the landscape. By forcing the man to succumb to the same optical illusion, Radcliffe reiterates that in *A Sicilian Romance*, women who resemble each other are more likely to survive. The novelist

---

130 Radcliffe, *A Sicilian Romance*, 93–94. Reproduced by permission of Oxford University Press.
131 See Miles, *The Great Enchantress*, 80 and Milbank, Introduction to Radcliffe's *A Sicilian Romance*, xx.
132 Radcliffe, *A Sicilian Romance*, 94.

makes the cavalier's approach terrifyingly familiar, persuading the heroine to see the man storming into the room as the Duke rather than who he is: a complete stranger. The surprise attack leaves Julia 'almost lifeless'.[133] Even if visual duplication empowers both women, they become victims of paranoia. Though 'finding herself unexpectedly at liberty', Julia remains terrorized.[134] In the novelist's sublime panoramas, female agency and elation are always temporary.

In *The Mysteries of Udolpho*, Radcliffe continues to treat landscape as a visual signifier of male power but shifts from reverie to recollection. She uses the sublimity of the Alps to awe the heroine with new sights that nonetheless strike her eyes as vaguely familiar. Though the heroine cannot see the resemblance between the temperament of the landscape and her memories of Valancourt, Radcliffe uses the impressions to project and reflect the heroine's ambivalent feelings:

> And here such scenes of sublimity opened upon them as no colours of language must dare to paint! Emily's mind was even so much engaged with new and wonderful images, that they sometimes banished the idea of Valancourt, though they frequently revived it.'[135]

The novelist's criticism of the insufficiencies of language links the sublimity of nature with the 'idea of Valancourt'. The single means of escape that the novelist allows Emily is through her eyes. Only by transforming into another type of woman – a peasant of the Piemonte – would she be 'free' from the burden of being subjected to the whims of patriarchal society. As much as she longs for Valancourt, she also longs to be at liberty to spend 'careless' hours in such 'romantic landscapes'.[136]

Radcliffe does not overindulge Emily in the idylls of nature. She uses the optical illusion of distance to suggest that, like love, the abuse of power knows no borders. Fixing her heroine's mind's eye on a far-off horizon, Radcliffe invites her to contemplate the panoramic scope of her helplessness: 'she considered that she was as much in his power at Venice as she could be elsewhere'.[137] The 'fairy' city of Venice stimulates fanciful images that usurp her mind:

---

133 Ibid.
134 Ibid., 112.
135 Radcliffe, *The Mysteries of Udolpho*, 167–68. Reproduced by permission of Oxford University Press.
136 Ibid.
137 Radcliffe, *The Mysteries of Udolpho*, 216–17. Reproduced by permission of Oxford University Press.

She indulged herself in imagining what might be the manners and delights of a sea-nymph, till she almost wished to throw off the habit of mortality, and plunge into the green wave to participate [*sic*] them.[138]

While Emily 'indulges' her imagination, the 'habit of mortality' covers her eyes, preventing her from actually 'picturing' as a sea nymph.[139] Broadwell similarly warns that a woman who has not consciously experienced death cannot understand it: 'Like the Jungian Shadow, it is the distance between the actual and the potential, between the ego as actualized self and what the person wants to achieve.'[140] For Radcliffe's heroine, the only obstacle preventing her vicarious transubstantiation is the 'the habit of mortality'. Visual opacity prompts her to turn inwards: 'and, anxious to escape from serious reflections, she now endeavoured to throw her fanciful ideas into a train, and concluded the hour with composing the following lines'.[141] The words of her poem 'The Sea-Nymph' allow her to turn from the unimaginable to the imaginable.

The novelist pairs Emily's self-perceptions with Montoni's deprecatory view of her as an outcast:

'by the right of my will; if you can elude that, I will not enquire by what right you do so. I now remind you, for the last time, that you are a stranger, in a foreign country, and that it is your interest to make me your friend; you know the means; if you compel me to become your enemy – I will venture to tell you, that the punishment shall exceed your expectation.'[142]

The man's articulation of his supreme power affects the heroine's self-perceptions. Even if Radcliffe mentions how 'a consciousness of misery was all that remained in her mind', Emily never falls entirely sense-less, as Julia does in *A Sicilian Romance*. The novelist insinuates that though Montoni threatens Emily, the heroine does not submit herself to intimidation. While Montoni acknowledges that she speaks

---

138 Radcliffe, *The Mysteries of Udolpho*, 178. Reproduced by permission of Oxford University Press. See also George E. Haggerty's article, 'Fact and Fancy in the Gothic Novel', *Nineteenth-Century Fiction* 39, no. 4 (March 1985): 379–91.
139 Radcliffe, *The Mysteries of Udolpho*, 178.
140 Broadwell, 'The Veil Image in Ann Radcliffe's *The Italian*', 79–80.
141 Radcliffe, *The Mysteries of Udolpho*, 178. Reproduced by permission of Oxford University Press.
142 Radcliffe, *The Mysteries of Udolpho*, 216–17. Reproduced by permission of Oxford University Press.

'like a heroine', his message suggests that she must show that she can suffer in order to become one.[143] Until then, she remains in his power.

By endowing Emily with an artist's eye, Radcliffe intensifies the role of chiaroscuro in the novel. The heroine's sensitivity to visual nuance makes her susceptible to the conflation of light and shadow that perpetually confronts her gaze in natural panoramas. As well as representing aesthetic tension, *chiaro* and *scuro* become the novelist's language of moral disjunction:

> Emily looked with some degree of terror on the savage countenances of these people, shewn by the fire, which heightened the romantic effect of the scenery, as it threw a red dusky gleam upon the rocks and on the foliage of the trees, leaving heavy masses of shade and regions of obscurity, which the eye feared to penetrate.[144]

Radcliffe contrasts the fiery glow of the setting sun with the 'dusky gleam' of the fire. The oxymoronic pairing of 'dusky' and 'gleam' projects visual tension into the surroundings. As much as the fire represents a source of literal and metaphorical enlightenment, it only illuminates a landscape that creates 'some degree of terror'. Rather than throwing light on every object, the fire's 'gleam' is selective. Bohls argues that the novelist provides a 'parable of women kept literally and metaphorically in the dark' by men.[145] To Emily's overwhelmed eyes, the 'red dusky gleam' appears to declare war on its complementary hue – verdant green. The scene epitomizes the novelist's technique of using natural panoramas to convey the way in which her fictional women are subjected to fears that oscillate between the *chiaro* and the *scuro*, the revealed and the concealed.

Fifth Visual Realm of Male Power: The Obscure

In her fifth and final concentric realm, Radcliffe departs from man-made and natural contexts of patriarchal power to show that women are 'framed' within the obscure. Radcliffe juxtaposes the defined and the undefined, sound and sight in various forms. Her novels show that women's fears of immaterial matter are as well founded as those of material threats. Her heroines' tendencies to sensibility and flights of fancy allow the novelist to make the obscure nightmarishly visible within material worlds of male power. The terrors of the visually undefined enter her heroines' eyes and resurface in their dreams.

---

143 Ibid., 381.
144 Radcliffe, *The Mysteries of Udolpho*, 40. Reproduced by permission of Oxford University Press.
145 Bohls, *Women Travel Writers and the Language of Aesthetics, 1716–1818*, 218.

By inducing fits of irrationality through encounters with the inexplicable, the novelist unlocks the futurity-induced hysteria that Burney, Edgeworth and Austen leave politely to the imagination. As Radcliffe writes in *A Sicilian Romance*, 'It is painful to know, that we are operated upon by objects whose impressions are variable as they are indefinable.'[146] The psychological consequences of oppression force women into a permanent state of insecurity and instability. As Terry Castle contends, the trope of 'spectralisation' conflating the living and the dead contradicts the reality of dying.[147] Though what appears to represent death is often an optical delusion, the obscure elicits a response from the unconscious. For Radcliffe, the 'blot' within her heroines' perceptions is actually woman herself – veiled from her own penetration.

David Morris's discussion of Sigmund Freud's 'The Uncanny' in Gothic fiction explains the awakening of the unconscious in Radcliffe's writing. His analysis of Gothic psychology identifies the uncanny as that which is simultaneously ordinary and extraordinary, natural and supernatural; it 'defeats our efforts to separate ourselves from it'.[148] To borrow Freud's definition, the uncanny '"is in reality nothing new or alien, but something which is familiar and old-established in the mind and which has become alienated from it only through the process of repression"'.[149] What Radcliffe depicts in her plots is a representation of women's fears that 'no colours of language'[150] can capture.

Rather than reducing mortality to a physical experience, Radcliffe uses it as a psychological metaphor for the terrors of patriarchal power. Her metaphorical representations of death draw on Locke's construct of nothingness in *An Essay Concerning Human Understanding* (1689):

> There seems to be a constant decay of all our ideas, even of those which are struck deepest, and in minds the most retentive; so that if they be not sometimes renewed by repeated exercise of the sense, or reflection on those kinds of objects which at first occasioned them, the print wears out, and at last there remains nothing to be seen. Thus the ideas, as well as the children of our youth often die before us; and our minds represent to us those tombs to which we are approaching.[151]

---

146 Radcliffe, *A Sicilian Romance*, 51. Reproduced by permission of Oxford University Press.
147 See Terry Castle's 'The Spectralization of the Other in *The Mysteries of Udolpho*', *The New Eighteenth Century: Theory, Politics, English Literature*, ed. Felicity Nussbaum and Laura Brown (New York: Methuen, 1987), 231–53.
148 David Morris, 'Gothic Sublimity', 307.
149 Quoted in Miles, *Ann Radcliffe: The Great Enchantress*, 307. See also Sigmund Freud, *The Uncanny*, trans. David McLintock ([1917] New York: Penguin, 2003).
150 Radcliffe, *The Mysteries of Udolpho*, 163.
151 Locke, *An Essay Concerning Human Understanding*, 98.

The fear of 'nothingness' becomes visibly significant for the novelist's heroines. Miles concludes, 'No longer understood as a phase of a rational order, death now comes to figure the irrational itself, with the result that new strategies arise to hide, displace, or disguise death.'[152] Instead of deploying the Burkean threat of physical harm, Radcliffe explores more obscure matter. In wielding visuality as a methodology of psychological torture, she allows the sublime to surface anywhere; it is as visible to the eye of the body as it is to the eye of the mind.[153]

While the influence of landscape painting on Radcliffe's novels dominates scholarly discussion, Jayne Elizabeth Lewis is one of the few scholars to have also focused on the 'ink-blot' effect in her plots. While Lewis does not discuss the obscure in relation to inexpressibility, she proposes that in Radcliffe's novels, it distorts time and distance in order to signify that from which women cannot escape.[154] As Lewis has suggested, the novelist's visualizations of women's powerlessness against patriarchy draw their inspiration from her contemporary, the Russian-born émigré and leading watercolourist Alexander Cozens (1717–1786).[155] While working as a drawing master at Eton College, Cozens found that unintentional stains, or blots, stimulated his pupils' imaginations. His observations led him to see that the obscure 'dark matter' of washes could create 'invented' landscapes that took shape in the eyes of the beholder.[156] As Cozens summarizes in his *New Method of Assisting Invention in Drawing Original Compositions of Landscape* (1785), 'a blot in drawing is similar to the historical fact on which a poet builds his drama'.[157]

One of the most relevant of Cozens's etchings to examine alongside Radcliffe's treatment of obscurity, or that which lacks definition, is *22. Half Cloud Half Plain, the Clouds Lighter than the Plain Part, and Darker at the Top than the Bottom. The Tint Twice Over in the Plain Part, and Once in the Clouds*.[158] Unlike the novelist, whose descriptions also manipulate hue, Cozens experiments with *chiaro* and *scuro* in a monochromatic frame. By pairing identical

---

152 Miles, *Ann Radcliffe: The Great Enchantress*, 108.
153 Refer to my Introduction for a discussion on the eye of the body and the eye of the mind.
154 Jayne Elizabeth Lewis, 383. ' "No Colour of Language" ', 383.
155 Ibid.
156 For a comprehensive analysis of Cozens's techniques, see Charles A. Cramer's 'Alexander Cozens's New Method: The Blot and General Nature', *Art Bulletin* 79, no. 1 (March 1997): 112–29.
157 Quoted in Jayne Elizabeth Lewis, No Colour of Language" ', 170.
158 Alexander Cozens, *22. Half Cloud Half Plain, the Clouds Lighter than the Plain Part, and Darker at the Top than the Bottom. The Tint Twice Over in the Plain Part, and Once in the Clouds* (n.d.), etching on paper, Tate Museum (London), ref T11469; from *A New Method for Assisting the Invention in the Composition of Landscape*.

proportions of positive and negative space, Cozens tricks the eye into perceiving them as visually interchangeable. The piece's highly technical title suggests that the artist finds it as indescribable as it is visually indefinable. However, the title serves an important function: as a verbal prompt for the viewer, it decreases visual confusion, thereby eliminating the 'blot' that the technique produces.

Radcliffe distinguishes between defined and undefined domains of female oppression in a similar manner but denies her fictional women a means of differentiation. Instead, the viewer's interpretation of the obscure gives it a subjective definition. As she writes in *The Mysteries of Udolpho*,

> To a warm imagination, the dubious forms, that float half-veiled in darkness, afford a higher delight, than the most distinct scenery, that the sun can shew. While the fancy thus wanders over landscapes partly of its own creation, a sweet complacency steals upon the mind, and
>
> Redefines it all to subtlest feeling,
> Bids the tear of rapture roll.[159]

Devoid of figures, amorphous scenes like those found in Cozens's etchings and in Radcliffe's verbal sketches invite the beholder to 'see' the familiar within the undefined. Morris repeatedly grapples with Radcliffe's art of the obscure, arguing, 'in the system of the uncanny, a corpse cannot represent death (as it might in allegorical texts) but only our inability to know what death is'.[160] Though he alludes to the psychological paradox inherent in viewing the dead, he neglects to explore how Radcliffe, like Cozens, manipulates the obscure to communicate a particular effect. For the novelist, 'dark matter' – the negative space in Cozens's compositions – becomes a visual analogue for the metaphorical death that her heroines confront.

In order to understand how the obscure operates in Radcliffe's novels, it is necessary to examine how sensibility predisposes her fictional women to terror. As Nelson C. Smith writes in his article 'Sense, Sensibility and Ann Radcliffe',

> she takes the typical heroine of sentimental novels and, using the techniques of the Gothic novel, reveals how such a state of mind brings

---

159 Radcliffe, *Mysteries of Udolpho*, 598. Reproduced by permission of Oxford University Press.
160 David B. Morris, 'Gothic Sublimity', 311. © 1985 *New Literary History*, The University of Virginia. Reprinted with permission of Johns Hopkins University Press.

about many of the terrors which the heroine faces. The cure for such an attitude, Mrs Radcliffe makes clear, lies in a return to common sense.[161]

The common sense that Smith mentions suggests that reason and superstition are mutually exclusive.[162] While wandering around the abbey of St Augustin, the heroine of *A Sicilian Romance* recites Hippolitus's haunting composition, 'Superstition: An Ode'. Its 'uncanny' conclusion poeticizes the drama between the rational and the irrational, the natural and the supernatural raging within the psyche:

> Wide – wide the phantoms swell the loaded air
> With shrieks of anguish – madness and despair!
> Cease your ruin! spectres dire!
>   Cease your wild terrific sway!
> Turn your steps – and check your ire,
>   Yield to peace the mourning day![163]

Through Freudian repetition, Radcliffe subjects the heroine to the effects of 'spectralisation'. Her homonymic blurring of 'morning' with 'mourning' intimates that 'mourning' is as inescapable as 'morning'. In her heroines' eyes, the 'hope' that morning traditionally brings persistently crumbles into a self-delusion.

Rather than informing her readers of physiognomic particulars, Radcliffe directs attention to the way in which sensibility colours her heroines' temperaments and viewpoints. Whereas Emilia 'inherits' much of her mother's sense, Julia is of 'a more lively cast':

> An extreme sensibility subjected her to frequent uneasiness […] Her imagination was ardent, and her mind early exhibited symptoms of genius. It was the particular care of Madame de Menon to counteract those traits in the disposition of her young pupils, which appeared inimical to their future happiness.[164]

Radcliffe's portrait of Julia's disposition illustrates the heroine's weakness for the irrational. The tension between the 'natural' state of the heroine's mind

---

161 Nelson C. Smith, 'Sense, Sensibility and Ann Radcliffe', *Studies in English Literature, 1500–1900* 13, no. 4, Nineteenth Century (Autumn 1973): 577–90 (580).
162 Ibid.
163 Radcliffe, *A Sicilian Romance*, 117–18. Reproduced by permission of Oxford University Press.
164 Radcliffe, *A Sicilian Romance*, 4. Reproduced by permission of Oxford University Press.

and idealized rationality presages the drama that the obscure evokes in a landscape of supernatural gloom.

Radcliffe explores how Julia's extreme sensibility determines her visual perceptions. Even from the outside, the heroine's eyes suggest her tempered manner of looking: 'Her eyes were dark, and full of fire, but tempered with modest sweetness.'[165] Whereas Emilia shows a penchant for drawing subjects found in the visible world, her sister prefers to invent scenes in her mind's eye:

> and Julia, as she gazed on its glittering spires, would endeavour in imagination to depicture its beauties, while she secretly sighed for a view of that world, from which she had hitherto been secluded by the mean jealousy of the marchioness, upon whose mind the dread of rival beauty operated strongly to the prejudice of Emilia and Julia.[166]

By accessing Julia's private thoughts, the narrator confirms that the heroine is 'seeing'. Whereas Emilia tends to look with the eye of the body, Julia shows a greater propensity for invention. The term 'depicture' communicates Julia's attempt to preserve the picture of the 'beauties' of glittering spires in her imagination. Julia intuits that she and her sister are in danger of becoming a 'likeness' of Louisa de Bernini: they risk a future identity limited to two dimensions.

Radcliffe's method of presenting the obscure combines sound with sight. She uses mystifying sounds to translate her fictional women's sensibility into visible projections of fear. In *A Sicilian Romance*, ambiguous noises cause Julia and her more rationally inclined sister to invent conclusions: 'Deadly ideas crowded upon their imaginations, and inspired a terror which scarcely allowed them to breathe.'[167] Radcliffe turns the sisters' eyes and imaginations to the 'figure and the light' that 'kindled wild conjectures' in their imaginations.[168] Instead of bringing the metaphorical light of knowledge to life, the novelist leaves the sisters in the dark. She redirects their gazes to Madame de Menon – the only voice of reason present. Rather than dismissing their fears of disembodied spirits, Madame confirms their existence:

> 'Such spirits, if indeed they have ever been seen, can have appeared only by the express permission of God, and for some very singular purposes;

---

165 Radcliffe, *A Sicilian Romance*, 4. Reproduced by permission of Oxford University Press.
166 Radcliffe, *A Sicilian Romance*, 6. Reproduced by permission of Oxford University Press.
167 Radcliffe, *A Sicilian Romance*, 35. Reproduced by permission of Oxford University Press.
168 Ibid., 36.

be assured that there are no beings who act unseen by him; and that, therefore, there are none from whom innocence can ever suffer harm.'[169]

By drawing on Madame de Menon's authoritative perspective, Radcliffe communicates the coexistence of the supernatural and the obscure. Though the older woman reassures the sisters that their 'innocence' will protect them, the selective visibility of the invisible makes a lasting impression on their thoughts and fears.

Madame de Menon's evocative warning alters Julia's vision early on in the novel. No longer able to rely on the power of sight to inform her of her surroundings, she begins to see that which does not exist:

> Julia, whose fears conspired with the gloom of night to magnify and transform every object around her, imagined at each step that she took, she perceived the figures of men, and fancied every whisper of the breeze the sound of pursuit.[170]

As well as signifying the shade of the supernatural, 'gloom' serves as a means of visual magnification and transformation. The images that Julia's mind invents are tellingly significant. Her delusions communicate her worst imaginings: 'figures of men' and 'pursuit'. By arousing these forms, Radcliffe shows that male power does not need to be materially present to inspire fear. The heroines internalize male power in the way they see and hear; the threat of obscure patriarchal violence corrupts their senses.

In *The Italian*, Radcliffe uses the hero's sudden recourse to the imagination to contextualize Ellena's encounters with obscurity. The narrative illustrates that even a strong-willed male mind may be 'magicked' upon: 'His mind resembled the glass of a magician, on which the apparitions of long-buried events arise, and as they fleet away, point portentously to shapes half-hid in the duskiness of futurity.'[171] Vivaldi's unconscious releases repressed images and 'imperfect' thoughts that also infect Ellena's imagination. When he looks upon the 'shadowy countenance' of the mysterious stranger, the narrator agrees that it has the indescribable air that 'we attach to the idea of a supernatural being'.[172] Radcliffe's use of 'we' invites the reader to empathize with Vivaldi's ruminations:

> 'I have heard of the spirit of the murdered,' said he, to himself – 'restless for justice, becoming visible in our world –' But Vivaldi checked the

---

169 Radcliffe, *A Sicilian Romance*, 36. Reproduced by permission of Oxford University Press.
170 Radcliffe, *A Sicilian Romance*, 149. Reproduced by permission of Oxford University Press.
171 Radcliffe, *The Italian*, 320. Reproduced by permission of Oxford University Press.
172 Ibid., 318.

imperfect thought, and, though his imagination inclined him to the marvellous, and to admit ideas which, filling and expanding all the faculties of the soul, produce feelings that partake of the sublime, he now resisted the propensity, and dismissed, as absurd, a supposition, which had begun to thrill his every nerve with horror.[173]

Vivaldi halts his sensibility in mid-sentence. Where his contemplation ends, the narrator's explanation begins. While Vivaldi's perception becomes an 'absurd' supposition even more than an 'imperfect thought', Radcliffe shows that the damage has been done: the sight has forced him to feel the impact of 'horror' on another level of his existence. By subjecting Vivaldi to imaginary suppositions, the novelist shows that the obscure menaces both men and women.

In *The Mysteries of Udolpho*, Radcliffe again opens the novel with an admonition against sensibility in order to dramatize the heroine's reactions to the obscure. Instead of employing one perspective, she experiments with two. Her visual technique suggests that women's views of decorum had to comply with male perceptions. Here, the father figure serves as the first voice of reason. Radcliffe stresses the significance of St Aubert's warning by reserving it for his last earthly words:

> 'Above all, my dear Emily [...] do not indulge in the pride of fine feeling, the romantic error of amiable minds. Those, who really possess sensibility, ought early to be taught, that it is a dangerous quality, which is continually extracting the excess of misery, or delight, from every surrounding circumstance. And, since, in our passage through this world, painful circumstances occur more frequently than pleasing ones, and since our sense of evil is, I fear, more acute than our sense of good, we become the victims of our feelings, unless we can in some degree command them.'[174]

In St Aubert's view, sensibility warrants self-destruction. Whereas Madame de Menon sees in sensibility a threat to 'future happiness', St Aubert perceives it as a form of self-victimization. For Radcliffe and for Emily's father, the greatest dangers are self-inflicted. However, he cannot foresee the role that others will play in breaking down the borders between the real and the unreal for his daughter.

---

173 Radcliffe, *The Italian*, 347. Reproduced by permission of Oxford University Press.
174 Radcliffe, *The Mysteries of Udolpho*, 79–80. Reproduced by permission of Oxford University Press.

Radcliffe aggravates Emily's anxiety by protracting her father's dying words. He advocates a moderate sensibility to prevent distorted vision:

> 'I repeat it,' said he, 'I would not teach you to become insensible, if I could; I would only warn you of the evils of susceptibility, and point out how you may avoid them. Beware, my love, I conjure you, of that self-delusion, which has been fatal to the peace of so many persons; beware of priding yourself on the gracefulness of sensibility; if you yield to this vanity, your happiness is lost for ever.'[175]

St Aubert foresees that Emily will become the victim of her own feelings unless she can free herself from 'self-delusion'. From picturing the metaphorical death that sensibility causes, the narrative shifts to examining Emily's perceptions of her father's actual death. By removing St Aubert from view, the novelist begins to unleash the heroine's fears of the obscurity that awaits her. The sudden absence of her father leaves a void in the scenes of daily life.

In *The Mysteries of Udolpho*, Radcliffe continues to use men's perspectives to magnify the powers of the female imagination. Valancourt can only imagine the dangers that await Emily with a man as despicable as Montoni:

> But his imagination magnified to her the possible evils she was going to meet, the mists of her own fancy began to dissipate, and allowed her to distinguish the exaggerated images, which imposed on his reason.[176]

The narrative introduces an episode that calls to mind Cozens's ink-blot technique at work within Emily's mind's eye. The heroine holds her lover accountable for clouding her vision with the 'mists'. By decreasing the ephemeral vapours, Radcliffe suggests their impermanence. Though the heroine's rationality triumphs briefly, the passage presages other occasions, including her interpretation of the wax figure, when her fancy will be unconquerable.

In *The Mysteries of Udolpho*, the dangers of sensibility feed off the terrors of male power. Miles proposes that Radcliffe unites 'the sexual politics of sensibility and the supernatural through this simple donnée: a young girl in a patriarchal setting cannot control her imagination'.[177] Even if the 'donnée'

---

175 Radcliffe, *The Mysteries of Udolpho*, 80. Reproduced by permission of Oxford University Press.
176 Radcliffe, *The Mysteries of Udolpho*, 158. Reproduced by permission of Oxford University Press.
177 Miles, *Ann Radcliffe: The Great Enchantress*, 148.

reads as simple to Miles, the novelist complicates it on a perceptual level. She transforms the 'mists' of fancy into something more concrete:

> The solitary life, which Emily had led of late, and the melancholy subjects, on which she had suffered her thoughts to dwell, had rendered her at times sensible to the 'thick-coming fancies' of a mind greatly enervated. It was lamentable, that her excellent understanding should have yielded, even for a moment, to the reveries of superstition, or rather to those starts of imagination, which deceive the senses into what can be called nothing less than momentary madness.[178]

The 'thick-coming fancies' invading Emily's mind's eye remain obscure and suggest the influence of Cozens's ink blots. Radcliffe's repeated attempts to replace the phrase communicate the heroine's struggle to define that which resists definition. She abandons 'the reveries of superstition' for 'starts of the imagination' but can only settle for 'nothing less than momentary madness'. By concluding with an understatement, the novelist indicates that Emily's condition will induce far more than 'momentary' madness.

Radcliffe uses Madame Montoni's matter-of-fact prophecy to strengthen the sway of the irrational over the way in which the heroine perceives the obscure. The woman's manner of looking at Emily's future speaks of the 'temper' of her own hardships:

> Pray get rid of all those fantastic notions about love, and this ridiculous pride, and be something like a reasonable creature. But, however, this is nothing to the purpose – for your marriage with the Count takes place tomorrow, you know, whether you approve it or not.[179]

Whereas St Aubert warns against sensibility on his deathbed, Madame Montoni threatens the heroine on the eve of her metaphorical death. The woman's call for Emily to 'be something like a reasonable creature' is juxtaposed with its antithesis:

> For some time she sat so lost in thought, as to be wholly unconscious where she was; at length, raising her head, and looking round the room, its gloom and profound stillness awed her […] Her mind, long

---

[178] Radcliffe, *The Mysteries of Udolpho*, 102. Reproduced by permission of Oxford University Press.

[179] Radcliffe, *The Mysteries of Udolpho*, 221. Reproduced by permission of Oxford University Press.

harassed by distress, now yielded to imaginary terrors; she trembled to look into the obscurity of her spacious chamber, and feared she knew not what.[180]

By depicting Emily's marriage to the Count as a certainty, Radcliffe drives Emily to 'imaginary terrors' that are more substantial than flights of fancy. The visible and invisible 'obscurity' that torments Emily's mind's eye leaves her 'wholly unconscious' of actuality.[181] She 'yields' to invented terrors because the real ones have yet to be defined. Her reluctance to gaze into the obscure suggests that she would rather see fictive than actual sources of terror. The conflation of visible and invisible prospects of obscurity paralyses Emily's mind, plunging her into a nightmare from which she cannot wake.

In *The Mysteries of Udolpho*, Radcliffe continues to exploit the relationship between sound and the invisible, this time to compel the heroine to see her persecutor where he visibly is not. To reveal the discrepancy between what Emily foresees and what her eyes confront, Radcliffe contrasts the invented image of a stiletto-armed Bertrand with the appearance of the scene's harmless intruder, Maddelina. Miles explains that where fictive images take on the aspect of real ones, real ones in their turn threaten to dissolve into the illusory.[182] The novelist draws attention to the heroine's art of catharsis:

> and she was thus enabled to amuse herself with selecting some of the lovely features for the prospect, that her window commanded, and combining them in scenes, to which her tasteful fancy gave a last grace. In these little sketches she generally placed interesting groups, characteristic of the scenery they animated, and often contrived to tell, with perspicuity, some simple and affecting story, when as a tear fell over the pictured griefs, which her imagination drew, she would forget, for a moment her real sufferings.[183]

By blending fact with 'tasteful fancy', Emily relates 'pictured griefs' that look uncannily familiar. Even vicarious escape fails to free her from her situation. The tear which drops from Emily's eye onto the scene projects her real sufferings into pictured ones, as if to offer visible proof that they are her own. She becomes the ink blot in her illustration of female oppression. Radcliffe uses the

---

180 Radcliffe, *The Mysteries of Udolpho*, 221. Reproduced by permission of Oxford University Press.
181 Ibid., 141.
182 Miles, *Ann Radcliffe: The Great Enchantress*, 84.
183 Radcliffe, *The Mysteries of Udolpho*, 418. Reproduced by permission of Oxford University Press.

blotted composition to make the heroine's blurred vision and self-perceptions visible. The passage suggests the relationship that the novelist draws between obscurity and loss of consciousness. As Emily's drawing attests, she – the ink blot – is the most insoluble element of all.

In *The Mysteries of Udolpho*, Radcliffe positions the ultimate frontier of the undefined in Emily's psyche. The novelist moves fluidly from pictured griefs in the visible world to the griefs pictured in her dreams. On the eve of the heroine's self-sacrifice, the images that disturb her sleep carry the clarity of 'real' evils:

> Her unquiet mind had, during the night, presented her with terrific images and obscure circumstances concerning her affection and her future life. She now endeavoured to chase away the impressions they had left on her fancy; but from imaginary evils she awoke to the consciousness of real ones.[184]

Here, 'terrific images' – not 'imaginary terrors' – conspire with 'obscure circumstances' to give shape to the obscurity that the future holds for the heroine. Instead of empowering the self-determining gaze, Radcliffe assaults Emily with images that cannot be 'chased away'. Fancy's command over her perceptions attests to the permanence of the effects of trauma. As Bohls suggests, 'When Emily says she is afraid of losing her senses, she is really afraid [...] of losing her mind.'[185] For all of Radcliffe's heroines, sensibility ensures their tendency to perceive the obscure as a manifestation of patriarchal power that corrodes their own sense of self.

Radcliffe's use of visuality shows that her fictional realms of patriarchal abuse operate like concentric circles from which there is no escape. Her novels owe much of their psychological depth to her method of making the boundlessness of male power and female oppression visible. Allusions to man-made, natural and supernatural visual realms of sublime terror restructure Radcliffe's views of the world within and beyond the novel. Her heroines appear as imprisoned in two dimensions as they are in actuality. In conditions where the obscure renders wax and flesh indistinguishable, the novelist converts her heroines' perceptions into misapprehensions, life into death, and dreams into the undying nightmare that is womanhood itself.

---

184 Radcliffe, *The Mysteries of Udolpho*, 161. Reproduced by permission of Oxford University Press.
185 Bohls, *Women Travel Writers and the Language of Aesthetics, 1716–1818*, 223.

Chapter 3

THE GENDERED GAZE AND 'MADE-UP' WOMEN IN MARIA EDGEWORTH'S *CASTLE RACKRENT*, *ENNUI* AND *BELINDA*

Leaving behind the Gothic realms of Radcliffe's novels, this chapter investigates how Maria Edgeworth uses visuality in her fiction to show the ways in which costume, jewellery, cosmetics and masks become extensions of, if not replacements for, women's innermost selves. As a discerning critic of turn-of-the-nineteenth-century society who was intimately acquainted with Irish life, Edgeworth warns the reader that myopia exists on gendered, moral and cultural levels. Her fictional women frequently denature their subjectivity and selfhood in order to meet the male gaze. They are shown to endure the agonies of concealment and to be engaged in a theatrical performance of feminine roles for the benefit of male spectators who do not suspect or acknowledge the inner misery behind the 'painting'.

By combining male and female perspectives into what Marilyn Butler calls 'pseudo-journalistic' prose,[1] Edgeworth circumvents the strictures of 'social acceptability' and 'moral appropriateness' on the female observer.[2] In *Letters for Literary Ladies* (1798), the novelist identifies the limitations on vision that thwarted women's pursuit of knowledge, stating that 'we see things as they are; but women must always see things through a veil, or cease to be women'.[3] Her preoccupation with the seen and the unseen situates her novelistic concerns in line with those found in Radcliffe's oeuvre. Rather than inspiring terror and concentrating on correlatives of character exterior to the self, Edgeworth's visual technique shows that those who learn to see with 'connoisseur eyes' and

---

1 Marilyn Butler, *Maria Edgeworth: A Literary Biography*, 398.
2 See Jane Nardin, *Those Elegant Decorums: The Concept of Propriety in Jane Austen's Novels* (Albany: New York State University Press, 1973), 13.
3 Maria Edgeworth, *Letters for Literary Ladies*, ed. Claire Connolly ([1798] London: J. M. Dent, 1993), 3.

become 'acute observers of human affairs' can distinguish *le vrai* woman from her *vraisemblable* masks.[4]

After considering Edgeworth's visual technique in relation to thematic concerns in contemporary reviews and recent scholarship, the chapter explores the visible and invisible binary of self-invention, or the relationship between representation and perception, in her plots. The analysis focuses on *Castle Rackrent* (1800), *Ennui* (1809) and *Belinda* (1801) in order to show that the theatrical 'making up' of her women's characters occurs on material, perceptual and pictorial levels.[5] By isolating three distinct contexts of fashionable life, it becomes clear that Edgeworth's experimentation with male narrators and socio-economic viewpoints offers a feminist platform by projecting different ways of looking at women's relationships with their public selves.

The first section of the chapter discusses Edgeworth's use of male narrators in *Castle Rackrent* and *Ennui*. In both novellas, the image of the desirable wife transforms from a commodity pictured in the mind's eye to a woman who displays those material values. Accompanying the need for 'self-determination' was the persistent risk that women faced of subjective male depiction. The novelist's references to jewellery and dress make the similarities and differences between male and female perceptions obstinately visible to the reader. While husband and wife may share the value of materialism, they see its benefit to their own images differently.

From analysing elements of fashion as analogues for value and female identity, the study turns to considering Edgeworth's dialogic treatment of made-up women in *Belinda*, which comprises the second section of the chapter. The heroine-centric courtship plot realigns the reader with female subjectivity. Employing direct comparison and cross-dressing, the novelist transforms the constrictions of fashionable attire into visual metaphors for women's inability to move and speak freely within and beyond the glass-bound theatre of the domestic sphere. Lady Delacour and Belinda specialize in the complex matter of public performance, which allows them to deceive the observer by expressing who they are not, visually and verbally, but who they must seem to be. The 'inside' and 'outside' of a woman's self encourage the reader to see that the spaces in which women hide are at once 'architectural' and perceptual, culturally defined and individually shaped.

---

4 Maria Edgeworth, *Ennui*, ed. Jane Desmarais, Tim McLoughlin and Marilyn Butler ([1809; 1832] London: Pickering & Chatto, 1999), 1: 157–308 (268). From Boileau, *Art poétique*, chant III, 1: 48: 'Le vrai peut quelquefois n'être pas vraisemblable.'

5 This analysis uses the Pickering & Chatto editions, which are drawn from the *Collected Edition* of 1832–33 (18 volumes).

The implicit solution for the different forms of myopia in Edgeworth's novels is the 'connoisseur' gaze. In an 1834 letter to her youngest brother, Michael Pakenham, Edgeworth attributed her success as a shrewd observer of society to her *connoisseur eyes*'.[6] The novelist's identification of her gaze with that of the 'connoisseur' rejects the male connotations of the term, which were representative of the era in which she lived. According to Jonathan Richardson's essay *The Science of a Connoisseur* (1719), dedicated to Sir Joshua Reynolds, the 'connoisseur' is a male archetype:

> To be a connoisseur, a man must be as free from all kinds of prejudice as possible; he must moreover have a clear and exact way of thinking and reasoning; he must know how to take in, and manage just ideas; and throughout he must have not only a solid, but unbiased judgement.[7]

Edgeworth appropriates the notion of the connoisseur seeing clearly and exactly without prejudice. Her novels modernize Richardson's definition by allowing her fictional women to gaze freely and to judge wisely. Like Austen and Radcliffe, Edgeworth uses visuality to encourage her characters and readers to question appearances and perceptions, including their own. She advocates a path for the female sex that enables the 'connoisseur' and the 'accomplished woman' to become interchangeable.

Edgeworth's feminized model of clear vision ironically incorporates the qualities that Hannah More described in 1799. More asserted that women are biologically and theologically inclined to see the world from a 'lower eminence', literally and figuratively, and thus in a smaller and more detailed domestic compass:

> Both in composition and action they (women) excel in details; but they do not so much generalize their ideas as men, nor do their minds seize a great subject with so large a grasp [...] A woman sees the world, as it were, from a little elevation in her own garden, where she makes an exact survey of home scenes, but takes not in that wider range of distant prospects which he who stands on a loftier eminence commands.[8]

Edgeworth agreed that women's attentiveness to the minutiae within the domestic sphere constituted their characteristic perceptual advantage. As

---

6 Maria Edgeworth, 'Beginning of the Journey', 8 March 1834, *Maria Edgeworth: Chosen Letters*, ed. F. V. Barry (London: Jonathan Cape, 1931), 390; emphasis in original.

7 Jonathan Richardson, *The Works of Jonathan Richardson* ([1719] Strawberry Hill: [n.p.], 1792), 201.

8 Hannah More, *Strictures on the Modern System of Female Education* (London: [n.p.], 1799), 127.

More indicated, the concept of detail is inherently subjective and depends on the field of vision to which the viewer is accustomed.

In her article 'The Aesthetics of Ignorance: The Accomplished Woman in the Culture of Connoisseurship' (1993), Ann Bermingham evaluates the cultural forces that influenced gendered modes of viewing and perceiving. She writes:

> the more a culture organizes itself as a visual culture, and poses sexual difference as an experience of looking or being looked at, the more problematic the tactical modes of looking employed [...] become, and the more they have to be morally disavowed.[9]

While Bermingham explores the problematic relationship between the female 'experience of looking and being looked at' in Austen's novels, the theme also dominates Edgeworth's fiction. Whereas Austen negotiated the cultural restrictions on vision and expression by using physiognomic correlatives of character, the same strains within visual culture turned Edgeworth to the theatrical model that J. F. Marmontel outlines in his *Eléments de Littérature* (1789): '[the writer] must present to the mind's eye the scene, the dumb-show'.[10] In *Castle Rackrent*, *Ennui* and *Belinda*, the 'dumb-show' speaks for itself, inviting the novelist's characters and readers to make out women's complex relationships with their made-up selves.

Edgeworth evades restrictions on female expression by using visuality to theatrically depict the predicament of penetration and misinterpretation, sometimes through her imagined view of the male gaze. In her lifetime, she was recognized for drawing verbal 'sketches' that were realistic but ironically lacking in detail. Olyett Woodhouse's 1802 review of the first edition of *Belinda*, for instance, observed that there were few 'full-length portraits' in her writing:

> Miss Edgeworth has likewise been very successful in delineating English manners. Her *Modern Griselda*, *Leonora*, *Belinda*, and *Patronage*, are great works, consider them as we will. The ethical merit is not to be doubted, and the spirit of their characteristic sketches not to be exceeded. They contain, it is true, but few full-length portraits; but this is a defect amply compensated by the variety which distinguishes her picture gallery, and the general *vraisemblance* of the likenesses of which it is composed.[11]

---

9 Ann Bermingham, 'The Aesthetics of Ignorance: The Accomplished Woman in the Culture of Connoisseurship', *Oxford Art Journal* 16, no. 2 (1993): 3–20 (12). © Oxford University Press 1993. Reprinted by permission of Oxford University Press.

10 J. F. Marmontel, 'Eléments de Littérature', in *Œuvres Complètes*, 18 vols. (Paris, 1818), 12: 524–25.

11 Edgeworth, *Belinda*, 462.

Woodhouse used metaphors from the visual arts to describe Edgeworth's prose. He found the 'spirit' and 'variety' of the personae in her fiction superior in their replication of the actual characters within the 'gallery' of English society. His review implies that Edgeworth preserved the 'ethical merit' of her writing by adhering to the set of aesthetic expectations that Reynolds's *Discourses* made culturally instinctive. Reynolds warned the aspiring artist that 'a mere copier of nature can never produce any thing great; can never raise and enlarge the conceptions, or warm the heart of the spectator'.[12] In order for her visual technique to communicate that which could not be stated openly, Edgeworth turned her readers into spectators of lifelike characters who act out the strictures on seeing and being seen.

Other nineteenth-century critics highlighted the connection between national identity and gender identity in Edgeworth's oeuvre. In 1812, the essayist and one-time chief secretary for Ireland John Wilson Croker praised her skill in reconciling her fictional depictions of the Irish with how the Irish actually appeared. He remarked,

> we do not know that she has, in the whole circle of literature, a rival except the inimitable authors of *Gil Blas* and *Don Quixote*; and the discrimination with which the individuality of her persons is preserved through all the varieties of rank, sex and nation, gives to her story a combined charm of truth and novelty [and] creates an interest more acute than fiction (if fiction it can be called) ever excited.[13]

Both Woodhouse and Croker found that Edgeworth resisted a monolithic vision where everything is essentially alike. Instead, she sought to present the multiplicity of character and perspective that the 'genius' of the female sex and the Irish contain. Croker emphasized that, while many of Edgeworth's predecessors had attempted to achieve accurate imitations of Irishness, her portrayal resisted prejudicial typology:

> In the accurate discrimination of the various classes of Irish society [...] Other writers have caught nothing but the general feature, and in their description, everything that is Irish is pretty much alike [...] To Miss Edgeworth [...] it was reserved to separate the genus into its species and

---

12 Sir Joshua Reynolds, *Discourses on Art*, ed. Robert R. Wark (New Haven and London: Yale University Press, 1975), 41.
13 John Wilson Croker, 'Article VIII: "Miss Edgeworth's *Tales of Fashionable Life*"', *Quarterly Review*, 7 (1812), 330.

individuals, and to exhibit the most accurate and yet the most diversified views that have ever been drawn of a national character.[14]

Croker's personal acquaintance with Irish life makes his account of the novelist's attentiveness to character particularly informative. Although his conclusions relate to national character rather than gender, they reassert the way in which Edgeworth's attentiveness to certain details and singularities could be used to her rhetorical advantage.

From the twentieth century on, literary scholarship has continued to analyse the themes of gender and national identity in Edgeworth's novels but has yet to address her specific reliance on visuality as a choice methodology. Since the publication of Marilyn Butler's influential *Maria Edgeworth: A Literary Biography* (1972), critiques of her fiction have tended to explore its pedagogical intent and autobiographical influences, namely focusing on the patriarchal imbalances of her partnership with her father.[15] In her article 'Shot from Canons' (1995), Mitzi Myers investigates Edgeworth's skill in conveying accurate views of Irish life to a naive English readership.[16] She draws attention to her 'startling' ability to make seemingly unnatural incidents appear factual, explaining, 'Edgeworth loves to write "taken from fact", and the close reader of her life, letters, and work is as startled by her skill in making capital of the smallest events of her everyday life as by the breadth of her reading'.[17] As Myers rightly acknowledges, Edgeworth was determined to present a complex, sophisticated and exploited Ireland generally unseen or unacknowledged by English eyes, which complicated the task for a woman novelist to communicate efficiently and effectively without harming her reputation.

Esther Wohlgemut also explores Edgeworth's treatment of national identity, extending it to the question of multiple allegiances. In her article 'Maria Edgeworth and the Question of National Identity' (1999), Wohlgemut analyses the novelist's writing on Ireland in conjunction with Bruce Robbins's definition of 'positive cosmopolitanism', or the 'density of overlapping allegiances rather than the abstract emptiness of non-allegiance'.[18] Her study highlights the Burkean importance of local attachment: 'This figure of international cross-over will prove the cornerstone to Edgeworth's rewriting of Burkean nationness; and the notion of education supporting such a crossover links her

---

14 Ibid., 336.
15 See Marilyn Butler, *Maria Edgeworth: A Literary Biography* (Oxford: Clarendon Press, 1972).
16 Mitzi Myers, 'Shot from Canons; or, Maria Edgeworth and the Cultural Production and Consumption of the Eighteenth-Century Woman Writer', in *The Consumption of Culture*, ed. Ann Bermingham and John Brewer (London: Routledge, 1995), 193–214.
17 Ibid., 193.
18 Bruce Robbins, 'Comparative Cosmopolitanism', *Social Text* 31, no. 32 (1992): 169–86 (173).

rewriting to eighteenth-century cosmopolitanism'.[19] The conceptual shift in cosmopolitanism and the possibility of multiple national allegiances are points that Edgeworth's fiction demonstrates by dramatizing the way in which women's 'appearances' often resisted cultural definition.

Mary Poovey, Nancy Armstrong and Clíona Ó Gallchoir are among the many scholars who have addressed the implications of gender and domesticity in Edgeworth's novels.[20] In *Maria Edgeworth: Women, Enlightenment, Nationhood* (2005), Ó Gallchoir examines women's persistent exclusion from the public sphere in an era of patriarchal 'enlightenment':

> Definitions of femininity were altered, but the effect remained constant: women were excluded from the public realm. Mary Wollstonecraft compared this denial of rights to the conditions of slaves; yet the United Irishmen, for all their lofty talk of liberty refused to entertain the possibility of the admission of women to the body politic.[21]

The complexity of Edgeworth's allusions to France further demonstrates her discontentment with the 'accomplished' woman's declining social status.[22] Despite the male misconception that the domestic sphere was a hermetically sealed environment, literary women were gaining a textual locus of power.[23] Visuality, more than any other single language, allowed women novelists, like Edgeworth, to negotiate the gendered strictures on self-expression while simultaneously depicting women's need for self-invention.

Butler identifies the limitations of the propagandist argument's understanding of national identity as a detailed cosmopolitan entity. In 'Edgeworth's Ireland: History, Popular Culture and Secret Codes' (2001), she contends that 'characteristic themes' are pervasive in Edgeworth's writing, arguing that the titles of her novels often indicate the crossover between her fiction and other imaginary worlds.[24] According to her study, the novelist's perceptiveness of

---

19 Esther Wohlgemut, 'Maria Edgeworth and the Question of National Identity', *Studies in English Literature, 1500–1900* 39, no. 4, The Nineteenth Century (Autumn 1999): 645–58 (647).

20 See Mary Poovey's *The Proper Lady and the Woman Writer: Ideology as Style in the Works of Mary Wollstonecraft, Mary Shelley, and Jane Austen* (Chicago: University of Chicago Press, 1985) and Nancy Armstrong's *Desire and Domestic Fiction: A Political History of the Novel* (Oxford: Oxford University Press, 1987).

21 For a discussion on women's rights in the public sphere, see Clíona Ó Gallchoir, *Maria Edgeworth: Women, Enlightenment and Nationhood* (Dublin: University College Dublin Press, 2005), 4.

22 Ibid., 12.

23 Ibid., 18.

24 Marilyn Butler, 'Edgeworth's Ireland: History Popular Culture and Secret Codes', *NOVEL: A Forum on Fiction* 34, no. 2, The Romantic-Era Novel (Spring 2001): 267–92 (267–68).

the subtexts of character enabled her to offer her readers an index of cultural nuances and values:

> Edgeworth as a fiction-writer distinguishes her characters, with a new subtlety in relation to their gender, class and nationality, by what they have been reading. In her best most bookish fiction of upper-class life she introduces a novel kind of subtext that makes reading and conversations on reading an indicator of rationality and moral worth.[25]

Although Butler asserts that Edgeworth's characters reveal their ethical ideologies through the books that they read, the need to read a character's moral worth through an indirect code points to the existence of other communicative motifs in her fiction. The novelist's detailed references to fashion and disguise similarly function as a code that conveys complex messages about gender, culture and socio-economic factors through 'well-chosen' words.[26]

Other discussions of Edgeworth's fiction have alluded to the gender-specific advantages of using 'secret codes' and the dumbshow to communicate the drama of womanhood. Heather MacFadyen and Joe Bray, for instance, propose that Edgeworth encourages the viewer within and outside of *Belinda* to read 'characters' by their 'likenesses'. In her article 'Lady Delacour's Library: Maria Edgeworth's *Belinda* and Fashionable Reading' (1981), MacFadyen maintains that 'Lady Delacour's fashionable success is dependent on her ability to use her literary skill to support her fashionable status'.[27] MacFadyen's study of the novel considers the way in which 'types' of literature correspond with 'types' of women, allowing them to identify vicariously with other fictional women experiencing analogous difficulties. Meanwhile, Bray's '*Belinda, Emma,* and the "Likeness" of the Portrait' (2011) analyses the destabilization of the 'likeness' in the context of trends in visual portraiture.[28] His argument explores the increasing 'untrustworthiness' of visual portraiture in relation to Lady Delacour's and Emma's public selves, rightly concluding that both women must learn to negotiate the 'subjective slipperiness of interpretation' in order to survive.[29] MacFadyen and Bray allude to the disconnect between the ways in which *Belinda*'s fictional women see themselves and how

---

25 Ibid., 268.
26 Refer to my Introduction.
27 Heather MacFadyen, 'Lady Delacour's Library: Maria Edgeworth's *Belinda* and Fashionable Reading', *Nineteenth-Century Literature* 48, no. 4 (March 1994): 423–39 (425).
28 Joe Bray, '*Belinda, Emma* and the "Likeness" of the Portrait', *Nineteenth-Century Contexts* 33, no. 1 (February 2011), 1–15.
29 Ibid., 13.

others picture them but do not consider the similar function that dress, cosmetics, jewellery and disguise serve. In *Castle Rackrent, Ennui* and *Belinda*, these instruments of self-invention theatrically expose the difference between the 'inside' and 'outside' of a woman's self.

Although Edgeworth's writing is 'pseudo-journalistic',[30] to borrow Butler's phrase, the novelist stressed that 'I spare you all that you will see in the newspapers'.[31] Her penchant for magnifying the 'trivial' highlights what Michael Gamer has claimed to be the significance of the anecdote, which 'promises to deliver textual truths superior to history because of the particular kind of "reality" it claims to embody'.[32] Edgeworth's account of Queen Victoria's opening of Parliament in November 1843 helps clarify the anecdote's critical role in presenting 'dumbshows' from an overtly subjective vantage point:

> She did not go up the steps to the throne well – caught her foot and stumbled against the edge of the footstool, which was too high. She did not seat herself in a decided queenlike manner, and after sitting down pottered too much with her drapery, arranging her petticoats. That footstool was much too high! Her knees were crumpled up, and her figure, short enough already, was foreshortened as she sat, and her drapery did not come to the edge of the stool: as my neighbour Miss Fitzhugh whispered, 'Bad effect.'[33]

Edgeworth's position overlooking the 'black heads of the reporter gentlemen' enabled her to distance herself literally and metaphorically from male critics of the scene.[34] Her use of the anecdote serves a teleological end that stresses the subjectivity of vision and depiction, a premise that Gamer alludes to but does not pursue.[35]

While the subjective anecdote is fundamental to Edgeworth's factual and fictional characterizations, she, like Austen and Radcliffe, consciously resisted

---

30 Butler finds that Edgeworth's novels 'introduce the objective, pseudo-journalistic approach to the social scene which successive nineteenth-century novelists could build on' (*Maria Edgeworth: A Literary Biography*, 398).
31 Maria Edgeworth, 'Opening of Parliament by Queen', 2 February 1844, *Maria Edgeworth: Letters from England 1813–1844*, ed. Christina Colvin (Oxford: Clarendon Press, 1971), 438.
32 Michael Gamer, 'Maria Edgeworth and the Romance of Real Life', *NOVEL: A Forum on Fiction* 34, no. 2, *The Romantic-Era Novel* (Spring 2001): 232–66 (243).
33 Edgeworth, 'Opening of Parliament by Queen', 2 February 1844, *Maria Edgeworth: Letters from England 1813–1844*, 441. Reprinted by permission of Oxford University Press.
34 Ibid.
35 Ibid.

the temptation to copy individuals from life, claiming that for a woman to paint subjects in '*bodily* unaltered' form would prove '*de trop*':[36]

> Wherever, in writing, a real character rose to my view, from memory or resemblance, it has always been hurtful to me, because, to avoid resemblance, I was tempted by cowardice or compelled by conscience to throw in differences which often ended in making my character inconsistent, unreal.[37]

Edgeworth's determination to avoid resemblance helps to explain why she often capitulated to the 'temptation' to reach for the quixotic, inconsistent and unreal, particularly in *Castle Rackrent*, which contains the only character(s) that she openly acknowledges to have been drawn from life. By combining the 'real' with an untrustworthy perspective, the novelist was able to safeguard her reputation as a woman when the story's authorship became public knowledge.

In contrast to what many of Edgeworth's contemporary critics and recent scholars regard as her forte, the novelist considered her fondness for the 'diligent accumulation of particulars' to be her stylistic flaw. In 1834, she acknowledged her struggle between delineation and suggestion:

> I had often and often a suspicion that my manner was too Dutch, too minute; and very, very often, and warmly, admired the bold, grand style of the master hand and the master genius. I *know* I feel how much *more is to be done, ought to be* done, by suggestion than by delineation, by creative fancy than by facsimile copying – how much more by skilful observation of individuals, or diligent accumulation of particulars.[38]

As much as Edgeworth admired those geniuses whose techniques revolved around 'suggestion', she consistently demonstrated her preference for revisiting the scenes that had passed before her eyes. 'There is a security and sense of reality in studying from life', she wrote, 'which the most inventive imagination can never attain.'[39]

Despite the persistent interest in gender politics and the presentation of national identity in Edgeworth scholarship after 1990, it is clear that the novelist's reliance on visuality to depict women's ambivalent relationships with their

---

36 See Teresa Michals, 'Commerce and Character in Maria Edgeworth', *Nineteenth-Century Literature* 49, no. 1 (June 1994): 1–20 (3); emphasis in original.
37 Edgeworth, 'The Art of Fiction', *Maria Edgeworth: Chosen Letters*, 239.
38 Ibid., 238; emphasis in original.
39 See Myers, 'Shot from Canons', 193.

made-up selves remains underexplored. The novelist's treatment of female performance and concealment demonstrates that the fashionable woman's image is as much a function of the viewer's ideologies as it is a projection of the subject's. Rather than relying on dress as a visual metaphor for patriarchal domination, as Radcliffe does in her Gothic novels,[40] Edgeworth uses elements of fashion to dramatize the way in which different types of women see and are seen from contrasting cultural viewpoints and gender biases.

Male Narrators and Made-up Women

In *Castle Rackrent* (1800) and *Ennui*, published as part of the eight works that comprise *Tales of Fashionable Life* (1809 and 1812),[41] Edgeworth masks herself behind male narrators in order to comment on the 'look' of the made-up woman. In the late eighteenth and early nineteenth centuries, observation and connoisseurship were, as Bermingham agrees, implicitly understood to be male roles.[42] The young novelist declared in *Letters for Literary Ladies*, 'You despise the writings of women: – you think that they might have made a better use of the pen, than to write plays, and poetry, and romances'.[43] By manipulating male 'focalizers'[44] who comment on what they see, Edgeworth secured a unique means of rhetorical freedom in a climate where conservative attitudes towards women novelists prevailed.[45] According to Gerry H. Brookes, the novelist's motive was therefore 'to influence the reader's attitudes and beliefs toward what we perceive as fictional men in fictional situations and to urge us to make the same judgement of actual men in actual situations'.[46] Though true, Brookes's assertion overlooks the other component of the novelist's pedagogical intent. By using male narrators to her rhetorical advantage,

---

40 Refer to Chapter 2.
41 *Tales of Fashionable Life* appeared in two series. The first series, published in 1809, contained 'Ennui', 'Madame de Fleury', 'Almeria', 'The Dun', and 'Manoeuvering'. The second series was issued in 1812 and included 'Emilie de Coulanges', 'The Absentee' and 'Vivian'.
42 See Bermingham, 'The Aesthetics of Ignorance', 3.
43 Edgeworth, *Letters for Literary Ladies*, 25.
44 For a discussion on 'focalization', see Joe Bray's *The Epistolary Novel: Representations of Consciousness* (London: Routledge, 2003), 18. Bray explains that 'Gerard Genette replaces "point of view" with the term "focalization", which he claims avoids the "too specifically visual connotations" of the former; thus the "focalizer" is the person who sees, while the "narrator" is the person who speaks'.
45 See W. F. Gallaway, Jr.'s article 'The Conservative Attitude toward Fiction, 1770–1830', *PMLA* 55, no. 4 (December 1940): 1041–59.
46 Gerry H. Brookes, 'The Didacticism of Edgeworth's *Castle Rackrent*', *Studies in English Literature, 1500–1900* 17, no. 4, *Nineteenth Century* (Autumn 1977): 593–605 (601).

Edgeworth secured an unusual means through which to present the 'dumb-show' of how she imagined the male gaze to pictorialize women.

An appropriate beginning for theorizing Edgeworth's manipulation of *Castle Rackrent*'s 'honest' male narrative voices is the relationship between the 'look' of the novelist's writing and the 'look' of the characters that she 'drew from life'. Writing from Brussels on 15 October 1802, Edgeworth recounted her journey to Ghent with her father, Richard Lovell Edgeworth, Brian Edwards and his son.[47] While her father claimed to have a 'physiognomic eye',[48] Edwards boasted of his superior skill as a graphologist.[49] The young novelist insisted that he 'was positive that mine could not be the hand of a woman, and then he came off by saying it was the writing of a *manly* character!'[50] Edwards's Lavaterian reading of the novelist's penmanship is particularly salient. It indicates that during her lifetime, Edgeworth could pass for a man on the page, much in the way that many of her female characters, including *Belinda*'s Lady Delacour, often pass for what they are not, by employing a means of 'self-distortion' that is at once visible and psychological.[51]

Castle Rackrent's purportedly honest Thady supplied the author with a vehicle for critiquing Ireland's squirearchy from a native's perspective. In the preface to *Castle Rackrent* and in her letters, Edgeworth confessed that Thady was one of the few characters that she sourced from her surroundings:

> The only character drawn from the life in Castle Rackrent is Thady himself, the teller of the story [...] he seemed to stand beside me and dictate and I wrote as fast as my pen could go, the characters all imaginary.[52]

In publishing the book anonymously, Edgeworth made her simulations of the male gaze and the male narrative voice all the more persuasive. Whether or not *Castle Rackrent* was entirely her own work remains a subject of scholarly debate. As Brookes points out, 'Free of her father's restraining hand, this romantic argument goes, she could see life clearly and record it without comment.'[53]

---

47 Edgeworth, 'Brussels', 15 October 1802, *Maria Edgeworth: Chosen Letters*, 95–102.
48 On Lavater and the 'physiognomic eye', see Chapter 1.
49 Edgeworth, 'Brussels', 15 October 1802, *Maria Edgeworth: Chosen Letters*, 95–102.
50 Ibid.; emphasis in original.
51 Edgeworth revisits the theme of female handwriting in *Helen* (1834). She uses the resemblance between Lady Cecilia's and Helen's penmanship to show how truth and falsehood often look alike.
52 Maria Edgeworth, 'Letter to Mrs Stark', 6 September 1834; also cited in Butler's *Maria Edgeworth: A Literary Biography*, 240–41. Reprinted by permission of Oxford University Press.
53 Brookes, 'The Didacticism of Edgeworth's *Castle Rackrent*', 603.

In either case, the novelist had to 'imagine' the subjective way in which men perceived and commented on the women before their eyes.

The novel's subtitle – *An Hibernian Tale / Taken from Facts, and from the Manners of the Irish Squires before the year 1782* – allowed it to be read simultaneously as a factual and a fictional account of Irish life. The word 'facts' was clearly designed to be controversial, for the plot of the novel presents a story, not facts, though it is grounded in historical truths.[54] The *Monthly Review* placed its review of the novel under the heading of 'Ireland', categorizing it alongside political texts discussing the Union.[55] Praising the 'unknown author of these unusually pleasing pages', the anonymous reviewer claimed that 'from a due contemplating of these portraits, many striking conclusions may be drawn [...] respecting the necessity and probable consequences of an union between the two kingdoms'.[56] Even George III and William Pitt reputedly relied on *Castle Rackrent* for insight into the Irish and their perceptions.[57] Butler agrees that at the time of the novel's publication, such an honest portrayal of the Irish was problematic: it ran the risk of attracting the vehement disapproval of the Irish people.[58] Edgeworth's brother William, who lived in Cork, found that many people there were reading it as a '"straight" account of present-day Irish society, and disliked it with that criterion in mind'.[59] His observation provides an additional explanation for Edgeworth's decision to conceal her female identity by turning to a male narrator and publishing the text anonymously.

Like the woman behind 'his' perceptions, *Castle Rackrent*'s Thady is a collector of subjective anecdotes rather than a note-taker. In 1834, Edgeworth reminisced on her visual approach to writing dialogues:

> I never could use notes in writing Dialogues [...] for I could not write dialogues at all without being at the time fully impressed with the characters, imagining myself each speaker, and that too fully engrosses the imagination to leave time for consulting note-books; the whole fairy vision would melt away, and the warmth and the pleasure of invention be gone [...] my memory is inaccurate, has hold of the object only by one side – the side or face that struck my imagination.[60]

---

54 See Butler's 'Edgeworth's Ireland: History, Popular Culture, and Secret Codes', 267–70.
55 See Gamer, 'Maria Edgeworth and the Romance of Real Life', 250.
56 *Monthly Review*, 32 (1800), 91.
57 See Gamer, 'Maria Edgeworth and the Romance of Real Life', 250.
58 Butler, *Maria Edgeworth: A Literary Biography*, 359.
59 Ibid.
60 Edgeworth, 6 September 1834, *The Life and Letters of Maria Edgeworth*, 2 vols. (Middlesex: The Echo Library, 2007), 2: 139.

Edgeworth emphasized the importance of imagining herself as the voices, and subsequently the eyes, of her characters. She acknowledged that the 'fairy vision' would disappear if she were to fall out of character by attending to the inaccuracies of her visual memory.

In *Castle Rackrent*, Edgeworth uses the male narrator's actual and subjective names to encourage the reader to question the apparent accuracy of his viewpoint. While 'Quirk' suggests that Thady has a highly individual perspective, it does not prevent the family from referring to him as '*honest Thady*'.[61] By the time that Thady recounts the Rackrent family history, perceptions of him have changed. He assumes the retrospective gaze of '*old Thady*' and 'poor Thady', whose imperfect memory is for the reader to expect and excuse.[62] While Thady is blindly attached to Sir Kit, the novel's absentee landlord, he professes, paradoxically, to adhere to unvarnished 'truth'.[63] The narrator's inability to recognize his subjectivity, together with his blind loyalty to a landlord whose absenteeism is damaging to the estate, warns the reader that his view cannot be wholly respected.

In *Castle Rackrent*, the voice of an 'honest' male focalizer provides Edgeworth with an apparatus for typifying the way in which men viewed women's relationships with their material selves. When Sir Kit's Jewish bride, the wealthiest heiress in England, arrives in Ireland, Thady's role as steward of the estate enables him to be the first to witness her actual appearance:

> for when the carriage door opened just as she had her foot on the steps, I held the flame full in her face to light her, at which she shut her eyes, but I had a full view of the rest of her, and greatly shocked I was, for by that light she was little better than a blackamoor, and seemed crippled.[64]

Edgeworth's manipulation of perspective allows her to shed light, literally and metaphorically, on a 'full view' of the bride's unvarnished ugliness. Thady's subjective depiction shows that wealth may have enabled the woman to purchase diamonds, but jewellery cannot rectify her actual image. The light that exposes the woman as a seemingly crippled 'blackamoor', or dark-skinned heretic, forces her to shut her eyes. Her reaction conveys the 'dumbshow' of what Thady cannot, from his male perspective, describe: her instinctive resistance to the violence of male visual penetration.

---

61 Maria Edgeworth, *Castle Rackrent*, ed. Jane Desmarais, Tim McLoughlin and Marilyn Butler ([1809; 1832] London: Pickering & Chatto, 1999), 1: 9–67 (9); emphasis in original.
62 Ibid.; emphasis in original.
63 Ibid.
64 Ibid., 18.

Edgeworth uses jewellery to draw attention to the relationship between Sir Kit's need for financial assets and the 'enslavement' of the heiress, whose racial, cultural and physical impediments do not make her an attractive match. While the novel relates to high-class slavery within the gentry – not fashion and diamonds – jewellery showcases the perceptual differences between man and wife. The 'reliable' narrator specifies Jessica's possessiveness of her precious stones. Despite the 'full view' of the woman that he has, Thady, like Edgeworth, refrains from detailing physical appearances:

> but her diamond cross, it's worth I can't tell you how much; and she has thousands of English pounds concealed in diamonds about her, which she as good as promised to give up to my master before he married, but now she won't part with any of them, and she must take the consequences.[65]

Through the equivocation in the passage – 'as good as promised' – Edgeworth indicates that Jessica made no such promise. It is the men of the story who expect her to sacrifice all of her private assets and pleasures to be converted for their own self-seeking purposes. Jessica gains a husband and a title, while he, in return, gains a body and a fortune.

In *Castle Rackrent*, Edgeworth uses the male gaze to emphasize that Jessica's value is entirely visible and monetarily defined. The woman's refusal to part with 'any' of her diamonds reveals that she sees herself as more attached to her jewellery, literally and metaphorically, than to her husband.[66] She knows that they are the only items of value over which she retains any legal control and that as soon as she relinquishes them, she will lose her sole power and marketable asset in the marriage. Thady's frequent concessions of ignorance and inability to 'tell' strengthen the untrustworthiness and subjectivity of his commentary.[67] His consistent unreliability ironically contains a form of 'transparency': it allows the reader to see, as Elizabeth Harden proposes, 'the truth underneath the external statement and draw his own conclusions'.[68] Through the male narrator–focalizer's persistent inconsistencies and self-contradictions, the novelist dexterously conveys and clarifies universal truths.

In *Castle Rackrent*, Edgeworth uses Jessica's refusal to hand over her diamonds as a visual metaphor for her possessiveness of her value and values – monetary, cultural and religious. Thady speculates that she is not English

---

65 Ibid., 21.
66 Ibid.
67 Ibid.
68 Elizabeth Harden, 'Transparent Thady', in *Family Chronicles: Maria Edgeworth's* Castle Rackrent (Dublin: Wolfhound, 1987), 86–96 (91–92).

but may be a nabob from the Caribbean, perhaps the natural daughter of a wealthy businessman.[69] Sir Kit, meanwhile, calls her 'my pretty Jessica', the Shakespearean tag for any female Jew.[70] Throughout the novel, the woman's identity remains deliberately indistinct, allowing her attachment to her diamonds to define her character and view of money. In *Nabobs: Empire and Identity in Eighteenth-Century Britain* (2010), Tillman W. Nechtman explains, 'Nabobs had no connection to British honour, no sense of obligation to the nation. They were stingy with their diamonds.'[71] More than a form of 'stinginess,' Jessica's attachment to her diamonds serves as a reasonable form of self-defence against male despoliation.

Edgeworth shows that Jessica's acculturated view of her diamonds anticipates the way in which she perceives other objects. The woman's relentless 'misreading' of sights demands Thady's attention and stages their conflicting subjectivities:

> Where have you lived, my lady all your life, not to know a turf stack when you see it, thought I, but I said nothing. Then, by-and-bye, she takes out her glass, and begins spying over the country. 'And what's all that black swamp out yonder, Sir Kit?' says she. 'My bog, my dear,' says he, and went on whistling. 'It's a very ugly prospect, my dear,' says she. 'You don't see it, my dear,' says he, 'for we've planted it out, when the trees grow up in summer time,' says he. 'Where are the trees,' said she, 'my dear?' still looking through her glass. 'You are blind, my dear,' says he; 'what are those under your eyes?' 'These shrubs,' said she. 'Trees,' said he.[72]

Thady observes that the glass, which can correct vision, fails to remedy Jessica's cultural illiteracy. In the narrator's prejudiced view, the woman 'asked for it' – all of the 'misfortune' that befell her – by insulting her husband's land: 'at that very instant; but I said no more, only looked at Sir Kit'.[73] Edgeworth uses his gaze to show rather than speak of the sudden change that he observes in Sir Kit's perception of his wife. Through subjective anecdotes and the dumbshow, the narrative encourages the reader to see that Sir Kit's pride in his marshy, unimproved estate and his grasping, unloving behaviour are as 'myopic' as anything that Jessica says or does.

---

69 Edgeworth, *Castle Rackrent*, 20–21.
70 From William Shakespeare's *The Merchant of Venice*.
71 Tillman W. Nechtman, *Nabobs: Empire and Identity in Eighteenth-Century Britain* (Cambridge: Cambridge University Press, 2010), 161.
72 Edgeworth, *Castle Rackrent*, 19.
73 Ibid.

In *Castle Rackrent*, Edgeworth shows that the 'consequences' of Jessica's inexorable attachment to her jewellery and cultural identity impinge on her appearance. Thady contends that the woman's troubles began when she attempted to usurp her husband's power at the table: 'My lady came down herself into the kitchen, to speak to the cook about the sausages, and desired never to see them more at her table.'[74] For Jessica, the sight of the sausages is an insult. Since she refuses to relinquish her private possessions and religious views, knowing all the while that Sir Kit does not value her perspective, she has no choice but to confront the imprisonment, silence and neglect that Radcliffe's fictional women similarly endure though in disparate settings.

While Thady emphasizes that the table is 'hers', Sir Kit's patriarchal authority prevails over what his wife 'sees' on 'her' table. Jessica's powerlessness, even within the domestic realm, forces her to 'give up' by exiting the scene:

> she gave up, and from that day forward always sausages, or bacon, or pig meat in some shape or other, went up to table; upon which my lady shut herself up in her own room, and my master said she might stay there, with an oath: and to make sure of her, he turned the key in the door, and kept it ever after in his pocket.[75]

Edgeworth shows that Sir Kit's wife is 'shut' – perceptually, religiously and mentally. Even if the room to which Jessica retreats is similarly 'hers', Sir Kit has power over the duration of her invisibility: 'We none of us ever saw or heard her speak for seven years after that.'[76] Sir Kit may have control over her physical appearance, but he cannot weaken his wife's attachment to the asset that defines her:

> he tried all his arts to get the diamond cross from her on her death-bed, and to get her to make a will in his favour of her separate possessions; but there she was too tough for him.[77]

Sir Kit's 'arts' cannot break his 'stiff-necked Israelite' even when her body is reduced to 'skin and bone'.[78] Illness and imprisonment cause her body to decay, but the 'toughness' of her commodified identity remains.[79] Her

---

74 Ibid., 20.
75 Ibid.
76 Ibid., 21.
77 Ibid.
78 Ibid.
79 For a discussion on 'commodity fetishism' that can be applied to Edgeworth's visual technique, see Andrea Henderson's article 'Burney's *The Wanderer* and Early-Nineteenth-Century Commodity Fetishism', *Nineteenth-Century Literature* 57, no. 1 (June 2002): 1–30.

diamonds read as emblems of her vigorous 'self' control, calling to mind Mary Wollstonecraft's declaration, 'I do not wish [women] to have power over men; but over themselves'.[80]

In *Castle Rackrent*, Edgeworth delays Jessica's return to visibility and health until the final pages of the novel. When the Jewish heiress and her diamond cross are allowed to show themselves, they replace Sir Kit's visibility in the scene. Through her version of poetic justice, the novelist issues a feminist stance on the patriarchal abuses of the domestic sphere. The unloving husband must die before he can profit from Jessica's demise. As Thady attests, 'if it had not been all along with her, his honour, Sir Kit, would have now been alive in all appearance'.[81] The sentimental value of Jessica's diamonds increases following her husband's interment:

> We got the key out of his pocket the first thing we did, and my son Jason ran to unlock the barrack-room, where my lady had been shut up for seven years to acquaint her with the fatal accident. The surprise bereaved her of her senses at first, nor would she believe but we were butting some new trick upon her, to entrap her out of her jewels, for a great while, till Jason bethought himself of taking her to the window, and showed her the men bringing Sir Kit up the avenue upon the hand-barrow, which had immediately the desired effect; for directly she burst into tears, and pulling her cross from her bosom, she kissed it with as great devotion as ever I witnessed; and lifting up her eyes to heaven, uttered some ejaculation, which none present heard.[82]

Thady's recollection of Jessica's 'heavenward' gaze offers an ekphrastic testimony of the woman's gratitude. The episode encourages the reader to realize that which he does not observe, visually or verbally, about Lady Rackrent's appalling situation. His own subjectivity and attachment to Sir Kit have blinded him to the paradox inherent in Lady Rackrent's 'dumbshow'.

Edgeworth's depiction of Jessica's self-display calls to mind Alexander Pope's portrayal of Belinda in *The Rape of the Lock* (1712):

> Fair nymphs, and well-dress'd youths around her shone,
> But ev'ry eye was fix'd on her alone.

---

80 Mary Wollstonecraft, *The Vindications: The Rights of Men, the Rights of Woman*, ed. D. L. Macdonald and Kathleen Scherf (Ontario: Broadview, 1997), 179.
81 Edgeworth, *Castle Rackrent*, 21.
82 Ibid., 22.

On her white breast a sparkling cross she wore,
Which Jews might kiss, and infidels adore.[83]

In Edgeworth's novel, Lady Rackrent appears to see her diamond cross as an ironic talisman of 'divine' female power. 'Bereaved out of her senses,' she unconsciously 'opens up' to Thady, allowing him to witness the object of her devotion that has come to represent her 'material' heart. While the narrator–focalizer's loyalty is to Sir Kit, the reader is inclined to favour the exiled, mistreated and yet staunchly resistant woman who overcomes him. Jessica's 'fashionable' status is ephemeral, dependent on self-display, but the value of her diamond cross remains inestimable, attesting to the possibility of righteousness in a society dominated by patriarchal abuses.

In *Castle Rackrent*, Edgeworth juxtaposes Thady's account of Sir Kit's wife with a male English editor's annotations. Her dialogic method continues to encourage the reader to mistrust the accuracy of Thady's subjectivity:

> This part of the history of the Rackrent family can scarcely be thought credible; but in justice to honest Thady, it is hoped the reader will recollect the history of the celebrated Lady Cathcart's husband; he has lately seen and questioned the maid-servant who lived with Colonel McGuire during the time of Lady Cathcart's imprisonment.—
>
> Her Ladyship was locked up in her own house for many years; during which period her husband was visited by the neighbouring gentry, and it was his regular custom at dinner to send his compliments to Lady Cathcart, informing her that the company had the honour to drink her ladyship's health, and begging to know whether there was any thing at the table that she would like to eat? The answer was always – 'Lady Cathcart's compliments, and she has everything she wants.'[84]

The editor's presumptive tone insists that Thady's perspective of Irish life is superior to the reader's. It offers vicarious contact with a culture in a way that ironically produces a visual glossary of Irish typologies.

In his article 'Castle Nugent and Castle Rackrent: Fact and Fiction in Maria Edgeworth' (1996), W. A. Maguire draws attention to a point that the footnotes to the novel make explicit: the similarity between Lady Cathcart's lengthy imprisonment, publicized in her obituary in the *Gentleman's Magazine*

---

83 Alexander Pope, *The Rape of the Lock*, in *Alexander Pope The Major Works: including* The Rape of the Lock *and* The Dunciad, ed. Pat Rogers (Oxford: Oxford University Press, 2008), 77–100 (83), 2.5–8. Reprinted by permission of Oxford University Press.
84 Edgeworth, *Castle Rackrent*, 20.

in August 1789, and Jessica's circumstances.[85] While Edgeworth claims that apart from Thady, the novel's characters were pure invention, Maguire posits that the account of Lady Cathcart's lengthy imprisonment in Ireland inspired the novelist's portrait of Sir Kit's wife.[86] He writes, 'It appears, then, that Maria Edgeworth by good fortune read the story of the wicked colonel in the *Gentleman's Magazine* and later adapted it for her own use.'[87] An 1834 letter to Mrs Stark also evidences that the novelist was well acquainted with the story of Lady Cathcart's fastidious attachment to her diamonds, even if she knew 'nothing' else:

> Indeed, the real people had no resemblance, at all events, to my Sir Kit, and I knew nothing of Lady Cathcart, but that she was fond of money, and would not give up her diamonds.[88]

Maguire overlooks the characteristic 'resemblance' between Lady Cathcart and her fictional counterpart: both women regarded diamonds as sources of female power in the 'enslavement' of marriage. Edgeworth's visual technique of commenting on female subjectivity draws attention to the colonial approach to managing land and women as spaces to be exploited but that may ironically outlast and usurp their 'owners'.

In her later novella, *Ennui*, Edgeworth reuses her male narrator–focalizer technique to encourage the reader to investigate the male gaze by looking through it rather than at it. The text's publication under her name turned her to another means of confirming the tale's credibility and her own respectability. In the preface, she called upon her father's 'protection' in order to discredit the assumption that texts by male writers carried superior intellectual merit and moral worth:

> My daughter asks me for a Preface to the following volumes; from a pardonable weakness she calls upon me for parental protection: but, in fact, the public judges of every work, not from the sex, but from the merit of the author.[89]

Edgeworth's 'disguise' as a male narrator, together with her father's visible intervention, enabled her to liberate herself from the societal strictures that

---

85 Refer to the *Gentleman's Magazine*, 59 (August 1789), 766–67.
86 W. A. Maguire, '*Castle Nugent* and *Castle Rackrent*: Fact and Fiction in Maria Edgeworth', *Eighteenth-Century Ireland/Iris an dá chultúr* 11 (1996): 146–59 (146–48).
87 Ibid., 147.
88 Edgeworth, 'Letter to Mrs Stark', 6 September 1834, *Memoir* (1867), 3: 152–53.
89 Edgeworth, *Ennui*, 159.

complicated women's attempts to translate their thoughts into words, in literature and in actuality. As Claire Connolly reminds us in her introduction to *Letters for Literary Ladies*, 'to eschew language entirely was impossible, so its slipperiness remains a potential threat, skirting the edges of plain speech, disrupting the ordering of words'.[90] The novelist circumnavigates the threat of misinterpretation by describing people in the act of viewing. She communicates who they are through how they think.

In *Ennui*, Edgeworth relies on the man of leisure's gaze to show how a man might control the fashionable woman's 'image'. The French condition of *ennui* alters the alleged Earl of Glenthorn's vision, subjecting him to an apathy that leads to visual indifference: 'I was afflicted with [...] an aversion to the place I was in, or the thing I was doing, or rather to that which was passing before my eyes.'[91] Edgeworth links perceptions to ethics, describing his condition as 'a moral indigestion, caused by a monotony of situations'.[92] Even Sherwood Park, his majestic English country seat, loses its 'look' of beauty in its owner's eyes, and 'the idea of being the proprietor of this enchanting place soon palled upon my vanity'.[93] The novelist's treatment of the fictive male gaze emphasizes that, while he observes that it is seen by others as an 'enchanting place', his ailment has desensitized him to the non-quantifiable forms of beauty before him.

Edgeworth uses hyperbole and alliteration to dramatize the relationship between the Earl of Glenthorn's aesthetic detachment and his habit of picturing women in quantitative terms. His skewed perception of the 'woman of fashion' begins in his mind's eye: 'In my imagination young women were divided into two classes; those who were to be purchased, and those who were to purchase.'[94] The Earl of Glenthorn's perceptual flaw lies in his inability to picture the look of the 'all-accomplished' woman: 'Notwithstanding my usual indifference to the whole race of *very agreeable young ladies*, I remember trying to form a picture in my imagination of this all-accomplished female.'[95] His deluded eyes and 'man of measures' philosophy prompt him to picture his bride in numeric terms:

> I chose her by the numeration table: Units, tens, hundreds, thousands, tens of thousands, hundreds of thousands. I was content, in the language

---

90 See Claire Connolly's introduction to Maria Edgeworth, *Letters for Literary Ladies*, xxii.
91 Edgeworth, *Ennui*, 162.
92 Ibid.
93 Ibid., 163.
94 Ibid., 167.
95 Ibid., 288; emphasis in original.

of the newspapers, *to lead to the Hymeneal altar* any fashionable fair one whose fortune came under the sixth place of figures.[96]

Edgeworth's use of alliteration links 'fashionable', 'fair', 'fortune' and 'figures' to the female sex. The scene calls to mind Bermingham's assertion that 'in neither their passive nor active roles can women escape their commodification by the gaze.'[97] By calling upon 'the language of the newspapers', the Earl of Glenthorn reveals his 'objective' formula for choosing a wife. Even when the woman is invisible in the scene, she is a visible commodity in his imagination, implying the novelist's view that fashionable cynicism and worldliness encourage all men to objectify women.

In *Ennui*, the narrative turns to examining the visual relationship between the theatre of the marriage market and women's status as commodities. Edgeworth uses the bride's 100 wedding dresses, the work of a team of English and French dressmakers and milliners, to make her material value and grafted identity visible.[98] The public exhibition of the woman's cosmopolitan wardrobe produces subjective interpretations of her outer worth even before she appears in person:

> the most admired came to about five hundred pounds, and was thought, by the best judges in these matters, to be wonderfully cheap, as it was of lace such as had never before been trailed in English dust, even by the lady of a nabob. These things were shown in London as a *spectacle* for some days.[99]

The transition into the passive voice signifies a shift from the subjective to the 'objective' gaze, confusing the lavishness of 'the most admired' dress with the perception that it was 'wonderfully cheap'.[100] Even before the Earl of Glenthorn's bride wears the 'most admired' dress, it seduces his attention, becoming, in his eyes, a visible analogue for the woman's body. Edgeworth manages commerce and consumption by, as Wohlgemut puts it, 'a particular mode of subjectivity'.[101] By declaring the gown to be a '*spectacle*' in England, the novelist forewarns the reader that the wearer of the gown will attract an analogous degree of subjective interpretation.

---

96 Ibid., 167; emphasis in original.
97 Ann Bermingham, 'The Aesthetics of Ignorance: The Accomplished Woman in the Culture of Connoisseurship', *Oxford Art Journal* 16, no. 2 (1993): 3–20 (12). © Oxford University Press 1993. Reprinted by permission of Oxford University Press.
98 Edgeworth, *Ennui*, 167.
99 Ibid.; emphasis in original.
100 Ibid.
101 Wohlgemut, 'Maria Edgeworth and the Question of National Identity', 12–13.

Whereas dress provides the reader with a material representation of the Earl of Glenthorn's visual indifference, jewellery displays his wife's similar myopia. Her 'prodigiously fine' diamonds showcase the Earl of Glenthorn's view of how she sees happiness: '"Poor young creature! I believe her chief idea of happiness in marriage was the possession of the jewels and paraphernalia of a countess – I am sure it was the only hope she could have, that was likely to be realized, in marrying me."'[102] His 'fashionable indifference' enables him to overlook his wife's 'indifference' to the individual stones in her collection.[103] When asked where she had purchased her diamonds, Lady Glenthorn can only confess, '"Really [...] I cannot tell. I have so many sets, I declare I don't know whether *it's* my Paris, or my Hamburgh, or my London set."'[104] Her inability to 'tell' the provenance of her diamonds implies their sentimental triviality at a time when trends in jewellery were favouring miniatures and locks of hair over sizeable precious stones.[105] Lady Glenthorn's 'indifference' to jewellery's aesthetic distinctions and invisible sentimental value implies that she is not, in actuality, what the Earl of Glenthorn should see as a desirable wife: 'She was too frivolous to be hated, and the passion of hatred was not to be easily sustained in my mind. The habit of ennui was stronger than all my passions put together.'[106] His eyes need to be open to their own subjective indifference in order to evaluate women according to their invisible worth.

In *Ennui*, Edgeworth uses the subjectivity of 'fashionability' to depict the contrasting appearances of Lady Geraldine and Miss Tracey, her 'shadow'. While a 'glance of curiosity' reveals that Lady Geraldine has 'no regularity of feature', she sees herself as a 'regular' image of 'fashionable' womanhood.[107] Her self-perceptions influence her view of Miss Tracey's contrasting appearance: '"In the language of the bird-fanciers, she has few notes nightingale, and all the rest rubbish."'[108] Despite Miss Tracey's desperate attempts to mirror and mimic the *bon ton*, her confused perception of 'good' taste prevents her from seeing herself as other 'fashionable' women see her. Lady Geraldine plots the exposure of Miss Tracey's aesthetic illiteracy, promising her female companions that they will witness the woman in '"every thing that I have sworn to her is fashionable"':[109]

---

102 Edgeworth, *Ennui*, 168.
103 Ibid., 167.
104 Ibid.; emphasis in original.
105 On jewellery and sentimental value, see Bertero, *Modes du XVIIIème siècle sous Louis XVI et Marie-Antoinette*, 69.
106 Edgeworth, *Ennui*, 168.
107 Ibid., 210.
108 Ibid., 213.
109 Ibid.

'Nor have I cheated her in a single article: but the *tout ensemble* I leave to her better judgement; and you shall see her, I trust, a perfect monster, formed of every creature's best: Lady Kilrush's feathers, Mrs. Moore's wig, Mrs. O'Connor's gown Mrs. Lighton's sleeves, and all the necklaces of all the Miss Ormsbys. She has no taste, no judgement; none at all poor thing! But she can imitate as well as those Chinese painters, who, in their drawings, give you the flower of one plant stuck on the stalk of another, and garnished with the leaves of a third.'[110]

In 'generously' allowing Miss Tracey to acquire the 'complete collection' that is 'formed of every creature's best', Lady Geraldine ensures that her scheme will make the woman's poor judgement decisively visible. She foresees that her social inferior will appear 'a perfect monster', exhibiting a grafted form of beauty akin to that found in Chinese bird-and-flower paintings that feature flowers, birds, fish and insects.[111]

According to Bermingham, the accomplished woman's skills as a consumer – 'her taste and discrimination in choosing and displaying those commodities that would be an extension of her subjectivity'[112] – determine how she is 'consumed'. Edgeworth shows that even if Miss Tracey succeeds in '"fancying herself the mirror of fashion"', her skills as a consumer are deficient: she cannot see the difference between good and bad taste, truth and deception because, in Lady Geraldine's view, she has been '"Spoiled by bad company!"'[113]

Lady Geraldine reconfirms Miss Tracey's deluded perceptions by dramatizing her inability to discriminate between men of high rank and their mimics. Through comedic disclosure and Miss Tracey's poor judgement, Edgeworth differentiates the *vrai* and the *vraisemblable*, the fashionable Lord Craiglethorpe and his double.[114] Lady Geraldine's ability to 'draw or *speak* caricatures'[115] facilitates her efforts to make herself look superior by plotting the 'dumb-show' of Miss Tracey's admiration for '*the false Craiglethorpe*'.[116] As in Molière's *La Critique de l'École des femmes* (1662), she seeks to expose her victims – her

---

110 Ibid.
111 Ibid.
112 Ann Bermingham, 'The Aesthetics of Ignorance: The Accomplished Woman in the Culture of Connoisseurship', *Oxford Art Journal* 16, no. 2 (1993): 3–20 (13). © Oxford University Press 1993. Reprinted by permission of Oxford University Press.
113 Edgeworth, *Ennui*, 213.
114 Ibid., 213.
115 Ibid., 211.
116 Ibid., 215; emphasis in original.

friends – in order to '*faire rire les honnêtes gens*'.[117] Lady Glenthorn's theatrical amusement teaches her husband to 'perceive that there was some difference between woman and woman, beside the distinctions of rank, fortune, and figure'.[118] Edgeworth shows that Lady Glenthorn's motive is simultaneously moralizing and demoralizing, depending on one's point of view. Like Lady Delacour, Lady Glenthorn is clever and witty but also cruel. By masking herself behind a male perspective, the novelist encourages her readers to view women's need to display their good taste through their commodified images. Rather than arguing that fashion dominates and destroys women's relationships with their own subjective selfhood, Edgeworth reveals her position to be ambivalent, reflecting a certain enjoyment of the satire that fashion and its foibles make possible.

Looking at Made-up Women in *Belinda*

Portrayals and discussions of the 'woman of fashion' occupy a significant part of Edgeworth's attention in *Belinda* (1801), which Brookes and Hawthorne observe to have been heavily influenced by the novelist's overbearing father.[119] Edgeworth's third-person narrative technique and heroine-centric plot encourage the reader to empathize with the female viewpoint. Hawthorne explains that, while the novelist originally intended for Lady Delacour to die, 'Mr. Edgeworth insisted on keeping her alive in order to show the effect of reason on a dissipated lady of fashion.'[120] In the novel, it is the dissipated lady of fashion whose vision must reform so that she can survive within the frame of the moral tale. As Ó Gallchoir has proposed, Edgeworth's fictional women must reinvent their images in order to endure cultural pressures: 'In *Belinda*, women are threatened with the loss of self both through the irrational pursuit of fashion and through the subordination of femininity on which the radical philosophies of the eighteenth century rest.'[121] Whatever the 'irrational' dangers of fashion – an obsession with 'useless' beauty and superficial 'improvement' – the risks of naiveté and self-exposure are, for Edgeworth, still greater.

---

117 Edgeworth's satire resembles that found in Molière's *La Critique de l'École des femmes* (1662); emphasis in original.
118 Edgeworth, *Ennui*, 219.
119 See Brookes, 'The Didacticism of Edgeworth's *Castle Rackrent*', 603, and Mark D. Hawthorne's 'Maria Edgeworth's Unpleasant Lesson: The Shaping of Character', *Studies: An Irish Quarterly Review* 64, no. 254 (Summer 1975): 166–77.
120 Hawthorne, 'Maria Edgeworth's Unpleasant Lesson, 173–74.
121 Ó Gallchoir, *Maria Edgeworth: Women, Enlightenment and Nation*, 45.

In 1802, the *Monthly Review* complained that Belinda 'usurped the superior right for Lady Delacour to give the title to the work: for it is to the character and agency of the latter [...] that the tale owes its principal attractions'.[122] Seven years later, when she was reworking the text for Anna Laetitia Barbauld's *The British Novelists* (1810), Edgeworth confessed, '"I really was so provoked with the cold tameness of that stick or stone Belinda, that I could have torn the pages to pieces."'[123] While the untrustworthiness of Lady Delacour's appearance makes her the most fascinating character in the story, Belinda's role in reforming the 'woman of fashion's' perceptions makes her the moralizing observer in the novel. Edgeworth emphasizes the fact that while Belinda, the moral ingénue, is the notional heroine capable of correcting others' self-perceptions, Lady Delacour, her damaged, witty, worldly mentor and rival, is the more sympathetic, nuanced and active female lead. Edgeworth's visual technique shows that woman's ideal role in society is at odds with her actual perception of female desire and marital compromise.

In the masquerade scene near the novel's opening, Edgeworth uses fashion to demonstrate women's need to hide behind masks in order to thwart penetration and misinterpretation. Her tableau of Lady Delacour as Comedy and Belinda as Tragedy suggests the influence of Sir Joshua Reynolds's *Garrick between Tragedy and Comedy* (1761), which reinterprets Hercules vacillating between pleasure and virtue.[124] The novelist's feminized composition amplifies the urgency for Lady Delacour and Belinda to conceal their feelings behind the guise of a contrasting emotion. Edgeworth shows that preconceptions of the way in which 'comedy' and 'tragedy' should appear influence the readings of the disguises that the women adopt. Marriott repeatedly anticipates Lady Delacour's choice of display:

> 'people always succeed best when they take characters diametrically opposite to their own – Clarence Hervey's principle – Perhaps you don't think that he has any principles; but there you are wrong; I do assure you, he has sound principles – of taste.'[125]

Reasoning that Lady Delacour is, like the legitimate Lord Craiglethorpe in *Ennui*, taller than her 'inferior', Marriott contends that she must become the Tragic

---

122 'Review of *Belinda*', *Monthly Review*, 37 (April 1802), 368.
123 MacFadyen, 424. MacFadyen refers to a letter to Margaret Ruxton, December 1809, in *A Memoir of Maria Edgeworth with a Selection from Her Letters*, ed. Frances Edgeworth, 3 vols. (London: Joseph Masters and Son, 1867), 1: 229.
124 For a discussion on 'Choice' paintings, see Frances Borzello's *Seeing Ourselves: Women's Self-Portraits* (New York: Harry N. Abrams, 1998), 82.
125 Edgeworth, *Belinda*, 18.

Muse, as tragedy is seen as 'tall'.[126] Although Lady Delacour follows Clarence's logic, her choice of character in the scene baffles him. Clarence, whose eyes have become accustomed to seeing Lady Delacour as Tragedy, is blind to the volatility of her repressed emotions. In confiding to the Tragic Muse that Belinda is '"a composition of art and affectation"', he articulates his inability to discriminate between the facades that society pressures women to adopt and their natural selves.[127] In presuming that Lady Delacour is acting as Tragedy, he does not anticipate that he will behold Belinda playing 'her' part. The novelist performs, through the masque, the silent masquerade of women's emotional careers and the extent to which they repress feelings to pass socially.

In the episode of the Comic and Tragic muses, Edgeworth presents the need for women to deceive the eye as a form of suffocation. She links the contrived appearance of the masquerade to Lady Delacour's concealed cancer and melancholy. Belinda's initial attraction to Clarence turns her feelings to mortification upon hearing the way in which he sees her actual character. The heroine's ability to breathe freely and resume her natural self involves a metamorphosis that risks overexposing her feelings. Lady Delacour narrates Clarence's reaction to seeing Belinda as he has never seen her before:

> 'What now! This is not the first time Clarence Hervey has ever seen your face without a mask, is it? It's the first time indeed he, or any body else, ever saw it of such a colour, I believe.'[128]

Rather than allowing the reader to look at the heroine directly, Edgeworth negotiates cultural strictures on vision by using the novel's 'woman of fashion' to narrate Belinda's visual transformation. Lady Delacour observes that 'her face was during the first instant, pale; the next moment, crimsoned over with a burning blush'.[129] The 'burn' of Belinda's passion breaches cultural expectations of appropriate self-display. As Lynn Festa explains, '[colour] allows individuals to turn a subjective perception into a property of the object perceived. Because it cannot be isolated as an object, colour undoes spectatorial mastery.'[130] The unsettledness of Belinda's unmasked complexion subjects her blush to the possibility of 'spectatorial mastery' in the eyes of the viewer, calling

---

126 Ibid.
127 Ibid., 23.
128 Ibid., 24.
129 Ibid.
130 Lynn Festa, 'Cosmetic Differences: The Changing Faces of England and France', *Studies in Eighteenth-Century Culture* 34 (2005): 25–54 (43). © 2005 American Society for Eighteenth-Century Studies. Reprinted with permission of Johns Hopkins University Press.

to mind Burney's treatment of the blush in *Camilla*.[131] The rush of blood to the face also suggests erotic attraction, making 'natural rouge' both a marker of modesty and sexual awareness of the male gaze.

In this episode, Edgeworth provides Belinda with an opportunity to save her image by masking her emotions. Observing the shade of her companion's cheeks, Lady Delacour urges the heroine to adopt her method of maintaining her image and reputation:

> 'Now you'll meet those young men continually, who took the liberty of laughing at your aunt, and your cousins, and yourself; they are men of fashion – Show them you've no feeling, and they'll acknowledge you for a woman of fashion.'[132]

Lady Delacour's advice suggests that impenetrable masks can be donned by both material and immaterial means. Her theatrical cue '"if you will only dry up your tears, *keep on your mask*, and take my advice"' intimates that whereas men of fashion are free to appear as they please, 'fashionable' women must conceal their actual selves, selves known only to themselves.[133]

Here, Edgeworth reuses *Ennui*'s themes of dispassion, cynicism and disinterest that were associated with the *bon ton*. In both plots, she uses the 'dumbshow' to communicate to the reader that direct access to feeling is not a desirable emotional condition in a society of penetrating gazes. Edgeworth's specific emphasis on keeping on one's facade visually informs the reader of the mask's ability to preserve women's reputations by dictating how others ought to read their appearances. From Belinda's perspective, Lady Delacour is a woman of fashion by her own definition: 'Through the mask of paint which she wore, no change of colour could be visible; and as Belinda did not see the expression of her ladyship's eyes, she could not in the least judge of what was passing in her mind.'[134] Lady Delacour's determination to hide her natural colours and deflect the gaze aligns her method with culturally dictated self-sacrifice. Like Radcliffe's fictional women, she must veil her mind and heart, even from other women.[135]

Edgeworth shows that Lady Delacour can only suffer the character of the Comic Muse so long before she finds its falsity too suffocating to wear. While Lady Delacour stresses the improbability of a fate similar to that of J. F. Marmontel's

---

131 On Burney's use of colour codes, see Chapter 4.
132 Edgeworth, *Belinda*, 26.
133 Ibid., 25; emphasis in original.
134 Ibid.
135 See Chapter 2.

'la femme comme il y en a peu', Lady Anne predicts that the 'magic' of her companion's made-up character will wear off: '"enchantment will soon be at an end and she will return to her natural character. I should not be at all surprised, if Lady Delacour were to appear at once *la femme comme il y en a peu*."'[136] Edgeworth uses the only unpainted woman in the novel to warn of the mortality of Lady Delacour's 'fashionable' character. Referring to Westal's portrait of Lady Anne and her family rather than to their actual appearances, Belinda later remarks, '"how much more interesting his picture is to us, from our knowing that it is not a fancy-piece; that the happiness is real, not imaginary"'.[137] The removal of Lady Delacour's imaginary happiness exposes her face to natural light: she 'let fall her mask, and was silent. – It was broad daylight, and Belinda had a full view of her countenance, which was the picture of despair.'[138] Whereas Edgeworth makes Clarence witness Belinda's metamorphosis, here, it is the heroine who beholds the woman of fashion's transformation into the visual definition of a contrasting emotion: 'At a distance, Lady Delacour had appeared to Miss Portman the happiest person in the world; upon a nearer view, she discovered that her ladyship was one of the most miserable of human beings.'[139] Belinda's altered perspective affects her interpretation of the woman of fashion's need to screen her melancholy and its somatic source, or what she sees and believes to be a cancer in her breast.

In *Belinda*'s presentation of theatrical concealment, Edgeworth directs the reader's attention to the 'stage set' itself. She uses glass to represent the nexus between private and public dimensions of the domestic realm and, in turn, women's characters. The mirror in Lady Delacour's boudoir invites the woman of fashion to determine 'behind the scenes' the deceptive look that others will regard as an interpretive index of her health and happiness:

> She put on an unusual quantity of rouge; then looking at herself in the glass, she said with a forced smile –
>
> 'Marriott, I look so charmingly, that Miss Portman, perhaps, will be of Lord Delacour's opinion, and think that nothing is the matter with me. – Ah, no! – She has been behind the scenes, she knows the truth too well!'[140]

Lady Delacour emphasizes the fashionable woman's need to consult her reflection in order to *shade* her character. As Festa explains, 'Putting on "one's

---

136 Edgeworth, *Belinda*, 82; emphasis in original.
137 Ibid., 184.
138 Ibid., 26.
139 Ibid., 55.
140 Ibid., 206.

face" is a doubling that anticipates the encounter with another: the woman who makes herself up *preoccupies* the place to be assumed by the spectator.'[141] The glass makes Lady Delacour a spectator to her many faces. She is the sole witness to her process of self-invention, which suggests that she has a more intimate relationship with her mirror than with her husband. While she is certain that the male gaze will not be able to read her facade, Belinda's penetration into her boudoir has acquainted her eyes with the 'truth' that cosmetics mask. Only in the privacy of her boudoir can Lady Delacour express herself naturally: ' "I seem to you, and to all the world, what I am not." '[142]

In *Belinda*, Edgeworth combines gendered subjectivities to draw attention to the woman of fashion's need to embody the same properties as glass. From Mr Vincent's vantage point, Lady Delacour's eyes are reflective rather than penetrable: He fixes his gaze on Lady Delacour, 'in whose face, as in a glass, he seemed to study every thing that was passing'.[143] Her eyes are more mirrors of the world than windows to her soul. Even her Queen Elizabeth costume 'reflects' her fever of mind and body. Clarence learns to see Lady Delacour's character through that which she does not exteriorize: ' "my secret is quite simple. – Look through the door at the shadow of Queen Elizabeth's ruff – observe how it vibrates; the motion as well as the figure is magnified in the shadow." '[144] While shadows can reveal the beatings of the female heart, Lady Delacour's 'outside' proves an unreliable source of insight for *Belinda*'s men.

Edgeworth uses Belinda to reform Lady Delacour's self-perceptions in a way that elicits an eventual transformation in how the woman is seen by others, especially by her husband. The heroine encourages her mentor to look in a mirror so that she may see for herself the visibility of her distress. Tears have 'ruined' the woman of fashion's image by washing away the toxins of her painted cheeks:[145]

> The tears rolled fast down her painted cheeks; she wiped them hastily away, and so roughly that her face became a strange and ghastly spectacle. Unconscious of her disordered appearance, she rushed past Belinda, who vainly attempted to stop her, threw up the sash, and, stretching herself far out of the window, gasped for breath.[146]

---

141 Festa, 'Cosmetic Differences: The Changing Faces of England and France', 33. © 2005 American Society for Eighteenth-Century Studies. Reprinted with permission of Johns Hopkins University Press.
142 Edgeworth, *Belinda*, 27.
143 Ibid., 273.
144 Ibid., 90.
145 Ibid., 161–62. On the dangers of cosmetics, see Festa, 'Cosmetic Differences', 25–54.
146 Ibid.

Lady Delacour's sudden emotional transparency suggests that, although she feels the tears streaming down her cheeks, she is 'unconscious' of the 'strange and ghastly spectacle' that they make of her face. Only by 'stretching herself far out of the window' can she extricate herself from the glass-bound suffocation of domesticity.[147]

In the episode, Edgeworth uses Belinda's moralizing perspective to critique Lady Delacour's dramatic change of face. Attempting to rescue the woman of fashion from certain misinterpretation, the heroine warns her of her unsightly lack of rouge:

'The rouge is all off your face, my dear Lady Delacour! – you are not fit to be seen. Sit down upon this sofa, and I will ring for Marriott, and get some fresh rouge. Look at your face in this glass – you see –'[148]

Edgeworth's dialogic technique treats Lady Delacour and Belinda as pedagogical doubles. Whereas Lady Delacour has to warn Belinda of her excessive reddening, here, the heroine has to reprimand the woman of fashion for exhibiting the opposite extreme. Lady Delacour is 'not fit to be seen' but refuses to see her ailing reflection in public. Her disordered appearance presages her misinterpretation of Belinda's benevolent intentions. She retorts, '*Rouge! – not fit to be seen!*'[149] The dumbshow exhibits how women must keep up their masks in order to greet the public gaze, even within the domestic sphere.

Belinda's Lady Delacour is, like the subject of Reynolds's *Mrs Siddons as the Tragic Muse* (1784; 1789), a great actor.[150] As *The Times* described Sarah Siddons's performances, '"*The sudden transition from VIOLENT rage to affected indifference, was a MASTER-PIECE of acting; none but Mrs. Siddons could so well exhibit the two extremes.*"'[151] Edgeworth shows that Lady Delacour must exercise the same spontaneity in displaying a contrived self: 'With the promptitude of an actress she could instantly appear upon the stage, and support a character totally foreign to her own.'[152] The physical constraints of fashionable female attire make visible the

---

147 For a discussion on women's unprivileged status in the public sphere, see Ó Gallchoir, *Maria Edgeworth: Women, Enlightenment and Nation*, 4.
148 Edgeworth, *Belinda*, 162.
149 Ibid.; emphasis in original.
150 See Heather McPherson's article 'Picture Tragedy: Mrs Siddons as the Tragic Muse Revisited', *Eighteenth Century Studies* 33, no. 3 (2000): 401–30 (403). McPherson points out that when the painting featured in an exhibition at the Royal Academy in 1784, the catalogue titled it 'Portrait of Mrs. Siddons, whole length'.
151 Ibid.; emphasis in original.
152 Edgeworth, *Belinda*, 165.

same inhibited nature in which women were able to behave. The only recourse that Lady Delacour and her arch friend–enemy Mrs Luttridge have in resolving the murderous tension between them is by putting Clarence Hervey's feminist treatise – 'Upon the Propriety and Necessity of Female Duelling' – to the test.[153] They must dress as men in order to behave as men. Lady Delacour's ability to 'support' the physical and emotional weight of a character 'distant' from her own points to the way in which she embodies 'tragedy' and 'comedy': 'Life is a tragicomedy! – Though the critics will allow of no such thing in their books, it is a true representation of what passes in the world; and of all lives, mine has been the most grotesque mixture, or alternation I should say, of tragedy and comedy.'[154] Lady Delacour's unsettling conclusion echoes *The Winter's Tale*. Even with male 'armour' to protect her, she is vulnerable to the unintended blow from her own pistol; the bullet rips through male and female skins, burying itself deep within her breast. Her 'happy' violation against her femininity has left her with what she falsely believes to be the tragic end in her future.

In *Belinda*, Clarence must wear the woman of fashion's character in order to see the heroine through a 'female' lens of subjectivity. Lady Delacour's comedic dumbshow of hoop manoeuvres inspires him to try on the material constraints of women's appearances. She hints at the *robe à la française*'s enlargement of personal space: '"The ladies wore such large hoops that one of them kept as much room as four people like me."'[155] Not heeding her warning, Clarence boasts that 'he could manage a hoop as well as any woman in England, except Lady Delacour'.[156] He bets that Lady Boucher, even with the aid of her glass, would not be able to penetrate the mask of the Comtesse de Pomenars: '"she would not know my face, she would not see my beard, and I will bet fifty guineas, that I come into a room in a hoop, and that she does not find me out by my air – that I do not betray myself, in short, by my masculine awkwardness."'[157] He believes that not only would she not 'see' his obvious male physique, she would overlook his awkward imitation of female deportment. Ironically, it is his counter character's identity, more than his inability to act, that cues his self-exposure.

Edgeworth uses a pun on the word 'comb' to show Clarence for what he is: a coxcomb. The heroine's appearance inspires Lady Delacour to fancy a physiognomic likeness between her and Madame de Grignan: 'I have sometimes

---

153 Ibid., 45.
154 Ibid., 50.
155 Willett Cunnington, *Handbook of English Costume in the Eighteenth Century* (London: Faber & Faber, 1972), 320.
156 Edgeworth, *Belinda*, 60.
157 Ibid.

fancied – but I believe it is only my fancy […] that this young lady […] is not unlike your Madame de Grignan – I have seen a picture of her at Strawberry-hill.'[158] Through visual association, or what Myers refers to as factual inclusions,[159] Lady Delacour recalls that the Comtesse de Pomenars had possessed a lock of Madame de Grignan's lustrous hair. Re-enacting history, Lady Delacour lets drop the fateful comb that conceals Belinda's seductive tresses. She invites the Comtesse to evaluate the heroine's '"*belle chevelure*"':[160] 'the Comtesse de Pomenars was so much struck at the sight, that she was incapable of paying the necessary compliments'.[161] The 'striking' quality of the sight prevents him from the 'necessary' verbal response. Clarence's incapacity to speak presages his sudden inability to continue acting:

> Clarence Hervey suddenly stooped to pick it up, totally forgetting his hoop and his character. – He threw down the music stand with his hoop – Lady Delacour exclaimed 'bravissima!' and burst out laughing – Clarence Hervey acknowledged he had lost his bet – joined in the laugh, and declared that fifty guineas was too little to pay for the sight of the finest hair that he had ever beheld.[162]

Clarence's dramatic bow says what his silence does not. It signals the end of his act and displays his newfound deference to Belinda. Even if he destroys his trompe l'oeil, he has won the opportunity to witness an even greater spectacle: the previously invisible allure of Belinda's hair. His imitation of the Comtesse de Pomenars's character has reformed his myopic judgement of feminine 'charm'.

Edgeworth's visual technique insists that by entering imaginatively into womanhood, however briefly, Clarence begins a journey towards releasing his protégée from the chains of picturesque domestic enslavement. He had found Rachel–Virginia to be '"the most charming creature in the whole world"' because he '"had not seen Belinda Portman then"'.[163] Rachel–Virginia, like Thomas Day's Sabrina, is modelled on Jean-Jacques Rousseau's Sophie, a fictive ideal.[164] Clarence 'was charmed with the

---

158 Ibid.
159 See Myers, 'Shot from Canons', 193–214.
160 Edgeworth, *Belinda*, 61.
161 Ibid.
162 Ibid., 60–61.
163 Ibid., 307.
164 Thomas Day, author of *Sandford and Merton*, was suspicious of the female sex's moral inclinations and sought to 'cultivate' Sabrina Sydney according to the system of *éducation negative* that Rousseau's *Emile* (1767) advocates. On Rousseau and *Belinda*, see William Ray's 'Reading Women: Cultural Authority, Gender, and the Novel. The Case of Rousseau', *Eighteenth-Century Studies* 27, no. 3 (Spring 1994): 421–47.

picture of Sophia, when contrasted with the characters of the women of the world, with whom he had been disgusted'.[165] In beholding Belinda's unpinned beauty, Clarence realizes that he has exploited rather than cultivated Rachel–Virginia's mind, body and soul. He learns to appreciate that the most valuable expression of femininity is not naive but rather morally and aesthetically self-regulating.

In the episode, Edgeworth allows fashion's inherent changeability to serve a feminist purpose. The narrator observes, 'Fortunately for Belinda, "the glittering forfex" was not immediately produced, as fine ladies do not now, as in former times, carry any such useless implements about with them.'[166] The novelist's obvious allusion to Pope's *The Rape of the Lock* warns of the scripted end that the heroine evades:

> Then flashed the living lightning from her eyes,
> And screams of horror rend the affrighted skies.
> Not louder shrieks to pitying heaven are cast,
> When husbands, or when lapdogs breathe their last;
> Or when rich china vessels fallen from high,
> In glittering dust and painted fragments lie!
> 'Let wreaths of triumph now my temples twine',
> The victor cried, 'the glorious prize is mine!'[167]

Unlike Pope's Belinda, whose beauty is 'raped', Edgeworth's Belinda flees the male gaze with her modesty and tresses intact.[168] Belinda, like *Castle Rackrent*'s Jessica, receives poetic retribution: she survives the lesson that the novelist reserves for the hero of the novel and escapes unscathed.

Edgeworth's method of visuality theatrically depicts the ways in which gender and culture influence the subjectivity of viewing women's ambivalent relationships with their commodified selves. The novelist's dialogic method relies on references to fashion and the dumbshow to question the trustworthiness of appearances. As Belinda insists, '"And yet, how are we to judge of character? How can we form any estimate of what is amiable, of what will make us happy or miserable, but by comparison?"'[169] What

---

165 Edgeworth, *Belinda*, 280.
166 Ibid., 61.
167 Pope, *The Rape of the Lock*, 3.155–60. Reprinted by permission of Oxford University Press.
168 Edgeworth, *Belinda*, 61.
169 Ibid.

Edgeworth shows explicitly through her '*connoisseur* eyes' and what she invites the reader to infer reveal her distaste for a 'polite', unwholesome society in which women were necessarily split in two. As she later writes in *Helen*, ' "seeing characters:" ' – especially women – depends on ' "getting the right point of view" '.[170]

---

170 Maria Edgeworth, *Helen*, ed. Susan Manly and Clíona Ó Gallchoir ([1834] London: Pickering & Chatto, 2003), 112.

Chapter 4

OPTICAL ALLUSIONS IN FRANCES BURNEY'S *EVELINA* AND *THE WANDERER*

Turning from Edgeworth's pseudojournalistic fiction, this chapter explores how Frances Burney's acute self-consciousness as a woman novelist prompted her to rely on coded forms of visuality for rhetorical liberation. In her journal entries and courtship novels, she deployed type, surface and convention to depict the ways in which propriety of vision and the constraints on verbal expression affected women's lives. Her first and last novels – *Evelina: or, the History of a Young Lady's Entrance into the World* (1778)[1] and *The Wanderer; or, FEMALE DIFFICULTIES* (1814)[2] – demonstrate that her visual technique remained largely consistent throughout her lifetime. Burney's distinct reliance on typology underscores the need for women to deflect the gaze in order to preserve their appearances from the irreparable consequences of misinterpretation. Although attacks on female modesty and encounters with prostitutes populate her fiction, her heroines ultimately evade the perpetual threat of patriarchal abuse through good sense, fortune and sympathy. After subjecting them to a sequence of reputation-threatening trials, she allows them to be rescued by scopic understanding, which links the Romantic

---

1 The analysis uses the following version of *Evelina*, which is based on the third edition, produced in 1779. It was the first to incorporate the expanded subtitle 'The History of a Young Lady's Entrance into the World': Fanny Burney, *Evelina: or, The History of a Young Lady's Entrance into the World*, ed. Stewart J. Cooke ([1778] New York: W. W. Norton & Company, 1998).
2 The relationship between entering society and becoming visible is critical to my analysis. For that reason, the discussion of *The Wanderer* cites an edition that is based on Longman's first printing of the text, which captivated the public imagination even before it appeared in print: Fanny Burney, *The Wanderer; or, FEMALE DIFFICULTIES*, ed. Margaret Anne Doody, Robert L. Mack and Peter Sabor ([1814] Oxford: Oxford University Press, 1991). The first edition, of which there were 3,000 copies, sold out days before its publication. After the second edition that Longman printed weeks later, the novel did not reappear until 1988, when Pandora Press published an unannotated edition (xxxix).

conception of human sympathy to the Third Earl of Shaftesbury's theory of 'social affection', or the philosophy that 'natural' goodness is that which benefits the 'Nature' of the social system of which one is a part.[3] In epistolary form and third-person prose, Burney moves between public and private spaces in order to question the correlation between the appearance and the essence. While Burney is conventional in praising authenticity over fakery and modest looks over penetrating gazes, her novels, like those of Radcliffe and Edgeworth, actually highlight women's need to hide, paint, dissemble and look critically.

After surveying Burney's visual technique in relation to the dominant thematic concerns in recent scholarship, this study considers the manner in which the novelist's anxiety about her critical and social receptions heightened her self-consciousness and influenced her self-expression in literature and in life. As Gina Campbell contends, a woman's determination to publish a text 'undermined her moral authority' and modesty.[4] Burney's overt preoccupation with her 'image' and reputation made her particularly attentive to the strictures on language when depicting the interplay of character in her novels. The perpetual threat of misinterpretation in life and in print advances the discussion to the second section of the chapter, which addresses the relationship between *Evelina*'s epistolary structure and the authority of scopic dialogue. The epistolary viewpoint empowers the gaze over other modes of somatic communication, inviting the reader of the novel to see society through the heroine's eyes. Whereas 'sympathetic' glances enter into 'correspondence' with the heroine, the penetrating gazes of exploitative viewers threaten her virgin eyes. The third and final section of the chapter concentrates on the relationship between *The Wanderer*'s third-person perspective and the nuanced language of colour codes. In contrast to Evelina, who is a silent observer, the Incognita is more seen than seeing. Despite Juliet's attempts to hide her true colours and identity, she remains persistently visible, regardless of her disguise.

While feminist readings of the increasing 'darkness' of Burney's novels and discussions exploring female identity have dominated recent studies, the novelist's specific dependence on the coded languages of the eyes and colours remains largely underexplored. As previous chapters have shown, modest silence and what Kenneth Graham calls 'frustrated utterance' coexist in

---

3 Anthony Ashley Cooper, Third Earl of Shaftesbury, *Characteristiks of men, manners, opinions, times*, 107.
4 Gina Campbell, 'How to Read Like a Gentleman: Burney's Instructions to Her Critics in *Evelina*', in Burney, *Evelina*, 433.

the eighteenth-century novel.⁵ John Gregory's *A Father's Legacy to his Daughters* (1774) provides a coherent context for exploring the trope of inexpressibility that compels Burney, like Austen, Radcliffe and Edgeworth, to turn to visuality – a methodology linking visual and verbal modes of communication and understanding:

> This modesty, which I think so essential in your sex, will naturally dispose you to be rather silent in company, especially in a large one. People of sense and discernment will never mistake such a silence for dullness. One may take a share in conversation without uttering a syllable. The expression in the countenance shows it, and this never escapes the observing eye.⁶

Although the 'observing eye' may, as Graham conjectures, objectify the woman-on-view, it still has the potential to convey meaning. The heroine of Burney's *Evelina* informs the reader that '"The gentlemen [...] looked as if they thought we were quite at their disposal."'⁷ Their 'looks' speak that which their lips do not. As Wittgenstein proposes, viewers use what they can and cannot see to represent what cannot be said.⁸

Joyce Hemlow, Margaret Anne Doody and Kate Chisholm are among the many scholars who have identified the autobiographical influences in Burney's plots. In 'Fanny Burney and the Courtesy Books' (1950), Hemlow investigates the conduct books that influenced Burney's imagination and literary style, noting such works as James Fordyce's *Sermons to Young Women* (1766), Mrs Elizabeth Rowe's *Letters Moral and Entertaining* (1729–32), Edward Moore's *Fables for the Female Sex* (1771) and Madame de Genlis's *Adèle et Theodore* (1782).⁹ She surveys the numerous casual quotations that appear in Burney's *Early Diary* of 1773 and *Memoirs of Dr Burney*, claiming that their emphasis on female virtue permeated the novelist's consciousness.¹⁰ Hemlow proposes that the novelist transferred conduct books' insistence on stringent morals to the genre of the

---

5 Kenneth Graham, 'Cinderella or Bluebeard: The Double Plot of Evelina', in Burney, *Evelina*, 401.
6 John Gregory, *A Father's Legacy to His Daughters* (1774), in *Eighteenth-Century Woman: An Anthology*, ed. Bridget Hill (London: Allen, 1984), 19.
7 Burney, *Evelina*, 23.
8 Refer to my Introduction.
9 Joyce Hemlow offers a comprehensive discussion of these texts in her article 'Fanny Burney and the Courtesy Books', *PMLA* 65, no. 5 (September 1950): 732–61 (734).
10 Ibid., 735.

novel in order to educate the young lady at the point of her entrance into the world.[11] Unlike writers of conduct books, however, Burney used visuality in her courtesy novels to secure a degree of rhetorical freedom that preserved her heroines' reputations as well as her own. Her approach reflects her acute awareness of her image – literal, textual and metaphorical.

Lillian D. Bloom and Edward A. Bloom have explored the social influences on Burney's manner of looking and how she was pictured. In 'Fanny Burney's Novels: the Retreat from Wonder' (1979), they explain that as 'a silent observer, Burney was modest and retiring; physically small and rather plain, she was the prototype of her pseudonymous Miss Nobody'.[12] Even in the privacy of her diaries, which span 70 of the 88 years of her life, Burney offered few accounts of her appearance, merely hinting at her sister's superior beauty.[13] Of Fanny's 'look' in 1779, the year following *Evelina*'s publication, Mrs Thrale recalled,

> '[Dr Burney's] Daughter is a graceful looking Girl, but 'tis the Grace of an Actress not a Woman of Fashion [...] Her Conversation would be more pleasing if She thought less of herself; but her early Reputation embarrasses her Talk, & clouds her Mind with scruples about Elegancies which either come uncalled for or will not come at all.'[14]

While Lillian Bloom and Edward Bloom do not consider the relationship between Burney's acute self-consciousness and her reliance on visuality to articulate that which would 'not come at all', they point to the novelist's 'scruples about Elegancies' that she could and could not express.

Other scholars have discerned the feminist intrusions in Burney's fiction but do not contemplate how coded visuality provided the novelist with a form of rhetorical self-determination. Noteworthy discussions exploring the reassessment of female modesty and the intricacies of preserving the reputation include Mary Poovey's study of eighteenth-century anxieties in *The Proper Lady and the Woman Writer: Ideology as Style in the Works of Mary Wollstonecraft, Mary Shelley, and Jane Austen* (1985)[15] and Nancy K. Miller's study of the

---

11 Ibid.
12 Lillian D. Bloom and Edward A. Bloom, 'Fanny Burney's Novels: The Retreat from Wonder', *NOVEL: A Forum on Fiction* 12, no. 3 (Spring 1979): 215–35 (220).
13 See Fanny Burney, *The Early Diary of Frances Burney, 1768–1778*, ed. Annie Raine Ellis, 2 vols. (London: Bell, 1913). For a critique of Burney's self-depictions, see Chisholm, *Fanny Burney: Her Life*, 5–20.
14 Claire Harman, *Fanny Burney: A Biography* (London: Flamingo, 2001), 144. Reprinted by permission of HarperCollins Publishers Ltd. © Claire Harman, 2001.
15 Mary Poovey, *The Proper Lady and the Woman Writer: Ideology as Style in the Works of Mary Wollstonecraft, Mary Shelley, and Jane Austen* (Chicago: University of Chicago Press, 1985).

euphoric-dysphoric relationship that Burney's heroines have with society.[16] Rose Marie Cutting's 'Defiant Women: The Growth of Feminism in Fanny Burney's Novels' (1977) argues that the 'preoccupation with propriety in Fanny Burney's novels was balanced by another sort of development – a growing rebellion against the restrictions imposed upon women'.[17] Cutting contends that Burney compounds a veneration of social mores with an insistence on 'a philosophy of self-reliance' in settings of economic and patriarchal injustices.[18] Her assessment of the conflict between women's desire to rebel and the need to blend in uses Judith Butler's definition of gender, which treats sexuality as the dynamics between the psyche and the appearance.[19] Cutting's point that Burney's fictional women learn that there is more to character – including their own – than appearances suggest provides a useful framework for understanding the functional roles that scopic communication and colour codes of self-expression play in her novels.

The need to comply with the culturally imposed image of modesty has also been considered in relation to charity. In her article 'The Unaverted Eye: Dangerous Charity in Burney's *Evelina* and *The Wanderer*' (1997), Sharon Long Damoff addresses the many contradictions to which the modest woman had to conform. As Damoff contends, 'If a woman – especially a young, single beautiful woman – accepts money from a man, the world concludes she must be his mistress.'[20] The perpetual threat of misinterpretation subjected women to acute anxiety. Women were, as Damoff points out, particularly subject to the limitations on verbal and visual self-expression:

In the eighteenth century, virtue for women was always linked with chastity; the virtuous woman was 'pure,' and the distinction between spiritually pure and sexually pure was easily blurred. Especially for unmarried

---

16 See Nancy K. Miller's *The Heroine's Text: Readings in the French and English Novel, 1722–1782* (New York: Columbia University Press, 1980). For a study positioning Burney's oeuvre in relation to French literature, see her article 'Men's Reading, Women's Writing: Gender and the Rise of the Novel', *Yale French Studies* 75, 'The Politics of Tradition: Placing Women in French Literature' (1988): 40–55.
17 Rose Marie Cutting, 'Defiant Women: The Growth of Feminism in Fanny Burney's Novels', *Studies in English Literature, 1500–1900* 17, no. 3, Restoration and Eighteenth Century (Summer 1977): 519–30 (519).
18 Ibid., 520.
19 Refer to Judith Butler, *Bodies That Matter: On the Discursive Limits of 'Sex'* (London: Routledge, 1993), 234.
20 Sharon Long Damoff, 'The Unaverted Eye: Dangerous Charity in Fanny Burney's *Evelina* and *The Wanderer*', *Studies in Eighteenth-Century Culture* 26 (1997): 231–46 (241). © 1997 American Society for Eighteenth-Century Studies. Reprinted with permission of Johns Hopkins University Press.

women, virtue was frequently reduced to modesty – not speaking in company, not expressing opinions, keeping the face hidden, averting the eyes, and not conferring 'favours' (such as smiles).[21]

In *Evelina* and in Burney's later novels, a woman's presentation of modesty becomes a visible analogue for spiritual and sexual purity. Although Damoff's discussion does not identify the 'strategic' means by which the female sex was able to communicate, it directs attention to the contradictions within the feminine ideal.

Emily Allen's study also explores the double bind of female visibility. In her article 'Staging Identity, Burney's Allegory of Genre' (1998), Allen argues that Burney's fiction reveals her distinct preoccupation with her public performance:

> Burney's [...] anxiety about theatrical performance was driven by a fear of 'coming out,' which is the precise task that the heroine of Burney's first novel must perform. To come out properly, to make her entrance into the world,' Evelina must paradoxically stay inside: she must come to be valued for her fully interiorized subject position. The double bind she must negotiate, then, is how to come out and stay in at the same time.[22]

The interrelatedness of visibility and invisibility, of 'coming out' and 'staying in' that Damoff also mentions directs the acting and action of Burney's plots.[23] Allen theorizes that the novelist's stage fright and fear of appearing in public coloured her perceptions from a young age. Her article analyses the following extract from a journal entry on the eve of *Evelina*'s publication and Burney's rise to fame:

> Next came *my* scene; I was discovered Drinking Tea; – to tell you how *infinitely*, how *beyond measure* I was terrified at my situation, I really cannot, – but my fright was nearly such as I should have suffered had I made my appearance upon a public Theatre.[24]

---

21 Damoff, 'The Unaverted Eye: Dangerous Charity in Fanny Burney's *Evelina* and *The Wanderer*', 235. © 1997 American Society for Eighteenth-Century Studies. Reprinted with permission of Johns Hopkins University Press.
22 Emily Allen, 'Staging Identity: Frances Burney's Allegory of Genre', *Eighteenth-Century Studies* 31, no. 4, The Mind/Body Problem (Summer 1998): 433–51 (435–36).
23 Ibid.
24 Fanny Burney, *The Early Journals and Letters of Fanny Burney*, ed. Lars E. Troide (Kingston: McGill-Queens University Press, 1990), 2: 239; emphasis in original.

Allen's assessment of Burney's immeasurable terror at her persistently visible situation lends itself to a study of the coded means through which she necessarily expressed herself. Allen's focus on the novelist's preoccupation with her public image inspires my discussion on Burney's awareness of social theatricality and how it influences her writing about women's public and private lives.

Andrea Henderson evaluates the drama of display in Burney's fiction and the way in which a woman's occupation 'commodifies' her image. Henderson's 'Burney's *The Wanderer* and Early-Nineteenth-Century Commodity Fetishism' (2002) draws from Doody's theory that in *The Wanderer*, Burney is 'the first novelist to investigate at any depth the phenomenon now known to us as "alienation"; the wanderer, and "those not brought up to gain [money]", are alienated by the possibility that money has to be earned at all'.[25] Henderson engages with Doody's premise of dysphoric alienation, arguing that despite Juliet's spectacular qualities, her status as a nobody endures:[26]

> the women in Miss Matson's shop are quite deliberately put on display before the customers, and most of Juliet's 'jobs' – as music teacher, personal companion, and so forth – involve some element of display.[27]

Henderson's conclusions about the commodification of the woman-on-view help explain the persistent visibility of Burney's heroines. Nonetheless, she overlooks a fundamental paradox: even if Juliet's occupations work on her image, transforming her into a commodity in the eyes of Miss Matson's customers, the Incognita's enigmatic identity persists, regardless of the disguise that she wears.

Unsurprisingly, Burney's pronounced aversion to detailing appearances in her diaries and in her fiction is a subject that a number of scholars, including Kate Chisholm, have mentioned in passing. In *Fanny Burney: Her Life* (1998), Chisholm provides a series of extracts from Burney's early diary, addressed 'To Miss Nobody', which covers the period up until *Evelina*'s publication. Of Prince Aleksei Grigorevich Orlov, who was reputedly implicated in the assassination of the Russian Empress Catherine the Great's husband, Burney had remarked,

---

25 Margaret Anne Doody, *Frances Burney: The Life in the Works* (New Brunswick, NJ: Rutgers University Press, 1988), 356.
26 Andrea Henderson, 'Burney's *The Wanderer* and Early-Nineteenth-Century Commodity Fetishism', *Nineteenth-Century Literature* 57, no. 1 (June 2002): 1–30 (18).
27 Ibid., 17.

The Prince [...] immensely Tall & stout in proportion [...] is a handsome & magnificent Figure. His Dress was very superb. Besides a Blue Garter, he had a star of Diamonds, of prodigious brilliancy; he had likewise a *shoulder knot* of the same *precious Jewels*, & a Picture of the Empress hung from his Neck, which was set round with Diamonds of such magnitude & lustre that, when near the Candle, they were too dazzling for the Eye.[28]

Chisholm's analysis of Burney's 'pen-portrait' highlights the stylistic consistency between Burney's records of her personal encounters and her fictional personalities: 'Fanny was practising her skills as a scene-setter and student of character. She does not describe Orlov's actual physical appearance; her skill was in highlighting the salient features [...] and then adding just a few words giving us her own opinion.'[29] While Chisholm does not acknowledge the pattern of visual details that the novelist used as an efficient coded language, she highlights the connection between Burney's novelistic skill and her pronounced subjectivity.

With the exception of Joe Bray's studies of Burney's fiction in *The Female Reader in the English Novel* (2009), most discussions regard the novelist's references to the gaze and appearances as highly superficial.[30] However, superficial visual details are critical in Burney's novels: the languages of the eyes and colours enabled her to use a methodology of 'well-chosen words'[31] to her advantage. Coded visuality provided her with a discreet system of communication that simultaneously preserved her reputation while drawing attention to the implications of female inexpressibility. Burney's close friend Samuel Crisp[32] was one of many early readers who praised her 'painterly' efforts:

'If specimens of this kind had been preserved of the different *Tons* that have succeeded one another for twenty centuries past, how interesting would they have been! Infinitely more so, than antique statues, bas-reliefs, and intaglio's. To compare the vanities and puppyisms of the Greek and Roman, and Gothic, and Moorish, and Ecclesiastical reigning fine gentlemen of the day with one another, and the present age

---

28 *The Early Journals and Letters of Fanny Burney*, ed. Lars E. Troide and Stewart J. Cooke (Montreal: McGill-Queen's University Press, 2012), 2: 181; emphasis in original.
29 Kate Chisholm, *Fanny Burney: Her Life* (London: Vintage, 1998), 38–39.
30 See Joe Bray's *The Female Reader in the English Novel: From Burney to Austen* (New York: Routledge, 2009) and *The Epistolary Novel: Representations of Consciousness* (London and New York: Routledge, 2003).
31 Refer to my Introduction.
32 On Crisp's relationship with the Burneys, see Chisholm, *Fanny Burney: Her Life*, 39.

must be a high entertainment, to a mind that has a turn for a mixture of contemplation and satire; and to do you justice, Fanny, you paint well.'[33]

Crisp differentiated Burney's method of characterization from the classicized delineations found in the oeuvres of her male predecessors. He proposed that the stylized appearances that she depicted were 'infinitely more interesting' than detailed allegorical etchings.

Dr Samuel Johnson gave the novelist similar praise, declaring that '"no writer so young and inexperienced had ever seen so deeply into character or copied the manners of the time with more accuracy."'[34] He regarded the Branghtons' mobile lodger, Mr Smith, as a paragon of characterization through the portrait's simulation of his visible struggle to appear a man of a higher social standing than he actually was:

> [Mr Smith] is dressed in a very showy manner, but without any taste, and the inelegant smartness of his air and deportment, his visible struggle, against education, to put on the fine gentleman, added to his frequent conscious glances at a dress to which he was but little accustomed, very effectually destroyed his aim of figuring (making a distinguished appearance), and rendered all his efforts useless.[35]

In Johnson's view, '"Harry Fielding *never* drew so good a Character! – such a fine varnish of low politeness! – such a *struggle* to appear a Gentleman! – Madam, there is *no* Character better drawn any where – in *any* Book, or by *any* Author."'[36] His emphatic raptures attest to *Evelina*'s success in courting the male expectations of character description and depiction that previous chapters of this book have examined through complementary lenses.

In contrast to the appreciation that Crisp and Johnson shared for *Evelina*, the reception of *The Wanderer: or, Female Difficulties* was mixed. John Wilson Croker's 1814 review contained an acerbic analysis of the novelist's visual technique, accusing Madame d'Arblay of producing an inferior reproduction of Miss Burney's work:

> We are afraid that she is self-convicted of being what the painters technically call a *mannerist*; that is, she has given over painting from the life,

---

[33] Ibid.
[34] Joyce Hemlow, 'The Composition of Evelina', in Burney, *Evelina: or, The History of a Young Lady's Entrance into the World*, ed. Stewart J. Cooke ([1778] New York: W. W. Norton & Company, 1998), 372–94 (388). Reprinted by permission of Oxford University Press.
[35] Burney, *Evelina*, 182–83.
[36] W. H. Davenport Adams, *Women of Fashion and Representative Women in Letters and Society* (London: Tinsley Brothers, 1878), 25; emphasis in original.

and has employed herself in copying from her own copies, till, instead of a power of natural delineation, she has acquired a certain trick and habitual style of portraiture: – but the Wanderer is not only the work of a mannerist, but of a mannerist who is *épuisée*.[37]

Whereas Croker lauded Edgeworth's portraits, he found Burney to be torn between two conflicting artistic identities. Positing a shift in Madame d'Arblay's visual technique, he argued that the older, married novelist had exhausted her genius for 'natural delineation' and turned to formulaic presentation.

In using the French term 'épuisée' to describe the declining quality of Burney's visual technique, Croker unintentionally indicated her exile in France's influence on *The Wanderer*. The voluminous text was the product of a 14-year period that also included the trauma of her complete mastectomy in 1811.[38] The striking similarity between the novelist's 1812 return to England and the Channel-crossing episode at the start of the novel highlights how Burney's 'habitual' reliance on visual codes endured along with her preoccupation with women's images, literal and metaphorical.

Even after Burney's acquisition of spectacles – her professed 'Miracle Machine'[39] – in the 1790s, her characters' appearances continued to retain their 'vagueness'. The clarity with which she perceived the society around her was independent of the approach to characterization that she adopted out of gendered necessity, a point that William Hazlitt's 1819 critique of Burney's character sketches brings to light. His account distinguished between the 'perception of any oddity or singularity of character' and controlled attention:

> Women, in general, have a quicker perception of any oddity or singularity of character than men, and are more alive to every absurdity which arises from a violation of the rules of society, or a deviation from established custom. This partly arises from the restraints on their own behaviour, which turns their attention constantly on the subject [...] They have less muscular strength; less power of continued voluntary attention – of reason, passion, and imagination: but they are more easily impressed with whatever appeals to their senses or habitual prejudices.[40]

---

37 John Wilson Croker, 'Review of *The Wanderer* by Frances Burney', *Quarterly Review* 11 (April 1814), 124; emphasis in original.
38 See Doody's introduction to Fanny Burney, *The Wanderer*, ix.
39 Chisholm, *Fanny Burney: Her Life*, 40.
40 William Hazlitt, 'On the English Novelists', *The Collected Works of William Hazlitt*, ed. A. R. Waller (London: Dent, 1903), 123.

Hazlitt proposed that women's self-consciousness made them more 'alive' to 'every absurdity' that caught their wandering eyes because of its potential harm to their reputation. His confidence in the female sex's capacity to see detail implies that they often observed that which men, by 'nature', did not. The novelist's relentless anxiety about the 'muscular strength' of the male gaze underscores one of the most crucial difficulties that Burney's heroines, like their creator, must negotiate.

Applying his theory to Burney's fiction, Hazlitt found her heroes and heroines disappointing. He denigrated the 'slightly shaded' manner in which they were portrayed:

> Her characters, which are ingenious caricatures, are, no doubt, distinctly marked, and well kept up; but they are slightly shaded, and exceedingly uniform. Her heroes and heroines, almost all of them, depend on the stock of a single phrase or sentiment, and have certain mottoes or devices by which they may always be known. They form such characters as people might be supposed to assume for a night at a masquerade.[41]

Hazlitt posited a disjunction between her perceptiveness of the minutiae of characters that she observed and the details that she conveyed. His conclusions about the novelist's 'dependency' on 'stock' characters, or formulae, suggests that Burney used established codes in an original way through deploying them for feminist ends. By presenting 'not the whole-length figure, nor even the face, but some prominent feature',[42] she managed to create individual 'caricatures' from typologies.

Like those in her aesthetic circle, Burney relied heavily on types and models for inspiration. She was repeatedly quizzed: 'But where, Miss Burney, where can, or could you pick up such characters? Where find such variety of incidents, yet all so natural?'[43] The unassuming manner of her reply replicated the modesty of her gaze: 'O, Ma'am, any body might find, who thought them worth looking for!'[44] While she found models of female excellence in the Dowager Duchess of Portland and Mrs Delany, whom Burke's eulogy insists to be 'a perfect pattern of a perfect fine lady',[45] she did not seek to draw 'perfect characters':

---

41 Ibid., 125.
42 Ibid.
43 Harman, *Fanny Burney: A Biography*, 131. Reprinted by permission of HarperCollins Publishers Ltd. © Claire Harman, 2001.
44 Harman, *Fanny Burney: A Biography*, 131. Reprinted by permission of HarperCollins Publishers Ltd. © Claire Harman, 2001.
45 See Hemlow, 'Fanny Burney and the Courtesy Books', 737.

> I meant in Mrs Delvile to draw a great, but not a perfect character; I meant, on the contrary, to blend upon paper, as I have frequently seen blended in life, noble and rare qualities with striking and incurable defects.[46]

Burney's account suggests that she aspired to depict women whose natural defects made them 'great'. While Jeanne Fahnestock contends that heroines did not become 'human' until the nineteenth century,[47] Burney's confession demonstrates that women novelists were already altering expectations of heroines in the late eighteenth century. It is towards the typology of ideal *behaviour* – not *beauty* – that Burney ultimately directs her characters and readers.

The influence of aesthetic expectations on women's images also appears in portraits of Burney. In 1778, the year of *Evelina*'s publication, Edward Francisco Burney produced a vignette of his cousin dressed in a simple but stylish morning gown.[48] He chose to portray her reading, a pose that protected her gaze from public interpretation. Four years later, he completed an oil painting of his cousin wearing a fashionable Vandyke gown.[49] The portrait's complementary colours set off Fanny's blush-and-ivory complexion, making her eyes unreadable: her gaze contemplates a sight that the viewer can only imagine. In image and in print, Burney sought to be portrayed as modest, manifestly absorbed in inward thought.

Despite Sir Joshua Reynolds's praise of Edward Francisco Burney's technique, Fanny's opinion of the painting was less favourable because she saw it as flattering. As she explained to her sister Susan,

> I believe if I am not under written, no one would guess he ever saw me, much less that I sat for the Picture called mine. Never was Portrait so violently flattered. I have taken pains incredible to make him *magnify* the Features, and darken the complexion, but he is impenetrable in action, though fair and docile in promise […] I shall still, however, work

---

46 Burney, *The Early Journals and Letters of Fanny Burney*, 5: 31.
47 See Jeanne Fahnestock, 'The Heroine of Irregular Features: Physiognomy and Conventions of Heroine Description', *Victorian Studies* 24, no. 3 (Spring 1981): 325–50.
48 For a discussion of visual depictions of Fanny Burney, refer to T. C. Duncan Eaves's 'Edward Burney's Illustrations to *Evelina*', *PMLA* 62, no. 4 (December 1947): 995–99. As Chisholm explains in *Fanny Burney: Her Life*, 'Some scholars have suggested that the informal pencil and crayon drawing is of her sister Charlotte, but her casual dress and stylish bonnet all favour Fanny – as does the approximate date, 1778, the year of *Evelina*' (322).
49 See Fanny Burney in her 'Vandyke Gown', 1782, by Edward Francisco Burney (Parham Park, West Sussex).

at him for it really makes me uneasy to see a Face in which the smallest resemblance of my own can be traced looking almost *perfectly* handsome. In his 3 portraits of Mr. Crisp he has succeeded beyond all his former works; they are all different, yet all strikingly like, animated, expressive & handsome. I never saw likenesses more agreeable, yet all strikingly like, animated, expressive & handsome [...] His flattery, as I reproach him eternally, is all for *me*; not only in the phiz, but the back Ground, which he has made very beautiful; & as to my Dress, which I have left to himself, he has never been tired of altering & gracing it. It is now the black vandyke Gown, with slashed lilac sleeves, & very elegant.[50]

The novelist, like Austen's Mr Knightley, disapproved of 'violent flattery' for the sake of pleasing others' eyes. Burney's courtesy novels question the blush-and-ivory model to which society encouraged women to conform, whether through natural or artificial means. By pairing Edward's visible portraits with Fanny's self-perceptions, an accurate understanding of the novelist's recourse to visuality becomes apparent.

While propriety of vision is important in Burney's novels, there is much about her vision, not least the vision expressed in writing novels, that is quietly unorthodox, assertive and, in a sense, actively solicits the stare. In the words of Anna Laetitia Barbauld, 'Next to the Balloon, Miss Burney is the object of public curiosity.'[51] Barbauld's claim defines the degree of visibility that Frances Burney – novelist, diarist, playwright, Second Keeper of the Robes to Queen Charlotte and eyewitness at the Battle of Waterloo[52] – attained upon being unveiled as the author of *Evelina*. The young novelist heard of its publication fortuitously when, oblivious to its impending significance, Burney's stepmother read aloud the following advertisement:

> *This day was published,* In three volumes, 12 mo. Price seven shillings and sixpence sewed, or nine shillings bound, EVELINA; Or, A YOUNG LADY'S ENTRANCE into the WORLD.[53]

---

50 Hemlow, *The History of Fanny Burney*, 155–56. Reprinted by permission of Oxford University Press; emphasis in original.
51 Anna Laetitia Barbauld, *Memoir of Mrs. Barbauld, including letters and notices of her family and friends* (London: George Bell and Sons, 1874), 53. Also quoted in Constance Hill, *Juniper Hall: A Rendezvous of Certain Illustrious Personages during the French Revolution Including Alexandre D'Arblay and Fanny Burney* (London and New York: John Lane, The Bodley Head, 1904), 244.
52 See Chisholm, especially chapter 8.
53 Burney, *Evelina*, ix. The advertisement appeared in the *London Evening Post*, 27–29 January 1778; emphasis in original.

After that epiphany, Burney witnessed a dramatic reversal in her social visibility. From an anonymous 'incognita', who had relied on writing in a 'man-made' hand, she became a highly conspicuous figure. Burke deemed *Evelina* a 'page-turner', and Reynolds famously pledged to pay 50 pounds for information regarding the author's identity.[54] Even her publisher, Thomas Lowndes, avowed that he did not know the 'Gentleman's' name but knew that the novel had a 'secret History'.[55]

As the novelist viewed her 'balloon-like' rise into the public eye, 'the Literary World was favoured with the first publication of the ingenious, learned, & most profound Fanny Burney'.[56] On 19 February 1781, when the king enquired about Burney's motive for writing *Evelina*, she acknowledged her preoccupation with maintaining her 'image', even in print:

> *'I only wrote, sir, for my own amusement, – only in some odd, idle hours.'*
>   *'But your publishing – your printing how was that?'*
>   *'That was only, sir – only because –'*
>
> The *What!* *was then repeated, with so earnest a look that forced to say something, I stammeringly answered,*
>   *'I thought – sir – it would look well in print.'*[57]

For Burney, 'looking well' on paper was essential for elevating her reputation as a woman and as a novelist. As Lillian Bloom and Edward Bloom suggest, 'Since *Evelina* was to be published anonymously and she arranged to have no part in the negotiation of a sale agreement, she devised a scheme whereby she "was to become, if possible, a candidate for fame, without running any risk of disgrace."'[58] The tension between literary fame and perceptions of the female reputation led Burney to remark, 'I would a thousand times rather forfeit my character as a *Writer*, than risk ridicule or censure as a *Female*.'[59]

While at times Burney's novels embrace the convention of moral transparency, on other occasions they warn against trusting in appearances. Her diary entries indicate the influence of portraiture on her manner of depicting social types that see and are seen. From an early age, she was a frequent visitor at

---

54 Ibid.
55 Fanny Burney, *A Known Scribbler: Frances Burney on Literary Life*, ed. Justine Crump (Peterborough: Broadview Literary Texts, 2002), 152.
56 Ibid.
57 Fanny Burney, *The Diary and Letters of Madame D'Arblay* (1778–1840), ed. Charlotte Barrett, 6 vols. (London: Macmillan, 1904–5), 2: 322; emphasis in original.
58 Lillian D. Bloom and Edward A. Bloom, 'Fanny Burney's Novels', 221.
59 Burney, *A Known Scribbler*, 170.

Streatham, where she encountered the Thrale circle and Reynolds's portraits of the 'Streatham Worthies'. She noted the striking difference between Dr Johnson's eye-catching inner character and his less attractive '*exterior*':

> This man [...] who has the most extensive knowledge, the clearest understanding, & the greatest abilities of any Living Author, – has a Face the most ugly, a Person the most awkward, & manners the most singular, that ever were, or ever can be seen. But all that is unfortunate in his *exterior*, is so greatly compensated for in his *interior*, that I can only, like Desdemona to Othello, '*see his Visage in his mind.*'[60]

Burney's persistent use of superlatives – 'most ugly', 'most awkward' and 'most singular' – draws attention to three qualities that were conventionally associated with flawed inner character. Her attentiveness to the ambivalent relationship between the appearance and the essence, exteriors and interiors, is a theme that 'frustrated utterance' further complicates in her novels.

Scopic Dialogue and *Evelina*'s Epistolary Form

Burney's treatment of the interplay of character in *Evelina* demonstrates that the language of the eyes speaks more truly than verbal speech and other features of visible appearances. The novel's epistolary structure highlights the implications of the woman's simultaneous status as a viewer and a subject-on-view, allowing the novelist to reconfigure the boundaries of verbal and scopic expression. In her first novel, Burney blends together active, passive and sympathetic gazes into a reformed vision of correspondence that allows for silent understanding. Allen finds her treatment of the gaze indicative of Adam Smith's sympathetic reading of character, identifying in the novel two distinct forms of scopic activity:

> the novel distinguishes two kinds of scopic acts, spectating and reading, and offers a reformed vision of the voyeuristic gaze of the spectator: the sympathetic gaze of the reader. While the spectator's gaze objectifies the female body as erotic object, the affective and feminized gaze of the reader subjectifies the body as a text requiring interpretation. The goal of *Evelina* is precisely the construction of this affective reader as sentimental addressee, and the novel's thematized conflict between visual spectacle and literary works to reform its readership even as it forms an idea of the private middle-class subject.[61]

---

60 See Chisholm, *Fanny Burney: Her Life*, 60; emphasis in original.
61 Allen, 'Staging Identity', 438.

Allen's theory explains how Burney's choreographing of the gaze enables sympathetic characters to interpret somatic meaning in a way that affects the reader of the novel. More than presenting a model of reading, the epistolary novel creates the conditions for visual dialogue that, in contrast to reading, engage the active gaze of the subject being viewed. Differentiating between penetrating and sympathetic gazes, Burney's visual technique insists that eyes *speak*.

Evelina's epistolary form occasions the retrospection needed for the heroine to comment on the experience of being seen. Her third letter in volume 2 evidences the state of 'frustrated utterance' to which she is subjected in public: ' "But I was silent, for I knew not what I ought to say." '[62] By 'seeing herself' as she had then appeared, Evelina is able to re-view and express her rationale for inexpressibility. Ironically, her thoughts remain as silent on paper as they had been in public. Her confession to 'Miss Nobody' echoes the way in which Burney's own self-doubt and interiority influence her verbal speech: she fears not 'knowing' the proper words through which to convey her feelings. Evelina's increasing self-consciousness explains her heightened preoccupation with her 'image' and can be read alongside the theory that Bakhtin outlines in 'Epic and the Novel': 'a crucial tension develops between the external and the internal man', and 'the subjectivity of the individual becomes an object of experimentation and representation'.[63] By following the heroine's backward-looking gaze, Burney's reader – Allen's 'voyeuristic spectator' – infers more about Evelina's own subjectivity than descriptions of her appearance allow.

The novel's epistolary structure also destabilizes the 'rigid' divide between private and public spheres of female experience and self-exposure, allowing Burney to recalibrate the threshold as a flexible zone between the 'private–public' of country life and the 'public–private' of the London stage. *Evelina*'s subtitle – *or, A Young Lady's Entrance into the World* – first included in the third edition of 1799, warns the reader of the trials that the heroine will encounter as she progresses from invisibility to visibility. Evelina's mentors, Mr Villars and Lady Howard, agree that she must train her eyes in order for her perceptions to mature. Lady Howard is adamant that the heroine must 'see something of the world' – even if her gender prevents her from seeing 'all' of it – to enable reason to correct the delusions that her mind's eye 'paints':

> 'it is time that she should see something of the world. When young people are too rigidly sequestered from it, their lively and romantic

---

62 Burney, *Evelina*, 128.
63 Mikhail Mikhailovich Bakhtin, *The Dialogic Imagination: Four Essays*, ed. M. Holquist, trans. C. Emerson and M. Holquist (Austin: University of Texas Press, 1981), 37.

imaginations paint it to them as a paradise of which they have been beguiled; but when they are shown it properly, and in due time, they see it such as it really is, equally shared by pain and pleasure, hope and disappointment.'[64]

Lady Howard's remark draws from Fordyce, who reminds his female readership that 'your destination in life [...] does not require reasoning or accuracy, so much as observation and discernment'.[65] Burney emphasizes that contrary to Fordyce, Lady Howard recognizes that young ladies are *visual* learners: the experience of seeing and being seen leaves an indelible impression on their minds, encouraging them to outgrow their 'spirited' affinity towards the 'romantic imagination'. The woman's alliterative pairing of 'paint' and 'paradise' sets Evelina's childish perceptions of actuality in conflict with the world 'as it really is'. In order to save her image from the dangers of what Patricia Meyer Spacks has called the '*source* of sexual feeling',[66] the heroine needs to be shown the ways in which her imagination has beguiled her before she can see the actual difficulties of being a disinherited woman of little economic means.

In *Evelina*, Burney combines gendered subjectivities, or male and female biases, to insist upon the dangers of female visibility in a society that views women as legitimate prey. Villars immediately foresees that Evelina's striking countenance will attract considerable attention when she enters the 'circle of high life':

'The town-acquaintance of Mrs. Mirvan are all in the circle of high life; this artless young creature, with too much beauty to escape notice, has too much sensibility to be indifferent to it; but she has too little wealth to be sought with propriety by men of the fashionable world.'[67]

Villars's warning informs the novel's voyeuristic spectator that the 'artless' young lady's excessive sensibility will force her to become increasingly conscious of her appearance as a visual analogue for her reputation. Artlessness, as Joanne Cutting-Gray observes, is Evelina's material asset: 'it is also the charm of her appeal, the only marketable asset she has, and the greatest danger to maintaining her character'.[68] The visual 'loudness' of the heroine's beauty denies her of

---

64 Burney, *Evelina*, 13.
65 Fordyce, *Sermons to Young Women*, 1: 273.
66 Patricia Meyer Spacks, 'Evr'y Woman Is at Heart a Rake', *Eighteenth-Century Studies* 8 (1974): 27–46 (38); emphasis in original.
67 Burney, *Evelina*, 14.
68 Joanne Cutting-Gray, *Woman as 'Nobody' and the Novels of Fanny Burney* (Gainesville: Florida University Press, 1992), 44.

the capacity to 'escape notice' and interpretation. Villars shares Lady Howard's opinion that she must see something of the world but provides a different rationale for her need to 'contract her views': 'Destined, in all probability to possess a very moderate fortune, I wished to contract her views to something within it.'[69] Even if Evelina is able to acquaint her eyes and mind with the spectacular extravagance of fashionable London life, Villars knows that with her economic position, she cannot afford to perpetuate such visual expectations.

Burney's method of juxtaposing voices and viewpoints differs from Edgeworth's but provides the reader with a similarly 'objective' presentation of the heroine's impending visibility. While Lady Howard echoes Villars's admonition, her female subjectivity allows her to see Evelina's 'simplicity' for what it actually is – a trompe l'œil:

> Her face and person answer my most refined ideas of complete beauty: and this [...] is yet so striking, it is not possible to pass it unnoticed [...] Her character seems truly ingenuous and simple; and, at the same time that nature has blessed her with an excellent understanding, and great quickness of parts, she has a certain air of inexperience and innocence that is extremely interesting.[70]

Like Villars, Lady Howard predicts that Evelina's 'complete beauty' and aura of 'innocence' will make her 'extremely interesting' in a context of visual conformity.[71] By cueing the reader to the heroine's future visibility, Burney underscores its significance to the plot. Although 'interest' during this period tends to imply sympathy, here, Burney implies arousal. Evelina inspires affection in others, but those qualities that 'interest' people positively are also those that make her sexually vulnerable. Catherine Parke suggests that when Evelina 'crosses the threshold into London and into her future, for the first time in her life she is more seen than seeing'.[72] While the heroine's visual identity appears to shift her status from viewer to woman-on-view, the epistolary structure prevents her from falling into the scopic binary that Parke presumes. More than Samuel Richardson's Pamela, the heroine persistently *sees* that she is seen. Her 'feminine and disenfranchised perspective'[73] informs her that she must

---

69 Burney, *Evelina*, 15.
70 Ibid., 16.
71 Ibid.
72 Catherine Parke, 'Vision and Revision: A Model for Reading the Eighteenth-Century Novel of Education', *Eighteenth-Century Studies* 16, no. 2 (Winter 1982–83): 162–74 (167). © 1982 American Society for Eighteenth-Century Studies. Reprinted with permission of Johns Hopkins University Press.
73 Labbe, *Romantic Visualities*, ix.

adapt her image in order to become, like Pope's women in 'To a Lady; of the Characters of Women', a chameleon to her context.[74]

Burney explores the impact that Evelina's estrangement from Berry Hill has on her self-perceptions. The heroine's path to self-discovery and perceptual maturation intensifies the relationship between the 'seeing eye' and the 'eye-that-is-seen', the 'I' with an inherited name. Writing of *A Sentimental Journey*, Parke explains that the 'Name' and the 'I' represent two margins of orientation that are connotative of the eighteenth-century novel of education.[75] She proposes that the 'Name' calls attention to the way in which a character is seen rather than sees:

> Seeing our images reflected in the mirror of our fellows, hearing our voices resonate in the interspace of conversation, we become reflexively visible and audible to ourselves. This activity of reappearance affords us paradoxically the first and only original view of ourselves.[76]

In Burney's novel, the heroine must learn to wear the 'look' that she wishes to become in the viewer's eyes in order to mirror her invisible image – her reputation. Reflexive visibility's implicit participation of the active gaze lends itself to Adam Smith's *The Theory of Moral Sentiments*:

> we endeavour to examine our own conduct as we imagine any other fair spectator would examine it. If, upon placing ourselves in his situation, we thoroughly enter into all the passions and motives which influenced it, we approve of it, by sympathy with the approbation of this supposed equitable judge.[77]

By applying Smith's theory of self-regulation to the novel, it is clear that Evelina's 'activity of reappearance' requires scopic equilibrium. Through her treatment of the self-reflexive gaze, the novelist makes the heroine increasingly visible to society and to herself. Scopic equilibrium represents a moral balance between the awareness of the Other's visual construction of ourselves by appearances and our own related consciousness.

---

74 Refer to my Introduction.
75 Parke, 'Vision and Revision', 164.
76 Parke, 'Vision and Revision: A Model for Reading the Eighteenth-Century Novel of Education', 165. © 1982 American Society for Eighteenth-Century Studies. Reprinted with permission of Johns Hopkins University Press.
77 Adam Smith, *The Theory of Moral Sentiments*, ed. D. D. Raphael and A. L. Macfie ([1759] Oxford: Clarendon Press, 1976), 110. Reprinted by permission of Oxford University Press.

Burney uses Smith's 'actor/spectator' model to introduce the theme of 'meaning eyes' as a visual correlative for verbal speech.[78] She begins Evelina's visual education with a visit to Drury-Lane Theatre to witness David Garrick, one of Dr Burney's friends, perform Ranger, the hero of *The Suspicious Husband*.[79] The heroine's gaze directs the voyeuristic spectator to the actor's reliance on the ekphrastic language of facial expression and gesture to communicate:

> Such ease! such vivacity in his manner! such grace in his motions! such fire and meaning in his eyes![80]

Evelina's repeated exclamations and alliteration point to the lasting impression that Garrick makes in her eyes and mind. Whereas his motions are all 'grace', his eyes represent the site of ever-changing 'meaning'. Entirely absorbed in the actor's facial expressions, the direction of Evelina's gaze informs the reader that she is uninterested in following the play's verbal script. She listens by looking at the actor's countenance, where 'every look *speaks*',[81] or what Ingold defines as 'looking-and-listening'.[82] Her fascination with the language of the actor's eyes presages the analogous role that ekphrasis will play in correcting a 'suspicious' suitor's misinterpretation of her character in the drama of her own life.

Burney moves Evelina from a theatrical encounter with 'meaning eyes' to a social stage on which they continue to speak truly. Barbara Darby contends that Burney's heroine 'must discover the proper way to "act" for a given audience, and more often than not, she is performing for a male audience whose watchful gaze is emphasized in the narrative'.[83] Whereas the theatre liberates the female gaze, Burney shows that in life, the heroine must conceal the act of looking at men, which would risk exposing her affections. As Villars reminds Evelina, '"nothing is so delicate as the reputation of a woman: it is, at once, the most beautiful and most brittle of all human things." '[84] Although she relies on her eyes to interpret men's characters, she must perform the act

---

78 Ibid.
79 Burney, *Evelina*, 20. David Garrick (1717–1779) was the most illustrious actor of his day. *The Suspicious Husband* (1747) was a comedy composed by Benjamin Hoadly (1706–1757) to showcase Garrick's talent.
80 Ibid.
81 Ibid.; emphasis in original.
82 Refer to my Introduction.
83 Barbara Darby, *Frances Burney, Dramatist* (Kentucky: University Press of Kentucky, 1997), 165.
84 Burney, *Evelina*, 136.

of directing her attention elsewhere in order to preserve her 'most beautiful and most brittle' possession – her 'virtue' – which in Richardson is a direct correlative for 'virginity'.

In *Evelina*, propriety of vision remains in perpetual opposition to her yearning to 'see something of the world'. The strictures on looking and speaking that complicated Burney's life similarly impede the 'improvement' of the heroine's perceptions. According to Damoff, late eighteenth-century society's oxymoronic visual expectations problematized actual and fictional women's lives:

> Chaste, innocent women are not to see or understand too much of the male world. But by scriptural standards – and Burney's – one can be tainted by failing to see as well as by seeing; averted eyes can be an indicator of indifference, arrogance, selfishness, and hard-heartedness as well as innocence [...] With the conflicting choices of seeing or not seeing, averting the eyes or looking boldly into the face of another, Burney reveals the double bind of the female situation.[85]

For Damoff, the tension that Evelina confronts represents the 'double bind' of a young lady making her entrance into the world. However, the 'conflicting choices' that the heroine encounters are more complex and varied than he suggests. The novel insists that being seen by eyes that do not 'speak' the same language risks breaking a woman's 'brittle' reputation.

Burney uses Evelina's first ball to show the way in which the 'penetrating' male gaze infringes upon female virtue through inappropriate speech. The heroine recounts her experience of Mr Lovel's stare on entering into the overlapping worlds of the public eye and the marriage market:

> Not long after, a young man, who had for some time looked at us [...] advanced, on tiptoe, towards me; he had a set smile on his face, and his dress was so foppish, that I really believe he even wished to be stared at; and yet he was very ugly.[86]

Inexperienced though she is with the intricacies of ball etiquette, Evelina sees the inappropriateness of Mr Lovel's appearance and manner of looking. In 1781, the *Morning Herald* caricaturized a similarly 'impertinent' spectator:

> The impertinent custom of staring modesty out of countenance is now become so much the ton among the macaronies of the age [...] they

---

85 Damoff, 'The Unaverted Eye', 238.
86 Burney, *Evelina*, 23.

thrust their noses within a few inches of Cupid's Rostrum, and pull out their glasses, to shew that their sight is as defective as their manners.[87]

Burney uses the invariability of Mr Lovel's looks and the duration of his stare to display rather than narrate his faults. The appearance of the man's 'set smile' contrasts with Evelina's recollection of Garrick's animated expression. She finds that his 'foppish' attire and 'ugliness' attract her attention because they do not 'blend in' with the mannerisms of the majority. The novelist's use of a passive infinitive in the phrase 'he even wished to be stared at' intimates the threshold of respectability that women's eyes could not pass.

Several paragraphs later, Burney tests the heroine's discretion in interpreting the 'meaning' in Lord Orville's face during their first rencontre. Evelina explains, 'He seemed very desirous of entering into conversation with me; but I was seized with such a panic, that I could hardly speak.'[88] As Elliott proposes in relation to Radcliffe's novels, 'even as these passages undermine the representational capacities of words, they do so paradoxically *through* words'.[89] Burney links the heroine's sudden incapacity to speak to the way in which Lord Orville communicates to her. His countenance seeks to 'converse' through a language other than verbal expression: 'his person is all elegance, and his countenance, the most animated and expressive I have ever seen.'[90] As John Mullan insists in the context of Richardson's novels: 'The most "natural" expression of all is the one which does not need words.'[91] In choosing to see the 'expressiveness' of his face, Evelina risks having the naive attentiveness of her gaze misunderstood.

During the episodes at Vauxhall and Marylebone, Burney forces the heroine to see and experience the irrevocable consequences of being seen in disreputable company. Denying the heroine her female companions, the novelist abandons her to a labyrinth of false appearances, calling to mind Radcliffe's sublime panoramas where the predatory male gaze has the power to lurk unseen.[92] Evelina's sudden isolation reveals her eyes' ability to detect predatory

---

87 *Morning Herald* (19 May 1781), 4. See also John Brewer, *The Pleasures of the Imagination: English Culture in the Eighteenth Century* (Chicago: University of Chicago Press, 2000), 262–81. Lord Chesterfield's judgement of Lady Coventry's appearance suggests the need for personal space: He 'was near her enough to see manifest that she had laid on a great deal of white which she did not want'.
88 Burney, *Evelina*, 24.
89 Elliott, *Portraiture and British Gothic Fiction*, 207; emphasis in original.
90 Burney, *Evelina*, 24.
91 John Mullan, *Sentiment and Sociability: The Language of Feeling in the Eighteenth Century* (Oxford: Clarendon Press, 1988), 74. Reprinted by permission of Oxford University Press.
92 Burney, *Evelina*, 162–63. Refer to Chapter 2 for a discussion on Radcliffe's novels.

gazes that seek to enter into unwarranted dialogue. Rather than escorting the young lady back to the social environs in which she should be seen, Willoughby plunges her into the 'dark walks' frequented by prostitutes.[93] As well as having power over Evelina's physical person, he controls the young lady's exposure to sympathetic gazes. He wishes to 'own' her visibility by forcing her into a liminal space in which 'we shall be least observed'.[94] Whereas Richardson allows Robert Lovelace to rape Clarissa Harlowe in *Clarissa*'s analogous scene, Burney, like Radcliffe, avoids portraying the explicit, instead choosing to exhibit the paradox of female invisibility wherein concealment is a delusion. By projecting Villars's and Lady Howard's fears into the visible world, Burney stages for the heroine and her voyeuristic spectator the real dangers of being seen.

In *Evelina*, Burney shows how Evelina's panic and insecurity at Vauxhall alter her vision. The heroine's conscious awareness of her vulnerability prevents her from foreseeing the consequences of innocently sheltering herself behind two prostitutes. While Villars condones 'unwomanly' recourses to self-protection when 'occasion demands them', he neglects to furnish the visual examples that would have allowed Evelina to picture his view of 'exceptional circumstances' in her mind's eye:[95]

> 'Though gentleness and modesty are the peculiar attributes of your sex, yet fortitude and firmness, when occasion demands them, are virtues as noble and as becoming in women as in men: the right line of conduct is the same for both sexes, though the manner in which it is pursued, may somewhat vary.'[96]

Through Villars's voice, Burney presents a protofeminist view of the universality of 'appropriate' conduct. In *The Wanderer*, her position takes on a clearer feminist tone. Only the manner in which ideal behaviour is pursued differs between the sexes. Bold action, as Damoff observes, is always risky for women – 'and particularly so for women in a world governed not by charity but by uncharitable judgments'.[97] Evelina's persistent incapacity to speak and look assertively during confrontations with the male gaze increases the likelihood that her appearance will be misunderstood.

Burney uses Lord Orville's fortuitous entrance in the scene to reassert the plight of visibility that Evelina endures. His inability to 'picture' the young

---

93 Ibid., 163.
94 Ibid., 162.
95 Ibid., 217.
96 Ibid.
97 Damoff, 'The Unaverted Eye', 237.

lady alongside prostitutes encourages him to look at her without recognising her: 'he passed us without distinguishing me; though I saw that, in a careless manner, his eyes surveyed the party'.[98] His 'careless' manner of looking allows the heroine to view the man in a way that preserves her visual anonymity. Ironically, Evelina's disreputable female companions are the first to witness the exposure of her affections. They instantly detect the 'look' of recognition in her eyes, retorting, '"you have a monstrous good stare, for a little country Miss"'.[99] By allowing the heroine's 'stare' to attract the prostitutes' attention, Burney emphasizes the uncharitable way in which Evelina's breach of decorum and lack of self-regulation appear. Only when the heroine has the comparative fortune of rejoining the Branghtons is Lord Orville able to 'place' the young lady and judge her in a way that calls to mind Fordyce's words: 'Between the state of pure virgin purity and actual prostitution are there no intermediate degrees?'[100] Evelina can neither flee from the scene nor defend herself verbally: 'unhappily I caught his eye; – both mine, immediately, were bent to the ground'.[101] Her sole means of escaping his visual censure is through the lowering of her eyes.

Burney demonstrates that, even if the heroine thwarts Lord Orville's scopic penetration of her, she cannot undo what has been witnessed. As Nancy Armstrong has shown, the damage of 'female subjectivity', or the likelihood of misinterpretation, becomes increasingly irrevocable in the novel:

> It is a woman's participation in public spectacle that injures her, for as an object of display, she always loses value as a subject [...] she cannot be 'seen' and still be vigilant.[102]

Burney presents Evelina's visibility, 'vigilance' and value as inexorably intertwined. The danger of misinterpretation shows that female subjectivity can also inflict damage on other women. Even if the prostitutes are no longer visible in the scene, the lowering of the heroine's gaze implies their former presence.[103] Burney uses the parallax between the concealed and the revealed to convey that which cannot be said. Despite Evelina's attempts to 'silence' the meaning in her eyes, Lord Orville's determined advances compel her to look up: 'Good God, with what expressive eyes did he regard me! Never were surprise and concern so

---

98 Burney, *Evelina*, 195.
99 Ibid.
100 Ibid.
101 Ibid., 196.
102 Nancy Armstrong, *Desire and Domestic Fiction: A Political History of the Novel*, 77. Reprinted by permission of Oxford University Press.
103 See Cutting, 'Defiant Women', 596.

strongly marked, – yes, my dear Sir, he looked *greatly* concerned.'[104] His 'expressive eyes' remark his 'surprise' and '*great* concern' in a way that words cannot.

Burney uses scopic interplay to expose the way in which Evelina's contact with 'the world of misinterpretations' has affected her 'image' and manner of looking. When the heroine returns to Berry Hill – the region of her 'eye/I' – she sees that her fading image is immediately apparent to those who recall her former bloom. Observing the attention that her appearance attracts, she conceals its underlying cause: an impertinent letter purportedly from her 'grateful admirer, ORVILLE' – 'As to Miss Mirvan, she is my second self, and neither hopes nor fears but as I do. And as to me, – I know not what to say, nor even what to wish.'[105] Evelina opens her letter with 'Never, never again will I trust to appearances'[106] and concludes with 'Yet I cannot but lament to find myself in a world so deceitful, where we must suspect what we see, distrust what we hear, and doubt even what we feel!'[107] Her newfound mistrust of mankind dissolves her implicit faith in the correspondence between apparent and actual truths, speaking eyes and written speech. By displaying the letter for her second self to see, the heroine allows the text to 'speak for itself'.[108] The man's documented impertinence and exposure of 'his real disposition'[109] kindles in her a resolve to see 'no more' of the world unless she finds that 'the eyes of Lord Orville agree with his pen'.[110] His visual and verbal speech must be synonymous in order for her to marry her second reading of his character with her first impressions.

In *Evelina*, Burney emphasizes that the heroine must perceive Villars's attentive concern for her in order to reconsider others' similar interpretations of her changed appearance. As Evelina explains to her 'second self', 'I should be very indifferent to all such observations, did I not perceive that they draw upon me the eyes of Mr. Villars, which glisten with affectionate concern'.[111] The 'glisten' of his eyes tearfully speaks his 'affectionate concern' in a way that the heroine cannot reciprocate. Her gender prevents her from entering into the 'sympathetic' social intercourse that David Hume's *A Treatise of Human Nature* (1739–40) outlines: 'the easy communication of sentiments from one thinking being to another'.[112] Channelling his thoughts through visual and verbal

---

104 Burney, *Evelina*, 196; emphasis in original.
105 Ibid., 103.
106 Ibid., 213.
107 Ibid., 216.
108 Ibid., 214.
109 Ibid., 215.
110 Ibid., 229.
111 Ibid., 215.
112 David Hume, *A Treatise of Human Nature*, ed. L. A. Selby-Bigge ([1739–40] Oxford: Clarendon Press, 1978), 363.

speech, Villars exclaims, 'for I hoped that time, and absence from whatever excited your uneasiness, might best operate in silence: but alas! your affliction seems only to augment, – your health declines, – your look alters, – Oh Evelina, my aged heart bleeds to see the change!'[113] The 'bleeding' of his heart suggests that he *feels* the pain that he *sees* within her. He observes that she is as far from the image of her ego ideal as she has ever been: 'To see my Evelina happy, is to see myself without a wish.'[114] His desire posits a transition from sympathetic to empathic states.

In contrast to Villars, who effortlessly perceives the meaning of the heroine's introspective speech, Orville needs time to 'penetrate' Evelina's apparent two-dimensionality. Burney's depiction dramatizes the heroine's hesitation to let him meet her eyes: 'But, not once, – not a moment, did I dare meet the eyes of Lord Orville! All consciousness myself, I dreaded his penetration, and directed mine every way – but towards his.'[115] Burney's inclusion of the word 'consciousness' exemplifies Bakhtin's theory that consciousness is inseparable from language, a point that he makes explicit in 'From the Prehistory of Novelistic Discourse': 'To a greater or lesser extent, every novel is a dialogized system made up of the images of "languages", styles and consciousnesses that are concrete and inseparable from language.'[116] The need for consciousness to choose a language nonetheless is problematized in Burney's novel by Evelina's necessary preoccupation with the 'penetration' of the male gaze.[117] Evelina's acute self-consciousness prompts her to resist Hume's 'easy communication of sentiments';[118] her implicit terror prevents her from entering into a scopic tryst, compelling her instead to stay in Mrs Selwyn's physical protection.

In *Evelina*, Burney uses Willoughby's presence in the scene to occasion Orville's verbal account of his changed view of Evelina's character. He explains, 'She is not, indeed, like most modern young ladies, to be known in half an hour; her modest worth and fearful excellence require both time and encouragement to shew themselves.'[119] Orville's pairing of 'fearful' and 'excellence' indicates his understanding of the double bind of the young lady

---

113 Burney, *Evelina*, 221.
114 Ibid., 19.
115 Ibid., 287.
116 Bakhtin, *The Dialogic Imagination*, 49.
117 See Bray, *The Epistolary Novel*, 5. According to Bakhtin, 'consciousness finds itself inevitably facing the necessity of *having to choose a language*. With each literary–verbal performance, consciousness must actively orient itself amidst heteroglossia, it must move in and occupy a position for itself within it, it chooses, in other words, a "language."'
118 For an insightful study of Hume's philosophy, see Bray, *The Female Reader in the English Novel*, 28–57.
119 Burney, *Evelina*, 286–87.

entering the world. He continues, 'She does not, beautiful as she is, seize the soul by surprise, but, with more dangerous fascination, she steals it almost imperceptibly.'[120] The man's recognition of the 'imperceptible' manner in which Evelina has attracted him confirms the 'dangerous fascination' of her repressed inner beauty. Whereas the trope of 'frustrated utterance' and the duplicity of speech anticipate misinterpretation in the novel, Burney's use of scopic visuality shows that some appearances do speak truly, as long as the 'sparkle' of honesty may be found in the eyes.[121] The underlying tension in Burney's *Evelina* shows that goodness, while vulnerable to exploitation, will meet its just reward.

Narrative Perspective and Colour Codes in *The Wanderer*

In contrast to *Evelina*'s epistolary form, which underscores the role of scopic communication, *The Wanderer*'s third-person narrative structure relies more heavily on the language of colours to communicate the strains of visibility and inexpressibility on the female sex.[122] Dorrit Cohn explains the avoidance of psychonarration in *Transparent Minds: Narrative Modes for Presenting Consciousness in Fiction* (1983):

> While prolonged inside views were largely restricted to first-person forms, third-person novels dwelt on manifest behaviour, with the characters' inner selves revealed only indirectly through spoken language and telling gesture.[123]

Even if eyes continue to speak in *The Wanderer*, Burney necessarily focuses on reading 'manifest' appearances and behaviour. Unlike Evelina, who enters the world of leisure, the Incognita, who is exiled from it, must labour in order to survive. Juliet's flight from male persecution and her ambitions for self-sufficiency require her to exploit her powers of metamorphosis in order to resist blending in with her elevated social class. By juxtaposing the unpainted face and the painted visage, the novelist's portraits of the heroine convince the reader that the 'Incognita' is impenetrable: 'And can you, really [...] be

---

120 Ibid., 286.
121 Ibid., 231.
122 While Burney's *Cecilia* and *Camilla* also show the relationship between third-person narratives and the language of colours, this chapter seeks to pair the two novels that best demonstrate the shift in her feminist position.
123 Dorrit Cohn, *Transparent Minds: Narrative Modes for Presenting Consciousness in Fiction* (Princeton, NJ: Princeton University Press, 1983), 21.

allured by such an adventurer? A Wanderer, – without even a name?'[124] While Julia Epstein has proposed that 'to lack a name is to belong to no one, that is, to belong to oneself',[125] Burney shows that Juliet remains fettered to her visible image and commodified female identity.

Juliet's unconventional use of cosmetics to conceal natural beauty asserts what Cutting interprets as Burney's preoccupation with the conflict between the individual and society.[126] The novelist shows that motifs of 'self-sacrifice' ironically empower the heroine through colour-coded connotations. Burney's implicit sanction of cosmetics in *The Wanderer* suggests that she feels that women should have the right to paint themselves in order to protect their 'images' and reputations. For Juliet, whose value and beauty are inherent, cosmetics provide a 'French' means of protection that separates the authentic self from its external appearance. As Tassie Gwilliam explains in 'Cosmetic Poetics: Colouring Faces in the Eighteenth Century' (1994), artificial colours add painterly complexity to natural complexions, masking the indices of true feelings behind pigments that were often life-threatening.[127] Face-painting's ability to conceal the colour codes of emotions suspends the Incognita from public interpretation in a way that sacrificing her name cannot: it permits her, like Edgeworth's Lady Delacour, to become a subject that only she can understand.

In *The Wanderer*, Burney destabilizes personal identity's association with the named self and its appearance, moral essentialism and its aestheticized presentation. Her use of coded visuality encourages the heroine and the reader to question the assumption that Chevalier Louis de Jaucourt issued in the *Encyclopédie*:

> '[colour] does not designate a particular property of a body, but only a modification of our soul; whiteness, for example, redness, and so on, only exist within us, and not in the body to which we nevertheless attribute them through a habit acquired in our childhood: it is a very singular thing, and worthy of the attention of metaphysicians, this penchant we have for attributing to a material, divisible substance that which really belongs to a spiritual, simple substance.'[128]

---

124 Burney, *The Wanderer*, 33. Reprinted by permission of Oxford University Press.
125 Julia Epstein, *The Iron Pen: Frances Burney and the Politics of Women's Writing* (Madison: University of Wisconsin Press, 1989), 178.
126 Cutting, 'Defiant Women', 528.
127 Tassie Gwilliam, 'Cosmetic Poetics: Coloring Faces in the Eighteenth Century', in *Body and Text in the Eighteenth Century*, ed. Veronica Kelly (Stanford, CA: Stanford University Press, 1994), 144–59 (144).
128 Festa, 'Cosmetic Differences: The Changing Faces of England and France', 43. © 2005 American Society for Eighteenth-Century Studies. Reprinted with permission

While Jaucourt acknowledged the linkage between invisible and visible, immaterial and material, he proposed that colour's metaphysical properties were representative of the soul. Burney revises his definition, treating colour theory according to the premise that Locke's 'of Identity and Diversity' made explicit: 'So that *self is* not determined by Identity or Diversity of Substance, which it cannot be sure of, but only by Identity of consciousness.'[129] The novelist shows that the colours of emotions act as a nuanced language of what Jacqueline Lichtenstein has called 'contingent effect'.[130] Dissolving the relationship between the material and the spiritual, the narrative highlights the subjectivity of the heroine's ambiguous complexion.

Burney emphasizes culture's role in (re)making the heroine's face. She incorporates Francophilia and Francophobia, Anglophilia and Anglophobia in the broader framework of her novelistic presentation of subjectivity. Whereas overrouged cheeks were connotative of prostitutes in late eighteenth- and early nineteenth-century England, in France, the unadorned appearances of the English were revelatory of self-neglect.[131] Modifications in the visible world prompted the eye, mind and imagination to adjust to the cultural presentation of the 'norm'. Writing in 1787, William Barker documented the cult of visual congruity representative of Chevalier Louis de Jaucourt's pre-Revolutionary France:

> [The French] are very similar [...] when dressed for public appearance, for the fashion of wearing their rouge is systematical [...] Unless ladies have very striking personal singularities, it is difficult to distinguish them asunder.[132]

In a culture of visual conformity, Barker's 'very striking personal singularities' allowed for differentiation. As Philip Thicknesse had remarked two decades earlier, '[T]he quantity of *rouge* put on by the ladies [in France] is very singular [...]; the truth is, it steals upon them by degrees, their eyes become

---

of Johns Hopkins University Press. Here, Festa supplies her own translation of the French. See also *Encyclopédie*, qv. Couleur.

129 John Locke, *An Essay Concerning Human Understanding*, ed. P. H. Nidditch ([1700, 4th ed.] Oxford: Clarendon Press, 1975), 345. On Locke, see Bray, *The Epistolary Novel*, especially 11–16; emphasis in original.

130 Jacqueline Lichtenstein, 'Making Up Representation: The Risks of Femininity', trans. Katherine Streip, *Representation* no. 20 (Fall 1987): 77–87 (81).

131 Festa, 'Cosmetic Differences', 43.

132 Ibid., 29. Passage taken from William Barker's *Treatise on the Principles of Hairdressing* [c. 1786].

habituated to it.'[133] The Incognita's preoccupation with remaking her visual identity draws attention to her striking resistance to the aesthetic expectations that she perceives in her surroundings. By embodying a plethora of visual contradictions rather than conforming to a 'national image', the heroine distances herself from France and England. In using cosmetics to suppress her recognizable visual identity, she enables her appearance to become that of a cross-Channel wanderer. Her face does not fit in anywhere because it contains traits from everywhere that she has wandered.

Before *The Wanderer*'s heroine can return to her identity in face, name and nationality, she must fashion her own visible anonymity. As a penniless émigrée fleeing the dread of the guillotine and an unconsummated marriage, Juliet's initial route to overcoming her past and surviving the future involves a 'revolution' in colours:

> The wind just then blowing back the prominent borders of a French night-cap, which had almost concealed all her features, displayed a large black patch, that covered half her left cheek, and a broad black ribbon, which bound a bandage of cloth over the right side of her forehead.[134]

Burney's portrait exposes the complex layers of the heroine's appearance. The wind's partial victory over the French nightcap's 'prominent borders' provides a metaphor for her spatial and cultural progression in a way that calls to mind the Jacobins' headgear. Black patches were often used to conceal the marks of smallpox or, indeed, the 'great pox' – syphilis. Despite Juliet's efforts towards visual self-determination and autonomy, Burney, like Edgeworth, empowers nature over art. The Incognita's white teeth compete with her 'dingy complexion'[135] in the way that Bakhtin proposes in 'Epic and the Novel': 'a crucial tension develops between the external and the internal man' that makes 'the subjectivity of the individual […] an object of experimentation and representation'.[136] The elevation of interiority enables the Incognita to preserve her identity by disassociating it with its visible index. She disrupts the binary division between actual and contrived faces by making the distinction between material and immaterial colour difficult to perceive.

---

133 Philip Thicknesse, *Observations on the Customs and Manners of the French Nation, in a series of letters, in which the nation is vindicated from the misrepresentations of some late writers* (Dublin: W. Sleater, D. Chamberlaine and J. Potts, 1767), 95; emphasis in original.
134 Burney, *The Wanderer*, 20.
135 Ibid., 23.
136 Bakhtin, *The Dialogic Imagination*, 37.

Burney demonstrates that Juliet's attempts to conceal her personal identity ironically pique curiosity. Henderson observes that she 'is introduced to us, as to the people of Brighthelmstone, as an assemblage of strictly external features, and she immediately becomes a spectacle, a novelty, and an object of amusement'.[137] The Incognita is, to borrow Henderson's term, a 'novelty'; she is entirely 'made up' – in face, name and nationality. The women who behold her cannot 'make out' her origins because they cannot picture her within their culture's set of visual expectations. Juliet is at once an aristocrat, an Englishwoman, an émigrée from France, a wanderer and 'the' Incognita. Even if she elects to 'mar' her natural beauty rather than enhance it, she only does so to 'make up' an identity that defies all systems of definition.

In *The Wanderer*, Burney uses the colour-coded inconsistencies within the Incognita's 'made-up' image to presage a series of fairy-tale metamorphoses. Doody interprets the heroine's progressive transformations as her 'double and paradoxical objective: to sacrifice herself as a medium of exchange, if duty demands, and on the other hand to resist with all her power everything that threatens her independence'.[138] The heroine's ability to remake herself simultaneously liberates and commodifies her image in a way that relates to how women's scopic vulnerability inspires and requires them to act. Her value, like her appearance, cannot be fixed: '"you metamorphose yourself about so, one does not know which way to look for you."'[139] While the Incognita can control her gaze, her colouration is subject to involuntary fluctuations that 'evince' her efforts to conceal her conscious thoughts: 'frequent blushes crossed her cheeks, which, though they died away almost as soon as they were born, vanished only to re-appear; evincing all the consciousness that she struggled to suppress'.[140] Juliet's coloured responses to questions about her identity persistently burn through her exhibited self: 'A crimson of the deepest hue forced its way through her dark complexion: her very eyes reddened with blushes, as she faintly answered, "I cannot tell my name!"'[141] Juliet's 'blushing eyes' channel the deepest hue of her emotions through visual and verbal speech, confirming colour's status as the coded language through which a 'polyphony of fully valid voices'[142] expresses her conflicting selves.

Burney links hues of emotions with manners in order to intensify the tension between Juliet's suppressed and expressed selves. The Incognita's complexion is material and immaterial, somatic and emotional, active and passive.

---

137 Henderson, 'Burney's *The Wanderer*', 15.
138 Doody, *Frances Burney: The Life in the Works*, 18.
139 Burney, *The Wanderer*, 771.
140 Ibid., 179–80.
141 Ibid., 33.
142 Bakhtin, *The Dialogic Imagination*, 6.

Her feelings and conduct visually compete with her 'dusky skin' and 'mean apparel' in a style that attracts rather than deflects attention:

> Nevertheless, her manners were so strikingly elevated above her attire, that, notwithstanding the disdain with which, in the height of her curiosity, Mrs. Ireton surveyed her mean apparel, and shrunk from her dusky skin, she gave up her plan of seeking for any other person to wait upon her, during her journey to town, and told the Incognita that, if she could make her dress a little less shocking, she might relinquish her place in the stage-coach, to occupy one in a post-chaise.[143]

The novelist juxtaposes the dysphoric-euphoric colours within the Incognita's appearance and how she acts. Mrs Ireton 'shrinks' from 'the walnut-skinned gypsey',[144] is 'shocked' by the mysterious woman's dress and is 'struck' by her behaviour but in a contrasting way. The Incognita's 'strikingly elevated manners' visually intimate her exposure to 'high' society – a possibility that 'heightens' Mrs Ireton's curiosity and intensifies her scrutiny of the woman who appears out of place in a stagecoach. The 'impertinent spectator'/actor model allows the novelist to comment on the heroine's perplexing appearance by visually differentiating between the inappropriate and appropriate representations of female behaviour of the women involved.

Burney's use of coded visuality shows that unlike the removal of a mask, the Incognita's metamorphosis and visual rebirth require time and spatial confinement. Nature lightens the Incognita's countenance so as to recreate the 'most dazzling fairness' of her 'true' face:

> When, however, on the fourth day, the shutters of the chamber, which give it a more sickly character, had hitherto been closed, were suffered to admit the sunbeams of a cheerful winter's morning, Mrs. Ireton was directed, by their rays, to a full and marvellous view, of a skin changed from a tint nearly black, to the brightest, whitest, and most dazzling fairness. The band upon the forehead, and the patch upon the cheek, were all that remained of the original appearance.[145]

Burney's treatment of chiaroscuro in the passage conveys the way in which Juliet's surroundings anticipate the destruction of her natural appearance's artistic means of protection. In contrast to the 'sickly character' of the room's

---

143 Burney, *The Wanderer*, 41. Reprinted by permission of Oxford University Press.
144 Ibid., 52.
145 Burney, *The Wanderer*, 43. Reprinted by permission of Oxford University Press.

darkness, which anthropomorphizes the heroine's initial opacity, the sunbeams' sudden penetration emulates the change in her appearance. Juliet's natural self pierces the material that had 'shuttered' it from view: 'a tint nearly black', implying an emotional or moral change expressed in dubious racial terms.

Masked and unmasked, black and white, the Incognita remains a 'marvellous' sight that attracts the penetrating gaze. The third-person narrative offers secondhand views of the Incognita's transformation into what Henderson aptly calls 'fair Circassian, tawny Hottentot, and Grecian beauty all at once'.[146] Juliet embodies the plethora of visual contradictions that Lillian Bloom and Edward Bloom have claimed to be the novel's visual miracle of a 'princess in disguise'.[147] Harleigh cannot take his eyes off her: 'He now looked at her with an earnest gaze, that seemed nearly to draw his eyes from their sockets.'[148] Mrs Ireton's persistent inability to distinguish between contrived colours and colours of contingent effect finds in the Incognita's brilliant fairness a trompe l'oeil. She chides, ' "If I did not fear being impertinent, I should be tempted to ask how many coats of white and red you were obliged to lay on, before you could cover over all that black." '[149] The woman's deliberate misreading of the Incognita's true and false colours asserts that she does not fear being an impertinent spectator or speaker; she has been tempted against her better judgement to articulate that which should have passed unuttered:

> 'You have been bruised and beaten; and dirty and clean; and ragged and whole; and wounded and healed; and a European and a Creole, in less than a week [...] There is nothing that can be too much to expect from so great an adept in metamorphoses.'[150]

Mrs Ireton's evaluation of the heroine's skill at visual metamorphoses permits the reader to picture her enigmatic colours through an indirect means. By informing the reader of Mrs Ireton's impertinence, the novelist secures a method of voicing the otherwise unsayable.

In *The Wanderer*, Burney relies on Mrs Ireton to communicate the multiple connotations that English viewers would associate with the heroine's complexion. She turns from highlighting the opposed states of the Incognita's appearance to enumerating the negative perceptions surrounding cosmetics. Her attempt to 'penetrate' the heroine's complexion reveals that she sees cosmetics in economic terms:

---

146 Henderson, 'Burney's *The Wanderer*', 117.
147 Lillian D. Bloom and Edward A. Bloom, 'Fanny Burney's Novels', 233.
148 Burney, *The Wanderer*, 51. Reprinted by permission of Oxford University Press.
149 Burney, *The Wanderer*, 44. Reprinted by permission of Oxford University Press.
150 Burney, *The Wanderer*, 46. Reprinted by permission of Oxford University Press.

> 'And pray, have you kept that same face ever since I saw you in Grosvenor Square? Or have you put it on again only now to come back to me? I rather suppose you have made it last the whole time. It would be very expensive, I apprehend, to change it frequently: it can by no means be so costly to keep it only in repair.'[151]

Mrs Ireton persistently answers her own rhetorical questions, insinuating that the heroine's colours display her poverty, thriftiness and prostitution. She conjectures that rather than replacing her made-up colours, the Incognita repairs them. Mrs Ireton's explanation for the duration of the heroine's actual face reflects her inability to distinguish between colours that mask feelings and those that are feelings made visible.

Burney advances Mrs Ireton's denigration of the Incognita's thrifty red and white complexion to its association with the stage. As Kathleen Anderson observes, the narrative persistently 'teases the reader with the suspicion that Juliet's "real self" is indistinguishable from her performances', confusing art and nature in order to highlight their visual similarity.[152] Mrs Ireton next accuses the heroine of participating in the visual 'trade' of seduction that cosmetics allow:

> 'That red and white, that you lay on so happily, may just as well hide the wrinkles of two or three grand climacterics, as of only a poor single sixty or seventy years of age. However, these are secrets that I don't presume to enquire into. Every trade has its mystery.'[153]

Mrs Ireton associates the heroine's dramatic physiological transformations with those of the 'climeratics' at the onset of menopause, who must contrive a more attractive face to their viewers. She 'presumes' the Incognita's impasto application of colour and attempts to resolve the 'trade' of the heroine's identity. However, the 'mystery' of the Incognita's natural colours remains insoluble to eyes that are veiled by their own subjectivity. Through the dysphoric-euphoric interplay between material colours and those of contingent effect, Burney stages her point that art allows truth and deception to look alike. Juliet's painted and unpainted identities read as unwavering analogues for the strained relationship between self-determination and conformity, self-expression and reticence. Regardless of the colours that she wears, they display the analogous battle taking place within her image, or her mind

---

151 Burney, *The Wanderer*, 250. Reprinted by permission of Oxford University Press.
152 See Bray, *The Female Reader in the English Novel*, 50.
153 Burney, *The Wanderer*, 45–46. Reprinted by permission of Oxford University Press.

and selfhood, alerting the reader to the tension that the remainder of the plot must seek to resolve.

Burney's reliance on coded visuality enabled her to achieve rhetorical freedom within the conventions of language while preserving her 'image' in print and in life. Whereas *Evelina*'s epistolary structure invites the reader to look with the conduct book-inspired heroine at the need to maintain one's image and reputation, *The Wanderer*'s third-person narrative structure calls attention to Juliet's colour-coded identity crisis through others' eyes. Despite the apparent uniformity of her characters and the contrasting narrative viewpoints through which she depicts them, Burney, like Austen, Radcliffe and Edgeworth, leaves the reader to ponder, 'and to appearances are we not all either victims or dupes?'[154]

---

154 Ibid., 275.

CONCLUSION

This book has shown that the visual details in women's novels published between 1778 and 1815 are collectively more telling about the gender politics of the era spanning the start of the Anglo-French War and the Battle of Waterloo than scholars have previously acknowledged. Visuality, which functions as a coded continuum linking visual and verbal modes of communication and understanding, empowered women novelists at a time when self-expression was particularly constrained for their sex, allowing them to control the gaze and speak through pictures. My analysis of the novels of Jane Austen, Ann Radcliffe, Maria Edgeworth and Frances Burney has demonstrated that visuality provided them with a methodology capable of depicting and negotiating the ways in which women 'should' see, appear and think in a society in which the reputation was image based.

Many factors contributed to the proliferation of visual codes, metaphors and references to the gaze in women's fiction of the late eighteenth and early nineteenth centuries. The novels that this study has discussed underscore culture's role in shaping perceptions and calibrating gendered definitions of acceptable display. From the novelties of Vauxhall Gardens to the eye-catching sights at portraiture exhibitions, the act of looking became increasingly self-conscious and culturally choreographed. The era's preoccupation with Taste, popularized by Addison's discussions in the *Spectator*, reshaped the relationship between depiction and description, combining visual and verbal communication in ekphrastic representations that depicted one medium through another.[1] His claim that 'well-chosen' words produce a more convincing sight in the imagination than does the image itself helps explain how women used an economy of detail to their diplomatic advantage in order to speak 'freely' while preserving their reputations as respectable women.[2]

Society's absorption of Lavater's physiognomic principles and Reynolds's *Discourses on Art* influenced vision and depiction in a manner that produced

---

1 See Addison, 'On the Pleasures of the Imagination', 290–93.
2 Ibid., 292.

corresponding fluctuations in the level of detail deemed necessary, or appropriate, to communicate. Views of women also shifted. Women novelists seized upon the Enlightenment's campaign for human rights and looked to the French Revolution's model of questioning conventional perceptions of their sex. Wollstonecraft's call for 'a REVOLUTION in female manners' recognized that universal progress and rhetorical liberation would have to start in the domestic sphere.³

Degrees of 'inexpressibility' and systems of 'well-chosen' words differed dramatically by gender between 1778 and 1815. Thompson has observed that 'will not tell' and 'cannot tell' represent two distinct states of mind in Austen's novels.⁴ Women novelists were, like women readers of novels, seen as threats to a patriarchal regime of knowledge where men had power over women's perceptions of their surroundings and themselves. In fiction and in actuality, women had to negotiate four scopic forces that determined their 'looks' and manners of looking: the 'impartial' spectator, the male gaze, the public eye and the disenfranchised female gaze.⁵ For Wollstonecraft, such a matrix of control enslaved the female viewpoint, leading her to proclaim, 'I do not wish [women] to have power over men; but over themselves.'⁶ While the emancipation that she envisioned took time to attain, visuality, with its intrinsic connection to the dynamics between the observer and the observed, invited women novelists to conform to societal strictures by employing an approach that afforded concealed resistance within artful narration. Referring to Radcliffe's treatment of portraiture, Elliott writes, 'Even as these passages undermine the representational capacities of words, they do so paradoxically *through* words.'⁷ Women novelists used references to the visible and the invisible to express feelings that would have otherwise been impossible, if not unseemly, to voice.

Allusions to novel reading absolved women's novels from reputation-harming connotations. In *Letters for Literary Ladies*, Edgeworth insists that 'a literary lady is no longer a sight; the spectacle is now too common to attract curiosity; the species of animal is too well known even to admit of much exaggeration in the description of its appearance.'⁸ Women novel readers,

---

3   See Wollstonecraft, *The Vindications: The Rights of Men, the Rights of Woman*, 179.
4   James Thompson, 'Jane Austen and the Limits of Language', 517.
5   Refer to my Introduction for an investigation of the gaze.
6   Wollstonecraft, *The Vindications: The Rights of Men, the Rights of Woman*, 179.
7   Elliott, *Portraiture and the British Gothic Fiction: The Rise of Picture Identification, 1764–1835*, 207. © 2012 The Johns Hopkins University Press. Reprinted with permission of Johns Hopkins University Press; emphasis in original.
8   Edgeworth, *Letters for Literary Ladies*, 19.

however, remained a 'species' that was subject to criticism. As *Belinda*'s woman of fashion remarks,

> 'You are thinking that you are like Camilla, and I like Mrs. Mitten – novel reading, as I dare say you have been told by your governess, as I was told by mine, and she by hers, I suppose – novel reading for young ladies is the most dangerous –'[9]

Lady Delacour's accusation emphasizes that seeing like a character in a novel is, like novel reading, 'most dangerous'. It overwhelms reason with the flights of the imagination, preventing the female sex from seeing and perceiving the world as it actually is. In *Northanger Abbey*, Austen extends the stigma in an ironic way to Edgeworth's novels: ' "And what are you reading, Miss – ?" "Oh! It is only a novel […] It is only Cecilia, or Camilla, or Belinda." '[10] In fiction and in actuality, novel reading implied a breach of domestic femininity because of its power to influence eyes, hearts and minds.

Crary argues that in contrast to the eighteenth century, which preferred 'transparency to opacity', the nineteenth century esteemed detail and called appearances into question.[11] The novels that this book has examined, however, reveal that the shift in perceptions was taking place even earlier. Changes in textual depictions of women accompanied changing attitudes towards the reciprocity between the appearance and the essence. Descriptions of the heroine's appearance reveal that ideal beauty was becoming an increasingly invisible attribute, pertaining to inner rather than outer character. The prototype heroine that Austen satirizes in 'Plan of a Novel' (c. 1816) begins to allow for imperfections:

> Heroine a faultless Character herself, – perfectly good, with much tenderness and sentiment, & not the least Wit – very highly accomplished, understanding modern Languages & (generally speaking) everything that the most accomplished young Women learn, but particularly excelling in Music – her favourite pursuit – & playing equally well on the Piano Forte & Harp – & singing in the first stile. Her Person quite beautiful – dark eyes and plump cheeks.[12]

The self-referential coordinates in women's novels published between 1778 and 1815 demonstrate that even if heroines conform outwardly, they see and

---

9 Edgeworth, *Belinda*, 57.
10 Austen, *Northanger Abbey*, 31.
11 See Crary, *Techniques of the Observer*, 62.
12 Austen, *Minor Works*, 428–29.

think for themselves. While the forms and functions of visuality that women novelists employed to their rhetorical advantage vary, they channelled their thoughts through several distinct visual pathways: visible and 'invisible' likenesses, architectural metaphors, the 'made-up' social self and communicating countenances.

Women novelists of the period often negotiated the strictures on vision and depiction by redirecting the female gaze to visual analogues of character. Likenesses invited women to look attentively and 'picture' character in a way that did not endanger their irreparable reputations. Austen's treatment of portraiture in *Pride and Prejudice*, for instance, presents Mr Darcy's portrait and actual person as interchangeable. The large-scale painting on view at Pemberley complies with Lavater's definition of a 'striking likeness': 'It lives, it breathes! It is not a portrait; it is Nature!'[13] Mr Darcy's portrait 'fixes' Elizabeth's attention and prejudices in a way that encourages the reader to see the heroine's reformed perceptions. Austen's treatment of portraiture in *Emma*, meanwhile, calls attention to the way in which looking 'makes' the subject and the object.

Radcliffe also uses 'striking' portraits in her Gothic novels but, in contrast to Austen, seeks to inspire fear in the female viewer. In *The Mysteries of Udolpho*, Dorothée torments Emily's eyes, exclaiming, ' "there is her very self! Just as she looked when she came first to the chateau. You see, madam, she was all blooming like you, then – and so soon to be cut off!" '[14] Dorothée's reference to the Marchioness's 'very self' speaks more of a supernatural *nature morte* than a work of art. Unlike benevolent portraiture, it warns of female subjection, confusing the boundaries between life and death, past and present, fiction and actuality. Through emotional responses to speaking eyes, the novelist invites the reader to 'picture' what she leaves physiognomically indistinct.

Society's absorption of the Lavaterian habit of looking and Descartes's philosophy that the eyes of the body reify the eye of the mind anticipates the connection between portraiture and place, another visual channel of thought that late eighteenth- and early nineteenth-century women novelists used to great effect. Radcliffe's fluid transitions between the concentric visual realms of architecture, natural panoramas and the obscure 'paint' women's lives as endlessly enfolded nightmares. In her revision to the Burkean sublime, structures are not simply characters; rather, they are analogues for the permanence of patriarchal abuse. Whereas castles exteriorize evil and convents internalize it, architecture consistently serves as a visual metaphor for live burial. In contrast to Radcliffe, who negates the reciprocity between appearances and moral

---

13 Lavater, *Essays on Physiognomy for the Promotion of the Knowledge and Love of Mankind*, 2: 249.
14 Radcliffe, *The Mysteries of Udolpho*, 532.

ideology, Austen endorses it. In *Emma*, she introduces the threat of loss, first of Donwell and then of its owner, to encourage the reader to see that Emma's perception of happiness depends on being 'first' in Mr Knightley's mind and heart. Only the prospect of a Mrs Harriet Knightley and the separation of the estates can change her view of marriage.

The 'made-up' social self represents an additional visual channel of expression that women's novels published between 1778 and 1815 frequent. At the time, women were moving from cosmetics to a form of 'self-determination' that continued to deflect penetration and remove the female subject from public interpretation. Regardless of their contrived public faces, veils and disguises, women's inner selves often contrasted with their expressed identities, calling to mind Locke's theory 'of Identity and Diversity': 'So that *self is* not determined by Identity or Diversity of Substance, which it cannot be sure of, but only by Identity of consciousness'.[15] In Edgeworth's novels, cosmetics and elements of dress create a material barrier between contrived and actual characters. *Belinda*'s 'woman of fashion' resorts to dramatic costume changes and make-up to cloak her inner distress. The allegorical guise of the Comic Muse allows Lady Delacour to masquerade the prefabricated picture of gaiety. Only in the privacy of her boudoir can she expose herself as 'the picture of despair': '"I seem to you, and to all the world, what I am not."'[16] In Burney's *The Wanderer*, Juliet must remake her face with traits from everywhere in order to resist all cultural systems of definition.[17] Even if Burney is conventional in praising nature over art and truth over aesthetic ruses, she condones the heroine's use of cosmetics to deface her natural beauty for the purpose of escaping recognition. Despite her attempts to deflect penetration, the eponymous Incognita remains persistently visible, attesting to the 'double bind' of the female situation.

As well as treating their fictional women as subjects-on-view, late eighteenth- and early nineteenth-century women's novels point to the causal relationship between 'frustrated utterance' and speaking countenances. Burney's novels rely heavily on ocular dialogue and colour codes of emotions, confirming Daly's conjecture that women were subjected to '"an invisible tyranny"': the persistent threat of misinterpretation.[18] *Evelina*'s epistolary structure empowers the role of scopic communication, insisting that 'every look *speaks*'[19] in a

---

15 Locke, *An Essay Concerning Human Understanding*, 345. For a relevant discussion of 'reading' appearances, see Bray, *The Epistolary Novel: Representations of Consciousness*, esp. 11–16; emphasis in original
16 Edgeworth, *Belinda*, 25.
17 Refer to Chapter 4.
18 Quoted in LeRoy W. Smith, *Jane Austen and the Drama of Woman*, 23.
19 Burney, *Evelina*, 20; emphasis in original.

society where words often deceive. In contrast, *The Wanderer*'s third-person narrative structure avoids psychonarration by exploiting the similarities between colour codes of emotion and deception. Burney reveals that colours of emotion act as a nuanced language of what Lichtenstein has called 'contingent effect'.[20] Whereas the formation of a scopic tryst, or conversation between gazes, is voluntary, the circulation of the blood cannot be controlled, creating what Festa describes as 'the transparent visage through which a desiring masculine eye can peer'.[21] Rather than individualizing her heroines through their physiognomies, Burney's use of coded visuality invites the reader to look at the countenance through others' perceptions of it. Achieving a polyphony of valid voices through an economy of detail, Burney simultaneously depicts viewer and subject-on-view.

By journeying from projections of character exterior to the self to depictions of the communicative capacity of coded self-display, this book has illustrated the efficacy of visuality to women novelists during an era shaped by revolutions, the rise and fall of empires and changing attitudes towards freedom of expression. In doing so, it has simultaneously pointed to the interdependence of visual and verbal expression's enduring diplomatic applications and implications – in fiction and in life. This study thus offers an opportune starting point for research on visuality's inherence in works by other late eighteenth- and early nineteenth-century women writers. It also serves as a lens through which the evolution of strategic communications, visual and verbal portraiture and definitions of cultural identity can be viewed and interpreted.

---

20 Lichtenstein, 'Making up Representation: the Risks of Femininity', 81.
21 Festa, 'Cosmetic Differences: The Changing Faces of England and France', 26. © 2005 American Society for Eighteenth-Century Studies. Reprinted with permission of Johns Hopkins University Press.

SELECTED BIBLIOGRAPHY

I list here only the writings that have been of use in the making of this book. This bibliography is not intended to represent a complete record of all of the works I have consulted. It indicates the range of reading upon which I have formed my ideas about visuality's particular inherence in British women's novels published between 1778 and 1815 and is intended to serve as a convenient guide for those wishing to pursue related research.

Adams, W. H. Davenport. *Women of Fashion and Representative Women in Letters and Society*. London: Tinsley Brothers, 1878.
Addison, Joseph. 'On the Pleasures of the Imagination'. *Spectator*, no. 416 (27 June 1712): 290–93.
———. *Spectator*, no. 29 (3 April 1711).
———. *Spectator*, no. 405 (14 June 1712).
———. *Spectator*, no. 421 (3 July 1712).
Agius, Pauline. *Ackermann's Regency Furniture and Interiors*. Ramsbury: Crowood Press, 1984.
Aikin, John, and Anna Laetitia Barbauld. *Miscellaneous Pieces, in Prose*. London: J. Johnson, 1773.
Allen, Emily. 'Staging Identity: Frances Burney's Allegory of Genre'. *Eighteenth-Century Studies* 31, no. 4, The Mind/Body Problem (Summer 1998): 433–51.
Alliston, April. *Virtue's Faults: Correspondences in Eighteenth-Century British and French Women's Fiction*. Stanford, CA: Stanford University Press, 1996.
Altieri, Joanne. 'Style and Purpose in Maria Edgeworth's Fiction'. *Nineteenth-Century Fiction* 23, no. 3 (December 1968): 265–78.
Anon. 'Art V. *Northanger Abbey* and *Persuasion*'. *British Critic*, 2nd series, 9 (March 1818): 293–301.
———. *British Critic*, 4 (August 1794).
———. *The Ear-wig; or an Old Woman's Remarks on the Present Exhibition [...] of the Royal Academy*. London: [n.p.], 1781.
———. *Essay on Consciousness*. London: [n.p.], 1728.
———. *Gentleman's Magazine*, 59 (August 1789).
———. *Gentleman's Magazine*, 64 (September 1794).
———. *The Ladies' Monthly Museum or, Polite Repository of Amusement and Instruction*. London: [n.p.], 1819.
———. *The Language of Flowers*. Philadelphia: Carey, Lea & Blanchard, 1835.
———. *The Mirror of Graces or The English Lady's Costume*. London: B. Crosby, 1811.
———. *Monthly Magazine* 47, no. 1 (May 1819).
———. *Monthly Review*, 37 (April 1802).
———. *Morning Herald* (19 May 1781).
———. *The New Guide to Matrimony*. London: T. Hughes, 1809.
———. *Weekly Register* (6 February 1731).

———. *The Whole Duty of Woman or A Guide to the Female Sex*. Glasgow: W. M. Borthwick, 1809.
———. 'Women's Faces'. *Once a Week* (26 December 1868): 530–31.
Appleton, Jay. *The Experience of the Landscape*. New York: John Wiley, 1975.
Armstrong, Isobel. *Victorian Glassworlds: Glass Culture and the Imagination, 1830–1880*. Oxford: Oxford University Press, 2008.
Armstrong, Nancy. *Desire and Domestic Fiction: A Political History of the Novel*. New York and Oxford: Oxford University Press, 1987.
Arnaud, Pierre. *Ann Radcliffe et le fantastique*. Paris: Aubier Montaigne, 1976.
Assmann, Aleida. *Cultural Memory and Western Civilisation: Functions, Media, Archives*. Cambridge: Cambridge University Press, 2011.
Austen, Jane. *Emma*. Edited by Richard Cronin and Dorothy McMillan. Cambridge: Cambridge University Press, 2006.
———. *Jane Austen's Letters, New Edition*. Edited by Deirdre Le Faye. Oxford: Oxford University Press, 1995.
———. *Juvenilia*. Edited by Peter Sabor. Cambridge: Cambridge University Press, 2006.
———. *Love and Friendship and Other Early Works*. London: Chatto and Windus, 1922; repr. 1929.
———. *Mansfield Park*. Edited by John Wiltshire. Cambridge: Cambridge University Press, 2006.
———. *Minor Works*. Edited by R. W. Chapman. Oxford: Oxford University Press, 1954; repr. 1963.
———. *Northanger Abbey*. Edited by Barbara M. Benedict and Deirdre Le Faye. Cambridge: Cambridge University Press, 2006.
———. *Persuasion*. Edited by Janet Todd and Antje Blank. Cambridge: Cambridge University Press, 2006.
———. *Pride and Prejudice*. Edited by Pat Rogers. Cambridge: Cambridge University Press, 2006.
———. *Sense and Sensibility*. Edited by Edward Copeland. Cambridge: Cambridge University Press, 2006.
Austin, Linda Marilyn. 'Aesthetic Embarrassment: The Reversion to the Picturesque in Nineteenth-Century English Tourism'. *ELH* 74, no. 3 (Fall 2007): 629–53.
Bakhtin, Mikhail Mikhailovich. *The Dialogic Imagination: Four Essays*. Edited by M. Holquist. Translated by C. Emerson and M. Holquist. Austin: Texas University Press, 1981.
Ballantyne, Andrew. *Architecture, Landscape and Liberty: Richard Payne Knight and the Picturesque*. Cambridge: Cambridge University Press, 1997.
Banfield, Ann. 'The Influence of Place: Jane Austen and the Novel of Social Consciousness'. In *Jane Austen in a Social Context*, edited by David Monaghan, 28–40. Totowa, NJ: Barnes and Noble, 1981.
———. 'The Moral Landscape of Mansfield Park'. *Nineteenth-Century Fiction* 26, no. 1 (June 1971): 1–24.
———. *Unspeakable Sentences*. London and New York: Routledge, 1982.
Barbauld, Anna Laetitia. *Memoir of Mrs Barbauld, Including Letters and Notices of Her Family and Friends*. London: George Bell, 1874.
———. *Selected Poetry and Prose*. Edited by William McCarthy and Elizabeth Kraft. Peterborough, ON: Broadview Press, 2002.
Barchas, Janine. *Matters of Fact in Jane Austen: History Location and Celebrity*. Baltimore: Johns Hopkins University Press, 2012.
Bartsch, Shadi. *Decoding the Ancient Novel: The Reader and the Role of Description in Heliodorus and Achilles Tatius*. Princeton: Princeton University Press, 1989.

Battaglia, Beatrice, and Diego Saglia, eds. *Re-drawing Austen: Picturesque Travels in Austenland*. Napoli: Liguori, 2004.
Beaumont, Sir Harry. *Crito: or, A Dialogue on Beauty*. Dublin: [n.p.], 1752.
Beckett, J. C. *The Anglo-Irish Tradition*. London: Faber & Faber, 1976.
Beckford, William. *Vathek*. Edited by Richard Lonsdale. Oxford: Oxford University Press, 2008.
Benedict, Barbara M. 'Reading Faces: Physiognomy and Epistemology in Late Eighteenth-Century Sentimental Novels'. *Studies in Philology* 92, no. 3 (Summer 1995): 311–28.
Bermingham, Ann. 'The Aesthetics of Ignorance: The Accomplished Woman in the Culture of Connoisseurship'. *Oxford Art Journal* 16, no. 2 (1993): 3–20.
———. *Landscape and Ideology: The English Rustic Tradition, 1740–1860*. London: Thames & Hudson, 1987.
Bertero, Eve, Emmanuelle Lepetit and Andrea Mielle. *Modes du XVIIIème siècle sous Louis XVI et Marie-Antoinette*. Paris: Editions Falbalas, 2009.
Bloom, Lillian D., and Edward A. Bloom. 'Fanny Burney's Novels: The Retreat from Wonder'. *NOVEL: a Forum on Fiction* 12, no. 3 (Spring 1979): 215–35.
Bodenheimer, Rosemarie. 'Looking at the Landscape in Jane Austen'. *Studies in English Literature, 1500–1900* 21, no. 4 (Autumn 1981): 605–23.
Bohls, Elizabeth. *Women Travel Writers and the Language of Aesthetics, 1716–1818*. Cambridge: Cambridge University Press, 1995.
Borzello, Frances. *Seeing Ourselves: Women's Self-Portraits*. New York: Harry N. Abrams, 1998.
Botting, Fred. *Gothic*. London and New York: Routledge, 1996.
———. *Gothic Romanced: Consumption, Gender and Technology in Contemporary Fictions*. London and New York: Routledge, 2008.
Bradney, Jane. 'The Carriage-Drive in Humphry Repton's Landscapes'. *Garden History* 33, no. 1 (Summer 2005): 31–46.
Bray, Joe. '*Belinda, Emma* and the "Likeness" of the Portrait'. *Nineteenth-Century Contexts* 33, no. 1 (February 2011): 1–15.
———. *The Epistolary Novel: Representations of Consciousness*. London: Routledge, 2003.
———. *The Female Reader in the English Novel: From Burney to Austen*. London: Routledge, 2009.
Brennan, Teresa, and Martin Jay, eds. *Vision in Context: Historical and Contemporary Perspectives on Sight*. London: Routledge, 1996.
Brewer, John. *The Pleasures of the Imagination: English Culture in the Eighteenth Century*. Chicago: *University of Chicago Press*, 2000.
Brilliant, Richard. 'Editor's Statement: Portraits: The Limitations of Likeness'. *Art Journal* 46, no. 3 (1987): 171–72.
———. *Portraiture*. London: Reaktion Books Ltd., 1991.
Broadwell, Elizabeth P. 'The Veil Image in Ann Radcliffe's *The Italian*'. *South Atlantic Bulletin* 40, no. 4 (November 1975): 76–87.
Brookes, Gerry H. 'The Didacticism of Edgeworth's *Castle Rackrent*'. *Studies in English Literature, 1500–1900* 17, no. 4, Nineteenth Century (Autumn 1977): 593–605.
Brown, Julia Prewitt. 'The Feminist Depreciation of Austen: A Polemical Reading'. Review of *Jane Austen: Women: Politics and the Novel* by Claudia L. Johnson. *Novel: A Forum on Fiction* 23, no. 3 (Spring 1990): 303–13.
Brown, Martha G., 'Fanny Burney's "Feminism": Gender or Genre?'. In *Fetter'd or Free? British Women Novelists, 1670–1815*, edited by Mary Anne Schofield and Cecilia Macheski, 29–39. Athens: Ohio University Press, 1986.
Burke, Edmund. *A Philosophical Enquiry into the Origin of Our Ideas of the Sublime and the Beautiful*. Edited by Adam Phillips. Oxford: Basil Blackwell, 2008.

———. *Reflections on the Revolution in France*. Edited by Conor Cruise O'Brien. Harmondsworth: Penguin, 1986.
Burney, Frances. *Brief Reflections Relative to the Emigrant French Clergy*. London: [n.p.], 1793; repr. Los Angeles: William Andrews Clark Memorial Library, 1990.
———. *Camilla: or, A Picture of Youth*. Edited by Edward A. Bloom and Lillian D. Bloom. Oxford: Oxford University Press, 1972.
———. *Cecilia: or, Memoirs of an Heiress*. Edited by Margaret Anne Doody and Peter Sabor. New York: Oxford University Press, 1999.
———. *Complete Plays of Frances Burney*. Edited by Peter Sabor, Geoffrey M. Sill and Stewart J. Cooke. 2 vols. London; Pickering; Montreal: McGill-Queen's University Press, 1995.
———. *The Diary and Letters of Madame d'Arblay (1778–1840)*. Edited by Charlotte Barrett. 6 vols. London: Macmillan, 1904.
———. *The Early Diary of Frances Burney, 1768–1778*. Edited by Annie Raine Ellis. 2 vols. London: Bell, 1913.
———. *The Early Journal and Letters of Fanny Burney*. Edited by Lars E. Troide and Stewart J. Cooke. 5 vols. Montreal: McGill-Queen's University Press, 2012.
———. *Evelina: or, The History of a Young Lady's Entrance into the World*. Edited by Stewart J. Cooke. New York: W. W. Norton & Company, 1998.
———. *The Journal and Letters of Fanny Burney (Madame d'Arblay)*. Edited by Joyce Hemlow, with Curtis D. Cecil and Althea Douglas. 12 vols. Oxford: Clarendon Press, 1972–84.
———. *Memoirs of Doctor Burney*. London: Edward Maxon, 1832.
———. *The Wanderer; or, FEMALE DIFFICULTIES*. Edited by Margaret Anne Doody, Robert L. Mack and Peter Sabor. Oxford: Oxford University Press, 1991.
Butler, Harriet Jessie [Edgeworth], and Harold Edgeworth Butler, eds. *The Black Book of Edgeworthstown and other Edgeworth Memories, 1585–1817*. London: Faber & Gwyer, 1927.
Butler, Judith. *Bodies That Matter: On the Discursive Limits of 'Sex'*. London: Routledge, 1993.
Butler, Marilyn. 'Edgeworth, the United Irishmen and "More Intelligent Treason"'. Edited by Chris Fauske and Heidi Kaufman. *An Uncomfortable Authority: Maria Edgeworth and Her Contexts*. Newark: Delaware University Press, 2003.
———. 'Edgeworth's Ireland: History, Popular Culture, and Secret Codes'. *NOVEL: A Forum on Fiction* 34, no. 2, The Romantic-Era Novel (Spring 2001): 267–92.
———. *Jane Austen and the War of Ideas*. Oxford: Clarendon Press, 1987.
———. *Maria Edgeworth: A Literary Biography*. Oxford: Clarendon Press, 1972.
Byrne, Paula. *Jane Austen and the Theatre*. London: Hambledon Continuum, 2007.
Campbell, Gina. 'How to Read Like a Gentleman: Burney's Instructions to Her Critics in *Evelina*'. In Burney, *Evelina: or, The History of a Young Lady's Entrance into the World*, edited by Stewart J. Cooke, 431–53. New York: W. W. Norton, 1998.
Castle, Terry. *The Female Thermometer: Eighteenth-Century Culture and the Invention of the Uncanny*. New York: Oxford University Press, 1995.
———. 'The Spectralization of the Other in *The Mysteries of Udolpho*'. In *The New Eighteenth Century: Theory, Politics, English Literature*, edited by Felicity Nussbaum and Laura Brown, 231–53. New York: Methuen, 1987.
Cecil, David. 'Fanny Burney'. In *Poets and Storytellers*, 77–96. London: Constable, 1949.
———. 'Fanny Burney's Novels'. In *Essays on the Eighteenth Century Presented to David Nichol Smith*, 213–24. Oxford: Oxford University Press, 1945.
Chaplin, Sue. *Law, Sensibility and the Sublime in Eighteenth-Century Women's Fiction*. Aldershot: Ashgate, 2004.

Chard, Chloe. *Pleasure and Guilt on the Grand Tour: Travel Writing and Imaginative Geography 1600–1830*. Manchester: Manchester University Press, 1999.
Chico, Tita. 'The Arts of Beauty: Women's Cosmetics and Pope's Ekphrasis'. *Eighteenth-Century Life* 26, no. 1 (Winter 2002): 1–23.
Chisholm, Kate. *Fanny Burney: Her Life*. London: Vintage, 1998.
[Cicero, Marcus Tullius?]. *Rhetorica Ad. Herennium*. Translated by Harry Caplan. Cambridge, MA: Harvard University Press, 1981.
Clery, Emma. *The Rise of Supernatural Fiction: 1762–1800*. Cambridge: Cambridge University Press, 1995.
———. *Women's Gothic: From Clara Reeve to Mary Shelley*. Devon: Northcote House, 2000.
Cohen, Emily Jane. 'Museums of the Mind: The Gothic and the Art of Memory'. *ELH* 62, no. 4 (Winter 1995): 883–905.
Cohen, Louise D. 'Insight, the Essence of Jane Austen's Artistry'. *Nineteenth-Century Fiction* 8, no. 3 (December 1953): 213–24.
Cohen, Michèle. *Fashioning Masculinity: National Identity and Language in the Eighteenth Century*. London: Routledge, 1996.
Cohen, Murray. *Sensible Words: Linguistic Practice in England, 1640–1785*. Baltimore: Johns Hopkins University Press, 1977.
Cohn, Dorrit. *Transparent Minds: Narrative Modes for Presenting Consciousness in Fiction*. Princeton: Princeton University Press, 1983.
Cole, Jonathan. *About Face*. Cambridge, MA: MIT Press, 1999.
Colvin, Christina and Charles Nelson. ' "Building Castles of Flowers" Maria Edgeworth as Gardener'. *Garden History* 16, no. 1 (Spring 1988): 58–70.
Combe, William. *A Poetical Epistle to Sir Joshua Reynolds*. London: Printed for Fielding and Walker, No. 20, Pater-naster Row, 1777.
Conway, Alison. *Private Interests: Women, Portraiture, and the Visual Culture of the English Novel, 1709–91*. Toronto: Toronto University Press, 2001.
Copley, Stephen, and Peter Garside, eds. *The Politics of the Picturesque: Literature and Aesthetics since 1770*. Cambridge: Cambridge University Press, 2010.
Cottom, Daniel. *The Civilized Imagination: A Study of Ann Radcliffe, Jane Austen, and Sir Walter Scott*. Cambridge: Cambridge University Press, 1985.
Cramer, Charles A., 'Alexander Cozens's New Method: The Blot and General Nature'. *Art Bulletin* 79, no. 1 (March 1997): 112–29.
Crary, Jonathan. *Suspensions of Perception: Attention, Spectacle, and Modern Culture*. Cambridge, MA: MIT Press, 2001.
———. *Techniques of the Observer: On Vision and Modernity in the 19th Century*. Cambridge, MA: MIT Press, 1992.
Craven, Elizabeth. *The Miniature Picture*. London: G. Riley, 1781.
Croker, John Wilson. 'Article VIII: "Miss Edgeworth's Tales of Fashionable Life" ', *Quarterly Review*, 7 (1812), 330.
———. 'Review of *The Wanderer* by Frances Burney'. *Quarterly Review* 11 (April 1814): 123.
Croker, Temple H., Thomas Williams and Samuel Clarke. *The Complete Dictionary of Arts and Sciences*. 2 vols. London: [n.p.], 1765.
Crump, Justine, ed. *A Known Scribbler: Frances Burney on Literary Life*. Peterborough: Broadview Press, 2002.
Cunnington, C. Willett, and Phillis Cunnington. *Handbook of English Costume in the Eighteenth Century*. London: Faber & Faber, 1972.

Cutting, Rose Marie. 'Defiant Women: The Growth of Feminism in Fanny Burney's Novels'. *Studies in English Literature, 1500–1900* 17, no. 3, Restoration and Eighteenth Century (Summer 1977): 519–30.

Cutting-Gray, Joanne. *Woman as 'Nobody' and the Novels of Fanny Burney*. Gainesville: University Press of Florida, 1992.

Damoff, Sharon Long. 'The Unaverted Eye: Dangerous Charity in Fanny Burney's *Evelina* and *The Wanderer*'. *Studies in Eighteenth-Century Culture* 26 (1997): 231–46.

Darby, Barbara. *Frances Burney, Dramatist*. Lexington: University Press of Kentucky, 1997.

de Bay, Philip and James Boulton. *Garden Mania: The Ardent Gardener's Compendium of Design and Decoration*. New York: Clarkson Potter, 2000.

de Bolla, Peter. 'The Visibility of Visuality'. In *Vision in Context*, edited by Teresa Brennan and Martin Jay, 63–82. Abingdon: Routledge, 1996.

Deleuze, Gilles. *Foucault*. Translated by Seán Hand. London: Athlone Press, 1988.

Denvir, Bernard. *The Eighteenth Century: Art, Design and Society, 1689–1789*. London: Longman, 1983.

Despotopoulou, Anna. 'Fanny's Gaze and the Construction of Feminine Space in *Mansfield Park*'. *Modern Language Review* 99, no. 3 (July 2004): 569–83.

Deutscher, Guy. *Through the Language Glass: Why the World Looks Different in Other Languages*. London: Arrow Books, 2011.

Devlin, D. D. *Jane Austen and Education*. London and Basingstoke: Macmillan, 1975.

Diderot, Denis. *Diderot on Art*, Vol. 2: *The Salon of 1767*. Translated by John Goodman. New Haven: Yale University Press, 1995.

Dobbin, Marjorie W. 'The Novel, Women's Awareness, and Fanny Burney'. *English Language Notes* 22, no. 3 (1985): 42–52.

Doody, Margaret Anne. *Frances Burney: The Life in the Works*. New Brunswick, NJ: Rutgers University Press, 1988.

Douthwaite, J. 'Experimental Child-rearing after Rousseau: Maria Edgeworth, *Practical Education* and *Belinda*'. *Irish Journal of Feminist Studies* 2, no. 2 (1997): 35–56.

Dryden, John. *Of Dramatic Poesy and Other Essays*. Edited by George Watson. 2 vols. London: John Dent, 1962.

Duckworth, Alistair. *The Improvement of the Estate: A Study of Jane Austen's Novels*. Baltimore: Johns Hopkins University Press, 1971.

———. 'Mansfield Park and Estate Improvements: Jane Austen's Grounds of Being'. *Nineteenth-Century Fiction* 26, no. 1 (June 1971): 25–48.

Duffy, Joseph M. 'Emma: The Awakening from Innocence'. *ELH* 21, no. 1 (March 1954): 39–53.

Duquette, Natasha, ed. *Jane Austen and the Arts: Elegance, Propriety, Harmony*. Bethlehem, PA: Lehigh University Press, 2015.

Eagles, Robin. *Francophilia in English Society, 1748–1815*. Houndmills: Palgrave Macmillan, 2000.

Eagleton, Terry. *Rape of Clarissa: Writing, Sexuality and Class Struggle in Samuel Richardson*. Minneapolis: University of Minnesota Press, 1982.

Eaves, T. C. Duncan. 'Edward Burney's Illustrations to *Evelina*'. *PMLA* 62, no. 4 (December 1947): 995–99.

Edgeworth, Maria. *Letters for Literary Ladies*. Edited by Claire Connolly. London: Everyman, 1993.

———. *The Life and Letters of Maria Edgeworth*. 2 vols. Middlesex: The Echo Library, 2007.

———. *Maria Edgeworth: Chosen Letters*. Edited by F. V. Barry. London: Jonathan Cape, 1931.

———. *Maria Edgeworth in France and Switzerland: Selections from the Edgeworth Family Letters*. Edited by Christina Colvin. Oxford: Clarendon Press, 1971.

———. *Maria Edgeworth: Letters from England 1813–1844*. Edited by Christina Colvin. Oxford: Clarendon Press, 1971.

———. *The Novels and Selected Works of Maria Edgeworth*. Edited by Marilyn Butler and others. 12 vols. London: Pickering & Chatto, 1999–2003.

———. *Women, Education and Literature: The Papers of Maria Edgeworth, 1786–1849*. Marlborough, Wiltshire: Adam Matthew, 1995.

Edgeworth, Richard Lovell. *Memoirs of Richard Lovell Edgeworth*. Edited by Maria Edgeworth. 2 vols. Shannon: Irish University Press, 1969.

Edwards, John. *Multilingualism*. London: Routledge, 1994.

Eger, Elizabeth. *Women, Writing and the Public Sphere, 1700–1830*. Cambridge: Cambridge University Press, 2001.

Eger, Elizabeth, and Lucy Peltz. *Brilliant Women: 18th-Century Bluestockings*. New Haven: Yale University Press, 2008.

Elliott, Kamilla. *Portraiture and British Gothic Fiction: The Rise of Picture Identification, 1764–1835*. Baltimore: Johns Hopkins University Press, 2012.

Ellis, Kate Ferguson. *The Contested Castle: Gothic Novels and the Subversion of Domestic Ideology*. Urbana and Chicago: University of Illinois Press, 1987.

Epstein, Julia. *The Iron Pen: Frances Burney and the Politics of Women's Writing*. Madison: University of Wisconsin Press, 1989.

Fahnestock, Jeanne. 'The Heroine of Irregular Features: Physiognomy and Conventions of Heroine Description'. *Victorian Studies* 24, no. 3 (Spring 1981): 325–50.

Fauske, Chris, and Heidi Kaufman. *Jane Austen and the War of Ideas*. Oxford: Clarendon Press, 1987.

———. *Maria Edgeworth: A Literary Biography*. Oxford: Clarendon Press, 1972.

———. *An Uncomfortable Authority: Maria Edgeworth and Her Contexts*. Newark: Delaware University Press, 2003.

Fay, Elizabeth A. *Fashioning Faces: The Portraitive Mode in British Romanticism*. Durham, NH: University of New Hampshire Press, 2010.

Festa, Lynn. 'Cosmetic Differences: The Changing Faces of England and France'. *Studies in Eighteenth-Century Culture* 34 (2005): 25–54.

Fineman, Joel. 'The History of the Anecdote: Fiction and Fiction'. In *The New Historicism*, edited by H. Aram Veeser, 49–76. London: Routledge, 1989.

Fludernik, Monika. *The Fictions of Language and the Languages of Fiction: The Linguistic Representation of Speech and Consciousness*. London and New York: Routledge, 1993.

Fordyce, James. *Sermons to Young Women*. London: J. Williams, 1767.

Foster, Mandy and Danielle Perry. *Regency Era Fashion Plates, 1800–1819*. Charleston, SC: Timely Tresses, 2008.

Fox, Charles. *Locke and the Scriblerians: Identity and Consciousness in Early Eighteenth-Century Britain*. Berkeley and London: University of California Press, 1988.

Freud, Sigmund. *Beyond the Pleasure Principle*. New York: W. W. Norton & Company, 1990.

———. *The Uncanny*. Translated by David McLintock. New York: Penguin, 2003.

Fritzer, Penelope Joan. *Jane Austen and Eighteenth-Century Courtesy Books*. Westport, CT: Greenwood Press, 1997.

Galperin, William H. *The Historical Austen*. Philadelphia: University of Pennsylvania Press, 2003.

———. *The Return of the Visible in British Romanticism*. Baltimore and London: Johns Hopkins University Press, 1993.

Gamer, Michael. 'Maria Edgeworth and the Romance of Real Life'. *NOVEL: A Forum on Fiction* 34, no. 2, The Romantic-Era Novel (Spring 2001): 232–66.

Garstang, Devid, ed. *The British Face: A View of Portraiture 1625–1850*. London: P & D Colnaghi, 1986.

Genette, Gerard. *Narrative Discourse Revisited*. Translated by J. E. Lewin. Ithaca and London: Cornell University Press, 1988.

Genlis, Stéphanie Félicité (comtesse de). *Adèle et Théodore, ou lettres sur l'éducation*. Paris: M. Lambert & F. J. Baudouin, 1782.

Gilbert, Sandra M., and Susan Gubar. *The Madwoman in the Attic*. New Haven: Yale University Press, 1984.

Gilpin, William. *Observations on the River Wye, and Several Parts of South Wales, &c. Relative Chiefly to Picturesque Beauty; Made in the Summer of the Year 1770*. London: Cadell and Davies, 1800.

———. *Observations on the Western Parts of England Relative Chiefly to Picturesque Beauty*. London: Cadell and Davies, 1798.

Girouard, Mark. *Life in the English Country House: A Social and Architectural History*. New Haven: Yale University Press, 1993.

Gisborne, Thomas. *An Enquiry into the Duties of the Female Sex*. London: T. Cadell, 1797.

Gombrich, E. H. *Art and Illusion: A Study in the Psychology of Pictorial Representation*. New York: Phaidon, 2002.

Goudar, Ange. *The Chinese Spy; Or, Emissary from the Court of Pekin*. London: S. Bladon, 1765.

Graham, Kenneth. 'Cinderella or Bluebeard: The Double Plot of *Evelina*'. In Burney, *Evelina: or, The History of a Young Lady's Entrance into the World*, edited by Stewart J. Cooke, 400–11. New York: W. W. Norton & Company, 1998.

Green, Katherine Sobba. *The Courtship Novel 1740–1820: A Feminized Genre*. Lexington: University Press of Kentucky, 1991.

Gregory, John. *A Father's Legacy to his Daughters* (1774). In *Eighteenth-Century Woman: An Anthology*, edited by Bridget Hill, 16–17. London: Allen & Unwin, 1984.

Grootenboer, Hanneke. 'Treasuring the Gaze: Miniature Portraits and the Intimacy of Vision'. *Art Bulletin* (September 2006): 1–17.

Gwilliam, Tassie. 'Cosmetic Poetics: Coloring Faces in the Eighteenth Century'. In *Body and Text in the Eighteenth Century*, edited by Veronica Kelly and Dorothea von Mücke, 144–59. Stanford: Stanford University Press, 1994.

Haggerty, George E. 'Fact and Fancy in the Gothic Novel'. *Nineteenth-Century Fiction* 39, no. 4 (March 1985): 379–91.

Halsey, Katie. *Jane Austen and Her Readers: 1786–1945*. London: Anthem Press, 2012.

Handler, Richard, and Daniel Segal. *Jane Austen and the Fiction of Culture*. Tucson: University of Arizona Press, 1990.

Harden, Elizabeth. 'Transparent Thady'. In Cóilín Owens, *Family Chronicles: Maria Edgeworth's* Castle Rackrent, 91–92. Dublin: Wolfhound, 1987.

Hardy, John. *Jane Austen's Heroines: Intimacy in Human Relationships*. London: Routledge & Kegan Paul, 1984.

Harman, Claire. *Fanny Burney: A Biography*. London: Flamingo, 2001.

———. *Jane's Fame: How Jane Conquered the World*. Edinburgh: Cannongate Books, 2009.

Harris, John. *The Artist and the Country House: from the Fifteenth Century to the Present Day*. London: Sotheby's, 1995.

Hart, Francis R. 'The Spaces of Privacy: Jane Austen'. *Nineteenth-Century Fiction* 30, no. 3, Jane Austen, 1775–1975 (December 1975): 305–33.

Hartley, Lucy. *Physiognomy and the Meaning of Expression in Nineteenth-Century Culture*. Cambridge: Cambridge University Press, 2001.

Hawthorne, Mark D. 'Maria Edgeworth's Unpleasant Lesson: The Shaping of Character'. *Studies: An Irish Quarterly Review* 64, no. 254 (Summer 1975): 167–77.
Hayden, Ruth. *Mrs Delany: Her Life and Her Flowers*. London: British Museum Press, 2000.
Hazlitt, William. *The Collected Works of William Hazlitt*. Edited by A. R. Waller. London: Dent, 1903.
Heffernan, James A. *Museum of Words: The Poetics of Ekphrasis from Homer to Ashbery*. Chicago and London: University of Chicago Press, 1993.
Helm, W. H. *Jane Austen and Her Country-House Comedy*. London: Eveleigh Nash, 1909.
Hemlow, Joyce. 'The Composition of Evelina'. In Burney, *Evelina: or, The History of a Young Lady's Entrance into the World*, edited by Stewart J. Cooke, 372–94. New York: W. W. Norton, 1998.
———. 'Fanny Burney and the Courtesy Books'. *PMLA* 65, no. 5 (September 1950): 732–61.
———. *The History of Fanny Burney*. Oxford: Clarendon Press, 1958.
Henderson, Andrea K. 'Burney's *The Wanderer* and Early-Nineteenth-Century Commodity Fetishism'. *Nineteenth-Century Literature* 57, no. 1 (June 2002): 1–30.
———. *Romantic Identities: Varieties of Subjectivity, 1774–1830*. Cambridge: Cambridge University Press, 1996.
Hill, Constance. *Juniper Hall: A Rendezvous of Certain Illustrious Personages during the French Revolution, including Alexandre D'Arblay and Fanny Burney*. London and New York: John Lane, The Bodley Head, 1904.
Hogan, Charles Beecher. 'Jane Austen and Her Early Public'. *Review of English Studies* 1, no. 1 (January 1950): 39–54.
Hogarth, William. *Analysis of Beauty*. Edited by Ronald Paulson. New Haven: Yale University Press, 1997.
Hopkins, Brooke. 'Keats and the Uncanny: "This Living Hand"'. *Kenyon Review* 11, no. 4 (Autumn 1989): 28–40.
Howells, William Dean. *Heroine of Irregular Features*. 2 vols. London and New York: Harper Bros., 1901.
Hudson, Glenda A. 'Consolidated Communities: Masculine and Feminine Values in Jane Austen's Fiction'. In *Jane Austen and Discourses of Feminism*, edited by Devoney Looser, 101–14. New York: St Martin's Press, 1995.
———. *Sibling Love and Incest in Jane Austen's Fiction*. Basingstoke: Palgrave Macmillan, 1999.
Hume, David. *A Treatise of Human Nature: Being an Attempt to Introduce the Experimental Method of Reasoning into Moral Subjects*. Edited by Ernest C. Mossner. London: Penguin, 1985.
Hume, Robert D. 'A Revaluation of the Gothic Novel'. *PMLA* 84, no. 2 (March 1969): 282–90.
Hunt, Leigh. *New Monthly Magazine and Literary Journal* 14, pt. 2 (1825): 72.
Hyde, Melissa. 'The "Makeup" of the Marquise: Boucher's Portrait of Pompadour at Her Toilette'. *Art Bulletin* 82, no. 3 (2000): 453–75.
Ingold, Tim. *The Perception of the Environment: Essays on Livelihood, Dwelling and Skill*. London: Routledge, 2000.
Irigary, Luce. *Speculum of the Other Woman*. Translated by Gillian C. Gill. Ithaca, NY: Cornell University Press, 1985.
Jacobs, Eva, W. H. Barber, Jean H. Bloch and others, eds., *Woman and Society in Eighteenth-Century France*. London: Routledge, 1990.
Jenkyns, Richard. *A Fine Brush on Ivory: An Appreciation of Jane Austen*. Oxford: Oxford University Press, 2004.
Johnson, Claudia L. *Equivocal Beings: Politics, Gender, and Sentimentality in the 1790s – Wollstonecraft, Radcliffe, Burney, Austen*. Chicago: University of Chicago Press, 1995.

———. *Jane Austen: Women, Politics and the Novel*. Chicago: University of Chicago Press, 1990.
Johnston, Elizabeth. 'The Epistemology of the Gaze in Popular Discourse: A Re-Vision'. *The Eighteenth Century* 50, no. 4 (Winter 2009): 385–91.
Jones, Hazel. *Jane Austen and Marriage*. London: Continuum Books, 2009.
Jones, Vivien. ' "The Coquetry of Nature": Politics and the Picturesque in Women's Fiction'. In *The Politics of the Picturesque: Literature, Landscape and Aesthetics*, edited by Stephen Copley and Peter Garside, 120–44. Cambridge: Cambridge University Press, 1994.
Jones, Wendy S. 'Emma, Gender, and the Mind-Brain'. *ELH* 75, no. 2 (Summer 2008): 315–43.
Jonson, Ben. *The Complete Poems of Ben Jonson*. Harmondsworth: Penguin, 1975.
Kearns, Katherine. *Nineteenth-Century Literary Realism: Through the Looking-Glass*. Cambridge and New York: Cambridge University Press, 1996.
Keats, John. *Letters of John Keats*. Edited by Frederick Page. London: Oxford University Press, 1954.
Kelly, Gary, ed. *Bluestocking Feminism: Writings of the Bluestocking Circle, 1738–1785*. 6 vols. London: Pickering & Chatto, 1999.
Kiely, Robert. *The Romantic Novel in England*. Cambridge, MA: Harvard University Press, 1972.
Kilgour, Maggie. *The Rise of the Gothic Novel*. London and New York: Routledge, 1994.
Kirkham, Margaret. *Jane Austen, Feminism and Fiction*. Totowa, NJ: Princeton University Press, 2000.
Klein, Lawrence E. 'Gender and the Public/Private Divide in the Eighteenth Century: Some Questions about Evidence and Analytic Procedure'. *Eighteenth-Century Studies* 29, no. 1 (Fall 1995): 97–109.
Knight, Richard Payne. *An Analytical Inquiry into the Principles of Taste*. London: [n.p.], 1805.
Knox-Shaw, Peter. *Jane Austen and the Enlightenment*. Cambridge: Cambridge University Press, 2004.
Kowaleski-Wallace, Elizabeth. *Their Father's Daughters: Hannah More, Maria Edgeworth and Patriarchal Complicity*. New York: Oxford University Press, 1991.
Krämer, Sybille. 'The "Eye of the Mind" and the "Eye of the Body": Descartes and Leibniz on Truth, Mathematics, and Visuality'. In *Sensory Perception*, edited by F. G. Barth, 369–82. Vienna: Springer-Verlag, 2012.
Labbe, Jacqueline M. *Romantic Visualities: Landscape, Gender and Romanticism*. Houndmills: Palgrave Macmillan, 1998.
Lamont, Claire. 'Domestic Architecture'. In *Jane Austen in Context*, edited by Janet Todd, 225–32. Cambridge: Cambridge University Press, 2005.
Landes, Joan B. *Women and the Public Sphere in the Age of the French Revolution*. London: Cornell University Press, 1988.
Lascelles, Mary. *Jane Austen and Her Art*. Oxford: Oxford University Press, 1939.
Lavater, Johann Casper. *Essays on Physiognomy: For the Promotion of the Knowledge and the Love of Mankind. Illustrated by more than eight hundred engravings accurately copied; and some duplicates added from originals. Executed by, or under the inspection of, Thomas Holloway*. Translated from the French by Thomas Holcroft. 3 vols. 5 bks. London: John Murray, 1789–98.
Lewis, Jayne Elizabeth. ' "No Colour of Language": Radcliffe's Aesthetic Unbound'. *Eighteenth-Century Studies* 39, no. 3 (Spring 2006): 377–90.
Lichtenstein, Jacqueline. 'Making Up Representation: The Risks of Femininity'. *Representation* 20, Special Issue: Misandry and Misanthropy (Autumn 1987): 77–87.
Litvak, Joseph. 'Reading Characters: Self, Society, and Text in *Emma*'. *PMLA* 100, no. 5 (October 1985): 763–73.

Locke, John. *An Essay Concerning Human Understanding*. Edited by Roger Woolhouse. London: Penguin, 1997.
Lodge, David. *Language of Fiction: Essays in Criticism and Verbal Analysis of the English Novel*. London: Routledge and Kegan Paul, 1966.
Lukács, Georg. *The Theory of the Novel*. Translated by A. Bostock. London: Merlin Press, 1978.
Lynch, Deidre Shauna. *The Economy of Character: Novels, Market Culture and the Business of Inner Meaning*. Chicago: University of Chicago Press, 1998.
Lyons, J. O. *The Invention of the Self: The Hinge of Consciousness in the Eighteenth Century*. Carbondale and Edwardsville: Southern Illinois University Press, 1978.
MacDonald, Fraser. 'Visuality'. In *International Encyclopedia of Human Geography*, edited by Rob Kitchin and Nigel Thrift, 151–56. London: Elsevier Books, 2009.
MacFadyen, Heather. 'Lady Delacour's Library: Maria Edgeworth's *Belinda* and Fashionable Reading'. *Nineteenth-Century Literature* 48, no. 4 (March 1994): 423–39.
Maguire, W. A. '*Castle Nugent* and *Castle Rackrent*: Fact and Fiction in Maria Edgeworth'. *Eighteenth-Century Ireland/Iris an dá chultúr*, 11 (1996): 146–59.
Maillet, Arnaud. *Le Miroir noir: Enquête sur le côté obscure du reflet*. Paris: Editions Kargo, 2005.
Malins, Edward. *English Landscaping and Literature, 1660–1840*. Oxford: Oxford University Press, 1966.
Mandal, Anthony. *Jane Austen and the Popular Novel*. Houndmills: Palgrave Macmillan, 2007.
Manly, Susan. *Language, Custom and Nation in the 1790s*. London: Ashgate, 2007.
Marmontel, J. F. 'Eléments de Littérature'. In *Œuvres Complètes*, 12: 524–25. Paris, 1818.
Marsh, Honoria D., and Peggy Hickman. *Shades from Jane Austen*. London: Parry Jackman, 1975.
McIntyre, Clara Frances. *Ann Radcliffe in Relation to Her Time*. New Haven: Yale University Press, 1920.
McKechnie, Sue. *British Silhouette Artists and Their Work: 1760–1860*. London: Sotheby's, 1978.
McKendrick, Neil, John Brewer and J. H. Plumb. *The Birth of a Consumer Society: The Commercialisation of Eighteenth-Century England*. London: Europa, 1982.
McMahon, A. Philip. 'Francis Bacon's Essay Of Beauty'. *PMLA* 60, no. 3 (September 1945): 716–59.
McMaster, Juliet. 'The Silent Angel: Impediments to Female Expression in Frances Burney's Novels'. *Studies in the Novel* 21, no. 3 (1989): 235–52.
McMillan, Dorothy. 'The Secrets of Ann Radcliffe's English Travels'. In *Romantic Geographies: Discourses of Travel, 1775–1844*, edited by Amanda Gilroy, 51–67. Manchester: Manchester University Press, 2000.
McPherson, Heather. 'Picture Tragedy: Mrs Siddons as the Tragic Muse Revisited'. *Eighteenth-Century Studies* 33, no. 3 (2000): 401–30.
McWhorter Harden, O. Elizabeth. *Maria Edgeworth's Art of Prose Fiction*. The Hague: Mouton, 1971.
Michals, Teresa. 'Commerce and Character in Maria Edgeworth'. *Nineteenth-Century Literature* 49, no. 1 (June 1994): 1–20.
Michasiw, Kim Ian. 'The Nine Revisionist Theses on the Picturesque'. *Representations*, no. 38 (Spring 1992): 76–100.
Miles, Robert. *Ann Radcliffe: The Great Enchantress*. Manchester: Manchester University Press, 1995.
———. *Gothic Writing 1750–1820: A Genealogy*. Manchester: Manchester University Press, 2002.
Miller, Christopher R. 'Jane Austen's Aesthetics and Ethics of Surprise'. *Narrative* 13, no. 3 (October 2005): 238–60.

Miller, Nancy K. *The Heroine's Text: Readings in the French and English Novel, 1722–1782.* New York: Columbia University Press, 1880.

———. 'Men's Reading, Women's Writing: Gender and the Rise of the Novel'. *Yale French Studies* 75, The Politics of Tradition: Placing Women in French Literature (1988): 40–55.

Mitchell, W. J. T. *Picture Theory.* Chicago: University of Chicago Press, 1994.

Molière. *La Critique de l'École des Femmes.* Paris: Librairie des Bibliophiles, 1890.

Monk, Samuel H. *The Sublime: A Study of Critical Theories in XVIII-Century England.* Ann Arbor: University of Michigan Press, 1960.

Moore, Edward. *Fables for the Female Sex.* 4th ed. London: T. Davies, 1771.

More, Hannah. *Strictures on Female Education.* Oxford: Woodstock Press, 1995.

Morgan, Lady [Sydney Owenson]. *The Wild Irish Girl: A National Tale.* Edited by Claire Connolly and Stephen Copley. London: Pickering & Chatto, 2000.

Morris, David B. 'Gothic Sublimity'. *New Literary History* 16, no. 2, The Sublime and the Beautiful: Reconsiderations (Winter 1985): 299–319.

Morris, Ivor. *The Interplay of Character.* London: Athlone Press, 1999.

Mount, Harry. 'The Monkey with the Magnifying Glass: Constructions of the Connoisseur in Eighteenth-Century Britain'. *Oxford Art Journal* 29, no. 2 (June 2006): 167–84.

Mullan, John. *Sentiment and Sociability: The Language of Feeling in the Eighteenth Century.* Oxford: Clarendon Press, 1988.

Mulvey, Laura. *Visual and Other Pleasures.* Bloomington: Indiana University Press, 1989.

———. 'Visual Pleasure and Narrative Cinema'. *Screen* 16, no. 3 (Autumn 1975): 6–18.

Murray, Douglas. 'Spectatorship in Mansfield Park: Looking and Overlooking'. *Nineteenth-Century Literature* 52, no. 1 (June 1997): 1–26.

Murray, E. B. *Ann Radcliffe.* New York: Twayne, 1972.

Myers, Mitzi. '"Completing the Union": Critical *Ennui*, the Politics of Narrative, and the Reformation of Irish Cultural Identity'. *Prose Studies: History, Theory, Criticism* 18 (1995): 41–77.

———. 'Shot from Canons; or, Maria Edgeworth and the Cultural Production and Consumption of the Late Eighteenth-Century Woman Writer'. In *The Consumption of Culture, 1600–1800: Image, Object, Text*, edited by Ann Bermingham and John Brewer, 193–214. London: Routledge, 1995.

Myers, Sylvia H. 'Womanhood in Jane Austen's Novels'. *A Forum on Fiction* 3, no. 3 (Spring 1970): 225–32.

Nardin, Jane. *Those Elegant Decorums: The Concept of Propriety in Jane Austen's Novels.* Albany: SUNY Press, 1973.

Nattes, John. *Sydney Hotel: The Garden Façade* (c. 1805), Holburne Museum of Art, Bath (UK), no. A296.

Nechtman, Tillmann W. *Nabobs: Empire and Identity in Eighteenth-Century Britain.* Cambridge: Cambridge University Press, 2010.

Newcomer, James. 'Maria Edgeworth and the Critics'. *College English* 26, no. 3 (December 1964): 214–18.

Newton, Judith. '*Evelina*: Or, the History of a Young Lady's Entrance into the Marriage Market'. *Modern Language Studies* 6 (1976): 48–56.

———. 'Power and the Ideology of Woman's Sphere'. In *Jane Austen and Discourses of Feminism*, edited by Devoney Looser, 880–95. New York: Palgrave Macmillan, 1995.

Norton, Rictor. *Mistress of Udolpho: The Life of Ann Radcliffe.* London: Leicester University Press, 1999.

Novak, Maximillian E. 'Gothic Fiction and the Grotesque'. *NOVEL: A Forum on Fiction* 13, no. 1 (Autumn 1979): 50–67.

Ó Gallchoir, Clíona. *Maria Edgeworth: Women, Enlightenment and Nation*. Dublin: University College Dublin Press, 2005.
O'Neill, Marie. 'Maria Edgeworth Anglo-Irish Writer, 1768–1849. *Dublin Historical Record* 55, no. 2 (Autumn 2002): 196–207.
Oliphant, Margaret. 'Miss Austen and Miss Mitford'. *Blackwood's Edinburgh Magazine* 107 (March 1870): 290–313.
Outram, Dorinda. *The Body and the French Revolution: Sex, Class and Political Culture*. London: Yale University Press, 1989.
Palmer, Caroline. 'Brazen Cheek: Face-Painters in Late Eighteenth-Century England'. *Oxford Art Journal* 31, no. 2. (June 2008): 195–213.
Parke, Catherine. 'Vision and Revision: A Model for Reading the Eighteenth-Century Novel of Education'. *Eighteenth-Century Studies* 16, no. 2 (Winter 1982–83): 162–74.
Pascal, Roy. *The Dual Voice*. Manchester: Manchester University Press, 1977.
Pearl, Sharrona. *About Faces: Physiognomy in Nineteenth-Century Britain*. Cambridge, MA: Harvard University Press, 2010.
Penny, Nicholas. 'An Ambitious Man: The Career and Achievement of Sir Joshua Reynolds'. In *Reynolds*, edited by Nicholas Penny, 17–42. London: Royal Academy of Arts, 1986.
Pevsner, Nikolaus. 'The Architectural Setting of Jane Austen's Novels'. *Journal of the Warburg and Courtauld Institutes* 31 (1968): 404–22.
Picciotto, Joanna. 'Optical Instruments and the Eighteenth-Century Observer'. *Studies in Eighteenth-Century Culture* 29 (2000): 123–53.
Pikoulis, John. 'Jane Austen: The Figure in the Carpet'. *Nineteenth-Century Fiction* 27, no. 1 (June 1972): 38–60.
Pilcher, Donald. *The Regency Style, 1800 to 1830*. London: B. T. Batsford, 1946.
Pointon, Marcia R. *Strategies for Showing: Woman, Possession, and Representation in English Visual Culture 1665–1800*. Oxford: Oxford University Press, 1997.
Poovey, Mary. *The Proper Lady and the Woman Writer: Ideology as Style in the Works of Mary Wollstonecraft, Mary Shelley, and Jane Austen*. Chicago: University of Chicago Press, 1985.
Pope, Alexander. 'Epistle to a Lady'. In *Alexander Pope: Selected Poems*, edited by Pat Rogers, 106–13. Oxford: Oxford University Press, 1998.
———. *The Major Works; including* The Rape of the Lock *and* The Dunciad. Edited by Pat Rogers. Oxford: Oxford University Press, 2008.
Porterfield, William. *A Treatise on the Eye, the Manner and Phenomena of Vision*. Edinburgh: Hamilton and Balfour, 1759.
Price, Martin. 'Manners, Morals, and Jane Austen'. *Nineteenth-Century Fiction* 30, no. 3, Jane Austen 1775–1975 (December 1975): 261–80.
Punter, David. *Gothic Pathologies: The Text, the Body and the Law*. London: Macmillan; New York: St Martin's Press, 1998.
———. *The Literature of Terror: A History*. London and New York: Longman, 1980.
Radcliffe, Ann. *The Italian*. Edited by Frederick Garber. Oxford: Oxford University Press, 1968.
———. *The Mysteries of Udolpho: A Romance*. Edited by Bonamy Dobrée. Oxford: Oxford University Press, 1960.
———. *The Posthumous Works of Ann Radcliffe, comprising Gaston de Blondeville, A Romance; St Alban's Abbey, A Metrical Tale, with Various Poetical Pieces*. 4 vols. London: Henry Colburn, 1833.
———. *The Romance of the Forest*. Edited by Chloe Chard. Oxford: Oxford University Press, 1986.
———. *A Sicilian Romance*. Edited by Alison Milbank. Oxford: Oxford University Press, 1993; repr. 2008.

Raleigh, Sir Walter. *The English Novel*. New York: Charles Scribner's Sons, 1894.
Ray, William. 'Reading Women: Cultural Authority, Gender, and the Novel. The Case of Rousseau'. *Eighteenth-Century Studies* 27, no. 3 (Spring 1994): 421–47.
Reynolds, Frances. *An Enquiry Concerning the Principles of Taste, and of the Origin of Our Ideas of Beauty &c*. London, 1785.
Reynolds, Sir Joshua. *Discourses on Art*. Edited by Robert R. Wark. New Haven and London: Yale University Press, 1975.
Ribeiro, Aileen. 'Some Evidence of the Influence of the Dress of the Seventeenth Century on Costume in Eighteenth-Century Female Portraiture'. *The Burlington Magazine* 119, no. 897 (December 1977): 832, 834–40.
Richardson, Jonathan. *The Works of Jonathan Richardson*. Strawberry Hill: [n.p.], 1792.
Richardson, Samuel. *Clarissa: or, the History of a Young Lady*. Edited by John Butt. London: Dent, 1932.
Richetti, John J. 'Voice and Gender in Eighteenth-Century Fiction: Haywood to Burney'. *Studies in the Novel* 19, no. 3, Women and Early Fiction (Fall 1987): 263–72.
Robbins, Bruce. 'Comparative Cosmopolitanism'. *Social Text* 31, no. 32 (1992): 169–86.
Robson, William. *Grammigraphia*. London: W. Wilson, 1799.
Rogers, Deborah D. *Ann Radcliffe: A Bio-Bibliography*. Westport, CT, and London: Greenwood Press, 1996.
Rosenthal, Angela. 'She's Got the Look! Eighteenth-Century Female Portrait Painters and the Psychology of a Potentially "Dangerous Employment"'. In *Portraiture: Facing the Subject*, edited by Joanna Woodall, 147–66. Manchester and New York, 1997.
Rousseau, Jean-Jacques. *Emile*. Translated by Barbara Foxley. London: J. M. Dent, 1992.
Rovee, Christopher. *Imagining the Gallery: The Social Body of British Romanticism*. Stanford: Stanford University Press, 2006.
Sabor, Peter, and Paul Yachnin, eds. *Shakespeare and the Eighteenth Century*. Aldershot: Ashgate, 2008.
Sacks, Oliver. *Seeing Voices: A Journey into the World of the Deaf*. Berkeley: University of California Press, 1989.
Saint-Pierre, and Jacques-Henri Bernardin. *Paul et Virginie*. Paris: L. Curmer, 1838.
Sales, Roger. *Jane Austen and Representations of Regency England*. London: Routledge, 1996.
Schmitt, Cannon. 'Techniques of Terror, Technologies of Nationality: Ann Radcliffe's *The Italian*'. *ELH* 61, no. 4 (Winter 1994): 853–76.
Sedgwick, Eve Kosofsky. 'The Character in the Veil: Imagery of the Surface in the Gothic Novel'. *PMLA* 96, no. 2 (March 1981): 255–70.
———. *The Coherence of Gothic Conventions*. New York: Arno Press, 1980.
Seeber, Barbara K. *General Consent in Jane Austen: A Study of Dialogism*. Montreal: McGill-Queen's University Press, 2000.
Selwyn, David. *Jane Austen and Leisure*. London: Hambledon Press, 1999.
Sennett, Richard. *The Fall of Public Man*. New York: Alfred A. Knopf, 1977.
Shaftesbury, Earl of (Anthony Ashley Cooper). *Characteristiks of Men, Manners, Opinions, Times*. Cambridge: Cambridge University Press, 1999.
Shannon, Jr., Edgar F. '*Emma*: Character and Construction'. *PMLA* 71, no. 4 (September 1956): 637–50.
Shaw, George, and James Francis Stephens. *General Zoology: or, Systematic Natural History*. London: G. Kearsley, 1800.
Shepherd, Lynn. *Clarissa's Painter: Portraiture, Illustration and Representation in the Novels of Samuel Richardson*. Oxford: Oxford English Monographs, 2009.

Shookman, Ellis, ed. *The Faces of Physiognomy: Interdisciplinary Approaches to Johann Caspar Lavater*. Columbia, SC: Camden House, 1993.
Smith, Adam. *The Theory of Moral Sentiments*. Edited by D. D. Raphael and A. L. Macfie. Oxford: Clarendon Press, 1976.
Smith, LeRoy W. *Jane Austen and the Drama of Woman*. London: Macmillan Press, 1983.
Smith, Mack. *Literary Realism and the Ekphrastic Tradition*. University Park: Pennsylvania State University Press, 2008.
Smith, Nelson C. 'Sense, Sensibility and Ann Radcliffe'. *Studies in English Literature, 1500–1900* 13, no. 4, Nineteenth Century (Autumn 1973): 577–90.
Spacks, Patricia Meyer. 'Evr'y Woman Is at Heart a Rake'. *Eighteenth-Century Studies* 8, no. 1 (Autumn 1974): 27–46.
———. *Imagining a Self: Autobiography and Novel in Eighteenth-Century England*. Cambridge, MA, and London: Harvard University Press, 1976.
Staël, Germaine de. *The Influence of Literature upon Society*. 2 vols. London: H. Colburn, 1812.
Stafford, William. 'The Gender of the Place: Building and Landscape in Women-Authored Texts in England of the 1790s'. *Transactions of the Royal Historical Society* 6, no. 13 (2003), 305–18.
Stalnaker, Joanna. *The Unfinished Enlightenment: Description in the Age of the Encyclopedia*. New York: Cornell University Press, 2010.
Stanhope, Louisa Sidney. *Striking Likenesses; or, The Votaries of Fashion: A Novel*. 4 vols. London: J. F. Hughes, 1808.
Staves, Susan. '*Evelina*; or, Female Difficulties'. *Modern Philology* 73, no. 4, pt. 1 (May 1976): 368–81.
Steegman, John. *The Rule of Taste: From George I to George IV*. London: Macmillan, 1968.
Steele, Valerie. *Paris Fashion: A Cultural History*. London: Berg Publishers, 1998.
Stemmler, Joan K. 'The Physiognomical Portraits of Johann Caspar Lavater'. *Art Bulletin* 75, no. 1 (March 1993): 151–88.
Stokes, Myra. *The Language of Jane Austen*. Houndmills: Macmillan, 1991.
Straub, Kristina. *Divided Fictions: Fanny Burney and feminine strategy*. Lexington: University Press of Kentucky, 1987.
Sutherland, Kathryn. *Jane Austen's Textual Lives: From Aeschylus to Bollywood*. Oxford: Oxford University Press, 2005.
Tandon, Bharat. *Jane Austen and the Morality of Conversation*. London: Anthem Press, 2003.
Tauchert, Ashley. *Romancing Jane Austen: Narrative, Realism, and the Possibility of a Happy Ending*. Houndmills: Macmillan, 2005.
Thicknesse, Philip. *Observations on the Customs and Manners of the French Nation, in a series of letters, in which the nation is vindicated from the misrepresentations of some late writers*. Dublin: W. Sleater, D. Chamberlaine and J. Potts, 1767.
Thomas, Sophie. *Romanticism and Visuality: Fragments, History, Spectacle*. Abingdon: Routledge, 2008.
Thompson, Helen. 'How the Wanderer Works: Reading Burney and Bourdieu'. *ELH* 68, no. 4 (Winter 2001): 965–89.
Thompson, James. 'Jane Austen and the Limits of Language'. *Journal of English and Germanic Philology* 85, no. 4 (October 1986): 510–31.
Tobin, Beth Fowkes, ed. *History, Gender & Eighteenth-Century Literature*. Athens: University of Georgia Press, 1994.
Todd, Janet. *Sensibility: An Introduction*. London and New York: Methuen, 1986.
Tompkins, J. M. S. *The Popular Novel in England 1770–1800*. London: Methuen, 1969.

Trilling, Lionel. *The Liberal Imagination: Essays on Literature and Society*. London: Mercury Books, 1961.
Turberville, A. S. *English Men and Manners in the Eighteenth Century*. London: Oxford University Press, 1926.
Tytler, Graeme. *Physiognomy in the European Novel: Faces and Fortunes*. Princeton: Princeton University Press, 1982.
Von Feinaigle, Gregor. *The New Art of Memory: Founded upon the Principles Taught by M. Gregor Von Feinaigle to Which Is Prefixed Some Account of the Principal Systems of Artificial Memory, from the Earliest Period to the Present Time*. London: Sherwood, Neely and Jones, 1812.
Wagner, Jennifer A. 'Privacy and Anonymity in *Evelina*'. In Burney, *Evelina*, edited by Harold Bloom, 99–109. New York: Chelsea, 1988.
Wagner, Peter, ed. *Icons–Text–Iconotexts: Essays on Ekphrasis and Intermediary*. New York: de Gruyter, 1996.
Wahba, Magdi. 'Madame de Genlis in England'. *Comparative Literature* 13, no. 3 (Summer 1961): 221–38.
Wall, Cynthia. 'The Impress of the Invisible: Lodges and Cottages'. *ELH* 79, no. 4 (Winter 2012): 989–1012.
Walpole, Horace. *The Castle of Otranto*. Edited by W. S. Lewis. Oxford: Oxford University Press, 1982.
Ware, Malcolm. *Sublimity in the Novels of Ann Radcliffe: A Study of the Influence upon Her Craft of Edmund Burke's Enquiry into the Origin of Our Ideas of the Sublime and Beautiful, Essays and Studies on English Language and Literature 25*. Upsala: Lundequist, 1963.
Watt, Ian. *The Rise of the Novel: Studies in Defoe, Richardson and Fielding*. London: Chatto & Windus, 1957.
Weiskel, Thomas. *The Romantic Sublime: Studies in the Structure and Psychology of Transcendence*. Baltimore: Johns Hopkins University Press, 1976.
Wenner, Barbara Britton. *Prospect and Refuge in the Landscape of Jane Austen*. Bodmin, Cornwall: Ashgate, 2006.
West, Shearer. 'Portraiture: Likeness and Identity'. In *Guide to Art*, edited by Shearer West, 71–83. London: Bloomsbury, 1996.
White, Laura Mooneyham. 'Jane Austen and the Marriage Plot: Questions of Persistence'. In *Jane Austen and Discourses of Feminism*, edited by Devoney Looser, 71–86. New York: St Martin's Press, 1995.
Wieten, Alida Alberdina Sibbellina. *Mrs Radcliffe in Relation to Romanticism*. Amsterdam: H. J. Paris, 1926.
Williams, Neville. *Powder and Paint: A History of the Englishwoman's Toilet, Elizabeth I–Elizabeth II*. London: Longmans, Green and Co., 1957.
Willis, Lesley H. '*Mansfield Park, Emma, Persuasion*'. In *The Cambridge Companion to Jane Austen*, edited by Edward Copeland and Juliet McMaster, 58–83. Cambridge: Cambridge University Press, 2005.
———.'Object Association and Minor Characters in Jane Austen's Novels'. *Studies in the Novel* 7, no. 1, Jane Austen (Spring 1975): 104–19.
Winckelmann, Johann Joachim. *The History of Ancient Art*. Translated by G. Henry Lodge. 4 vols. Boston: J. R. Osgood, 1872.
Winkler, K. P. 'Locke on Personal Identity'. *Journal of the History of Philosophy*, no. 29 (1991): 201–26.
Wittgenstein, Ludwig. *Zettel*. Edited by G. E. M. Anscombe and G. H. von Wright. Berkeley: University of California Press, 1970. © 1967 Basil Blackwell.

Wohlgemut, Esther. 'Maria Edgeworth and the Question of National Identity'. *Studies in English Literature, 1500–1900* 39, no. 4, The Nineteenth Century (Autumn 1999): 645–58.
Wollstonecraft, Mary. *The Collected Letters of Mary Wollstonecraft*. Edited by Janet Todd. London: Columbia University Press, 2000.
———. 'Review of *The Italian*'. *Analytical Review*, 25 (1797), 516–20.
———. *A Vindication of the Rights of Woman*. Edited by Miriam Brody. Harmondsworth: Penguin, 1992.
———. *The Vindications: The Rights of Men, the Rights of Woman*. Edited by D. L. Macdonald and Kathleen Scherf. Ontario: Broadview, 1997.
Wood, Gillen D'Arcy. *The Shock of the Real: Romanticism and Visual Culture, 1760–1860*. Houndmills: Palgrave Macmillan, 2001.
Woodall, Joanna, ed. *Portraiture: Facing the Subject*. Manchester: Manchester University Press, 1997.
Worsley, Lucy. *If Walls Could Talk: An Intimate History of the Home*. New York: Faber and Faber, 2011.
Yaegar, Patricia. 'Toward a Female Sublime'. In *Gender and Theory: Dialogues on Feminist Criticism*, edited by Linda Kauffman, 191–212. Oxford: Oxford University Press, 1989.
Young, Kay. 'Feeling Embodied: Consciousness, Persuasion, and Jane Austen'. *Narrative* 11, no. 1 (January 2003): 78–92.

INDEX

The following entries have been emboldened to indicate their centrality to the text, making this index a more efficient tool for the reader to use: Austen, Jane; Burney, Frances; Edgeworth, Maria; Radcliffe, Ann; and visuality.

Addison, Joseph 1
   taste 14, 209
aesthetics
   classical 14
   colour and moral disjunction 117
   ethical ideologies 67, 68, 69, 70, 71, 109, 141, 209
   portraits of women 184
affection
   exposure of 196
anecdote
   significance of 145
Anglo-French War 3, 209
anonymity
   publication 186
   visual 21, 111, 196
appearance
   change in 197, 199
   mistrust of 170, 186, 197
   visual conformity 190
architecture 27, 32, 212
   Austen's physiognomic treatment of structures 28, 66
   castles 88, 110
   convents 88, 110
   Emma 82–4, 85
   The Italian 107–9
   Mansfield Park 78
   The Mysteries of Udolpho 106
   Pride and Prejudice 66–73
   Radcliffe's treatment of 91
   A Sicilian Romance 104–6, 109–11
   subjection 104
   windows 71, 107

artlessness 48, 189
associationism 96, 97, 169
   Locke, John 96
Austen, Jane 23, 24
   architecture 73–78, 82–85, 105
   Chawton 78
   dancing 56
   'dual voice' effect 45, 65
   Emma 7, 46–56, 78–85, 212, 213
   feminism 31
   free indirect discourse 45, 46, 50, 54, 65, 83
   interior design 62, 70, 74–76
   literary criticism 88–96
   Mansfield Park 73–8
   'The Mystery' 1
   Northanger Abbey 73, 79, 211
   Persuasion 39
   physiognomy 34, 39
   portrait gallery 66
   portraiture 40–44, 46–66
   Pride and Prejudice 37, 56–73, 212
   Sanditon 73
   Sense and Sensibility 23, 40–6

Barbauld, Anna Laetitia 21, 22, 94
Battle of Waterloo 24, 185, 209
beauty
   concept of 22
   physiognomic definitions of 60
Belinda. *See* Edgeworth, Maria
blindness
   metaphorical 80, 82
body language 106
Brontë, Charlotte 40

Burke, Edmund
    Evelina 186
    on the sublime and the beautiful 93
    terror 126
Burney, Edward Francisco
    portrait of Frances Burney 184
Burney, Frances 23, 25
    autobiographical influences 175–6
    Camilla 164
    diaries 176, 178, 179, 186
    Evelina 9, 184, 185–86, 187–99, 213
    literary criticism 175–82
    The Wanderer 19, 21, 108, 181, 182, 199–207, 213, 214
Byron, Lord 13

camera obscura 12
Camilla. *See* Burney, Frances
Carter, Elizabeth 21, 22
Castle Rackrent. *See* Edgeworth, Maria
character
    addition of 54
    deciphering of 58
    depiction of 179, 183
    duality of 17, 165
    illustration of 58
    improvements to 47
    individualisation of 17
    invention of 213
    physiognomic correlatives of 68, 140
    projections of 24
    reciprocity of 80
    relationship between the appearance and the essence 187
    self-invention 168
    sympathetic reading of 187
characterisation
    universal recognition 28
charity 177, 195
chiaroscuro
    in Radcliffe's novels 112, 116, 117, 119
    in *The Wanderer* 204
cinema
    male gaze 8
Coleridge, Samuel Taylor 89, 114
colour
    Radcliffe's preoccupation with 117
colour codes
    deception 214

The Wanderer 199–207
communication
    of character 51
    Hume, David 197
    impossibility of 104
    metacommunication 57
    somatic 174, 177, 187–207, 213
    system of 180
concealment 147, 165
conduct books 39, 51, 175, 176
consciousness
    language of 198
cosmetics
    Belinda 167
    cross-Channel perceptions of 201
    economics 205
    France 200
    interpretation of 163, 200
    self-determination 213
    views of 15, 205
    The Wanderer 200
courtesy novel 176, 185
courtship novel 24, 32, 173
Cozens, Alexander
    'ink blot' effect 88, 126, 132, 133
    manipulation of positive and negative space 127
Crisp, Samuel 180
culture
    shaping of perceptions 209

dancing
    Evelina 193
    Pride and Prejudice 56, 57
Day, Thomas 169
depiction 146, 179, 211
    of character 183
    drawing 48, 58, 106
    strictures on 212
    vagueness 182
Descartes, René 5, 28
detail
    economy of 209, 214
domestic sphere 143, 167
drawing. *See* depiction

economic security 30, 85, 179, 189, 190
Edgeworth, Maria 23, 25
    Belinda 3, 5, 10, 11, 109, 161–71, 211

INDEX

Castle Rackrent 146, 148–56
  Ennui 156–61
  fashion 156–61, 162–71
  jewellery 150–56
  Letters for Literary Ladies 137, 147, 210
  literary criticism 140–45
  male narrators 148–56, 161
ekphrasis
  definition of 11
  Radcliffe's use of 88, 106, 113
  scopic dialogue 192
  self-expression 94
  shift in gendered and stylistic associations 11
  visuality 11
Emma. See Austen, Jane
Enlightenment 11, 210
ennui
  French condition of 157
Ennui. See Edgeworth, Maria
epistolary novel 174, 188
  scopic dialogue 174, 187–99
estate 4, 150, 152, 157
  identification with 83
  primogeniture 66
ethics
  vision 32
Evelina. See Burney, Frances
eye colour. *See* physiognomy
eyes. *See* gaze

fame
  female reputation 186
  literary 186
fashion
  as analogue for value and identity 138
  Belinda 162–71, 213
  crinolines 168
  cross-dressing 23
  cultural identity 153
  Ennui 156–61
  fashionability 159
  feminism 170
  gowns 158, 184
  jewellery 43, 151, 152, 153, 159
  masks 164, 165
  as metaphor for patriarchal domination 147
  self-invention 168

female gaze 72, 102, 103, 161, 163, 196, 210, 212. *See* gaze
feminism
  in Austen's novels 31
  fashion 170
  female duelling 168
fiction
  self-invention 138
  visuality 1
focalizers 147, 150, 156
Fordyce, James 38, 189, 196
  Sermons to Young Women 2, 175
France 15, 143, 203
  cosmetics 200, 201
  influence on Burney 182
free indirect discourse. *See* Austen, Jane
French Revolution 3, 202, 210
Freud, Sigmund
  repetition 128

gardening. *See* landscape design
Garrick, David 192
gaze 5
  active, passive and sympathetic 187
  choreography of 188
  connoisseur 139
  control of 52, 209
  deflecting of 6
  expressiveness 197
  moral 7, 8
  penetrating 164, 174
  retrospective 150
  stare 193
  subjectivity 56
  sympathetic 174
gender
  definitions of 177
gender politics 4, 12, 26, 55, 90
Gilpin, William 60, 70
Gothic novel 23, 24, 87
  associationism 97
  landscape 115, 120, 122, 124, 135
  obscure 88, 124, 127, 128–31, 135
  portraiture 212
  Radcliffe's treatment of mortality 125
  repetition 88, 117, 118, 120
  sensibility 127
  sublime 93, 99, 106, 118, 126

supernatural 87, 98
superstition 128
terror 89, 126, 127
trauma 94
uncanny 125
undefined 88
Gothic novelists 117
Griffith, Elizabeth 22

handwriting. *See* physiognomy
Hays, Mary 38
Hazlitt, William 182, 183
heroine depiction 179, 211
    female typologies 5, 79, 135, 144, 147, 157, 161, 164, 183, 186
    self-discovery 191
    shift during Regency and Victorian periods 20
Hume, David 96
    A Treatise of Human Nature 197

image control 6, 21, 48
Industrial Revolution 12
inexpressibility. *See* self-expression
'ink blot' effect. *See* Cozens, Alexander
interior design
    Austen's treatment of 33
    Mansfield Park 74–76
    Pride and Prejudice 62, 70
invisibility
    where concealment is a delusion 195
invisible
    cultural anxiety 10, 134
Ireland 23, 137, 141, 142, 149, 150, 155, 156
    as perceived by the English 142
The Italian. *See* Radcliffe, Ann

jewellery. *See* fashion
Johnson, Samuel 23
    Burney's treatment of depiction 181
    morality 49
    portrait painting 48
Jonson, Ben
    country house poetry 68
A Journey through Holland, &c. made in the summer of 1794. *See* Radcliffe, Ann
Jung, Carl 123

Kauffmann, Angelica 22, 53
Keats, John 45
    on Radcliffe's use of repetition 117
Knight, Richard Payne 60

landscape design
    affective force of 73
    Austen's treatment of 69, 79
    gardening 67
    Mansfield Park 77
landscape painting
    Radcliffe, Ann 116
    seventeenth-century 88, 95, 116, 126
landscapes 32, 212
    memories 122
    The Mysteries of Udolpho 122–24
    psychological effect 116, 117
    Radcliffe's preoccupation with 94
    repetition 118
    A Sicilian Romance 118–22
language
    colour 117
    colour codes 174
    gendered constrictions of 14
    limits of 13, 88, 122
    somatic 180, 188
    threat of misinterpretation 174
    vocabulary of discrimination 16, 21, 27
Lavater, Johann Caspar
    beauty 60, 76, 78
    eye colour 48, 60
    handwriting 45
    ideological implications of 'beauty and deformity' 35
    intolerance 58
    'likeness' of the likeness 52
    Nature 67
    physiognomy and truth 39
    physiognomy as poetic feeling 35
    portraiture 39, 43
Lennox, Charlotte 22
Letters for Literary Ladies. *See* Edgeworth, Maria
likenesses
    metaphorical 56
    as a positive force for change 27
    trustworthiness of 41, 54
Linnaeus, Carl 16
literacy
    cultural 152

INDEX

Locke, John 97
  associationism 96
  construct of nothingness 125
  on identity and diversity 201
looking
  gender-specific modes of seeing and being seen 5
  manner of 5
Lorrain, Claude 95. *See* landscape painting

Macaulay, Catharine 22
male gaze 140, 152, 156, 157, 183, 210 *See* gaze
  in Austen's novels 28, 61
  cinema 8
  in Edgeworth's novels 137
  Emma 52
  Evelina 193, 194, 195
  female subjection 8
  The Italian 111
  penetrating 196
  Radcliffe's treatment of 107, 108
  A Sicilian Romance 121
male narrators 25, 147
  Castle Rackrent 148–56
  Edgeworth's use of 138
  Ennui 156–61
manners
  as a link between the visible and the audible 2
  class distinction 204
Mansfield Park. See Austen, Jane
Marmontel, Jean-François 140, 164
marriage 32, 39, 74, 82, 85, 134, 158, 202
marriage plots 29, 32
Marylebone 194
masks. *See* fashion
masquerade 162, 163
metacommunication 57
metamorphosis 202, 203
  The Wanderer 199
miniatures. *See* portraiture
mirrors 166
modesty 173, 174, 178
Montagu, Elizabeth 2, 3, 22
  portraiture 22
moral tale 161

morality 49
More, Hannah 22
  women's perceptual advantage 139
Mulvey, Laura
  the male gaze 8
myopia 137
The Mysteries of Udolpho. See Radcliffe, Ann

nabobs 152
Napoleonic Wars 3. *See* Battle of Waterloo
narrative perspective 161, 174
  colour codes 207
  epistolary structure 188, 190
  male narrators 25
  scopic dialogue 187–99
national identity 141, 142, 143
  multiple allegiances 142
Nattes, John-Claude 35
Nature. *See* Lavater, Johann Caspar
Northanger Abbey. See Austen, Jane
novel-reading
  allusions to in women's novels 210

objectification
  of women 158
obscure. *See* Gothic novel
optics
  level of detail deemed necessary to communicate 40

patriarchal abuse
  concealment of 99
  metaphors for 106, 111
patriarchal power 9, 88, 91, 110, 113, 135, 153
  metaphors for 125
  panoramas of 115, 116, 119, 124
  visibility of 91, 121, 124, 126, 173
perception
  gendered 140
  transformation in 81
performance 147, 178
  cosmetics 206
perspective 65
Persuasion. See Austen, Jane
physiognomy

affective force of 35
communication of character 51
eye colour 47, 48, 60
hair 43, 169
handwriting 45
improvements and the 'Addition of Character' 54
influence on vision and depiction 209
Lavaterian habit of looking 28
'likeness' of the likeness 52
limits of language 49
morality 15
resemblance 85
silhouettes 47
symmetry 77
visual culture 21
The Wanderer 21
Winckelmann's views of 20–21
picturesque
   Austen's treatment of 32, 75
   improvements 67, 70
   irregularity of appearance 60
   relation to beauty 60
   Romantic poets 13
Pope, Alexander 6
   Aristotelian golden mean 78
   An Essay on Criticism 75
   The Rape of the Lock 154, 170
   'To a Lady' 16–19, 191
portrait gallery
   Pride and Prejudice 63–6
portraiture 27, 32, 184, 187
   affective power of 40–44, 55, 63, 65, 66
   benevolent 'disproportion' 54, 56
   Emma 46–56
   exhibitions of 5, 37
   flattery 184
   influence of 186
   The Italian 101–2
   'likeness' of the likeness 52
   miniatures 40, 41, 62, 64, 99, 101
   miniaturists 40
   The Mysteries of Udolpho 98–99
   perceptual differences 51, 55
   Pride and Prejudice 56–66, 212
   Radcliffe's treatment of 88, 212
   Sense and Sensibility 40–46

A Sicilian Romance 102–4
   vocabulary of discrimination 20
Poussin, Nicolas 95
Price, Sir Uvedale 60
prostitutes 173, 195, 196, 201
psychonarration 199, 214
public eye 210
publication
   self-consciousness 176

Radcliffe, Ann 23, 24
   architecture 104–6, 109–11
   colour 117
   A Journey through Holland, &c. made in the summer of 1794 118
   landscapes 118–24
   literary criticism 88–96
   portraiture 27, 97, 98–99, 101–4, 107
   The Italian 101–2, 107–9, 111–14, 130–31
   The Mysteries of Udolpho 96–101, 106–7, 114–15, 122–24, 127, 135, 212
   The Romance of the Forest 79
   A Sicilian Romance 11, 104–6, 109–11, 118–22, 130
   treatment of obscurity 126, 127, 128–31, 135
   veils 111–15
rape 195
readership
   female 189
religion
   Austen's religious background 49
   Edgeworth's treatment of 153
   Radcliffe's views of 109, 110, 112
repetition. *See* Gothic novel
   Freudian 128
Repton, Humphry 70, 74
   improvements 67
reputation 174
   fragility of 9, 192
   image-based 3, 196, 209
   preservation of 164, 200
   visual analogues for 189
Reynolds, Frances 3, 63
Reynolds, Sir Joshua 3, 167, 184
   archetype of the connoisseur 139
   classical features 22

Discourses on Art 209
Evelina 186
imitation 141
portraiture 7, 187
Richardson, Samuel 190, 193, 194, 195
Robson, William 46
The Romance of the Forest. *See*
    Radcliffe, Ann
Romantic poets 13
Rosa, Salvator. *See* landscape painting
Rousseau, Jean-Jacques 169
Russia 179

Samuel, Richard
    drawing 39
    The Nine Living Muses of Great
        Britain 21, 53
Sanditon. *See* Austen, Jane
scopic dialogue. *See* communication,
    somatic
Scott, Sir Walter 74
    on Radcliffe's landscape technique 116
self-consciousness 183, 188
    as a woman artist 22
    as a woman novelist 173, 174, 176
self-expression 14, 174
    frustrated utterance 112, 174,
        187, 188
    inexpressibility 14, 175, 188, 194, 210
self-perceptions
    heroine depiction 191
Sense and Sensibility. *See* Austen, Jane
sensibility 131, 132, 135
Shaftesbury, Third Earl of (Anthony
    Ashley Cooper)
    Characteristicks 14
    human sympathy 15
    Taste's universal applications 15
Shakespeare, William 95, 152, 168
Sheridan, Elizabeth 22
A Sicilian Romance. *See* Radcliffe, Ann
Siddons, Sarah 167
sight. *See* vision
silhouettes
    Austen's approach to depiction 36
    handwriting 45
    influence of landscape trends 35
    physiognomy 47, 51

Smith, Adam
    moral gaze 7
    self-regulation 191
    sympathetic reading of character 187
    The Theory of Moral Sentiments 6, 8, 191
social mobility 50
spectacles 10, 152
    clarity of vision 182
spectator
    female 88
    impartial 6, 8, 210
    impertinent 193, 204
spectatorship
    polyphony of valid viewpoints 9
stare. *See* gaze
sublime. *See* Gothic novel
supernatural. *See* Gothic novel
superstition. *See* Gothic novel

Tales of Fashionable Life. *See*
    Edgeworth, Maria
Taste. *See* aesthetics
terror. *See* Gothic novel
theatricality
    female gaze 192
    heroine performance 192
    male gaze 192
    scopic dialogue 192
Thrale, Hester 176, 187
Treaty of Alliance 16
Treaty of Amity and Commerce 16

uncanny
    Freud's definition of 125
United States of America 16

Vauxhall Gardens 5, 194, 195
veils 22
    constraints on female vision 137
    The Italian 111–14
    The Mysteries of Udolpho 99, 100,
        114–15
    psychological functioning of 88, 100
    visual anonymity 111
viewing. *See* looking
viewpoints
    multiplicity of 53
visibility

dangers of 189, 195
inescapability of 178
recognition 196
of the self 33
as a woman novelist 185, 186
vision 5
  duality of spectatorship and display 10
  envisioning 10
  gendered 140
  propriety of 185, 193
  strictures on 212
visual culture 3, 10, 15, 140, 141
visuality
  in Britain 5
  change in the conception of language 13
  changed expectations of 90
  coded 173, 176, 179, 180, 199, 204, 207
  creating attachments 30
  definitions of 4
  ekphrasis 16
  fashion 147
  forms and functions of 20, 209, 212
  free indirect discourse 24, 65
  heroine depiction 22
  as methodology 3, 12, 175, 209
  optics 12
  overview of 3
  pedagogical intent 147
  psychological effect 87, 115, 135
  rhetorical freedom 14

self-expression 143
self-invention 146
theatricality 137, 140, 163, 170
visibility of 4
visual culture and the social body 10
visual description and verbal depiction 11
women novelists 23–6
women's novels 6

Walpole, Horace 117
The Wanderer. See Burney, Frances
Wedgwood, Josiah
  likenesses 22
Winckelmann, Johann 20
windows. *See* architecture
Wittgenstein, Ludwig 37, 175
  ekphrasis 16
  Lavater, Johann Caspar 38
  visual and verbal communication 16
Wollstonecraft, Mary 9, 89, 210
women artists 22
women novelists 2, 3, 23, 26, 212
  self-consciousness 173
  self-expression 143, 209
  as threat to patriarchal regime of knowledge 210
women's novels 5, 8, 18
  allusions to novel reading 210
  visuality 6
Wordsworth, William 13

www.ingramcontent.com/pod-product-compliance
Lightning Source LLC
Chambersburg PA
CBHW021824300426
44114CB00009BA/307